T0329897

EURO-AUSTERITY AND WELFARE STATES

Comparative Political Economy of Reform during the Maastricht Decade

European Union Studies

European Union Studies features the latest research on topics in European integration in the widest sense, including Europe's role as a regional and international actor. This interdisciplinary series publishes the research of Canadian and international scholars and aims at attracting scholars working in various disciplines such as economics, history, law, political science, and sociology. The series is made possible in part by a generous grant from the European Commission.

The first series of its kind in Canada, and one of only a few in North America, *European Union Studies* is unique in looking at the EU "from the outside," making sense not only of European integration but also of the role of the European Union as an international actor.

GENERAL EDITORS:

Randall Hansen
Professor of Political Science
Director, Centre for European, Russian, and Eurasian Studies
University of Toronto

Amy Verdun
Professor of Political Science
Jean Monnet Chair Ad Personam Founding
Director, European Studies Program
University of Victoria

For a list of books published in the series, see page 271.

H. TOLGA BOLUKBASI

Euro-Austerity and Welfare States

Comparative Political Economy of Reform during the Maastricht Decade

UNIVERSITY OF TORONTO PRESS
Toronto Buffalo London

ISBN 978-1-4875-0776-3 (cloth)   ISBN 978-1-4875-3690-9 (EPUB)
                                  ISBN 978-1-4875-3689-3 (PDF)

European Union Studies

Library and Archives Canada Cataloguing in Publication

Title: Euro-austerity and welfare states : comparative political economy
    of reform during the Maastricht decade / H. Tolga Bolukbasi.
Names: Bolukbasi, H. Tolga, author.
Series: European Union studies.
Description: Series statement: European Union studies | Includes
    bibliographical references and index.
Identifiers: Canadiana (print) 20200345680 | Canadiana (ebook) 20200345982 |
    ISBN 9781487507763 (cloth) | ISBN 9781487536909 (EPUB) |
    ISBN 9781487536893 (PDF)
Subjects: LCSH: Welfare state – Belgium – Case studies. | LCSH: Belgium –
    Appropriations and expenditures – Case studies. | LCSH: Welfare state –
    Greece – Case studies. | LCSH: Greece – Appropriations and expenditures –
    Case studies. | LCSH: Welfare state – Italy – Case studies. | LCSH:
    Italy – Appropriations and expenditures – Case studies. | LCGFT:
    Case studies.
Classification: LCC HV303 .B65 2021 | DDC 330.12/6094 – dc23

University of Toronto Press acknowledges the financial assistance to its
publishing program of the Canada Council for the Arts and the Ontario
Arts Council, an agency of the Government of Ontario.

 Canada Council   Conseil des Arts
for the Arts   du Canada

 ONTARIO ARTS COUNCIL
CONSEIL DES ARTS DE L'ONTARIO
an Ontario government agency
un organisme du gouvernement de l'Ontario

Funded by the   Financé par le  Canadä
Government   gouvernement
of Canada   du Canada

Contents

Tables and Figures

Preface

People of my generation are all children of austerity – we were born around the time of the first oil shock. Many memories of my childhood and teenage years are coloured by *kemer sıkma politikaları* (belt-tightening), which I remember asking my parents about back in the early 1980s. As I grew up and started reading the newspapers, I noticed stories of austerity everywhere. And just like that, I continued reading about austerity for three decades and counting.

My interest in austerity – what it is, what it is good for, and at what price – crystallized during my late teenage years. I was majoring in economics at the Middle East Technical University (METU) but was also interested in questions of who gets what, when, and how – not exactly the typical questions economics majors would ask at the height of the Conservative Revolution. I do not think there were any courses on the welfare state at METU, but I remember taking advanced courses on political economy and institutions. I continued taking courses on economic policy and distribution in my economics master's program at Ankara University. These courses taught me about how institutions are designed to distribute resources (and therefore power) to particular groups of actors and not to others. I was all eyes and ears about how austerity was commonly institutionalized and what its distributive consequences were for different groups in society. My master's work, therefore, *had* to be on austerity and its social consequences.

Going through one IMF austerity package after another, my native Turkey would be an ideal test case; but, unlike my peers and professors, the contrarian in me did not want to work on my own country. The late 1990s was a time when Europe's leaders were hammering out the final details of the Economic and Monetary Union (EMU). There was no match for this experiment on the institutionalization of austerity on such a scale for a research project, I thought. And I was obviously interested in its future social consequences. To predict these, I had to learn where the euro came from. Given my training at the kitchen table and onwards, the answer was self-evident: the EMU was nothing but the institutionalization of orthodox macroeconomic principles for its own overarching economic governance. Convergence on these principles had already begun in some EU member states. The EMU would seal the fate of the remaining others by collectively locking in the process of conversion to macroeconomic discipline (read: austerity) across Europe. Since the EMU was institutionalizing austerity at the highest level, member states would have no choice but to bear the brunt of falling wages, rising unemployment, and other social disruptions.

What I read hints of, while learning about all this, was how *politicized* the project was. In the simplest terms, the euro was the economic means to political ends. These ends included building disciplined economic governance along with a multi-level policy-making state. Having been trained as an economist up to that point, and despite having read Karl Polanyi, I could hardly see the *politically constructed* nature of institutionalizing the euro. But as I learned more about the politics behind the euro, I realized that economic policymaking was nothing but "an essentially political process" (Hall 1986). I became increasingly interested in what I learned to be the "political sociology of political economy" (Gourevitch 1986).

My interest in the social and political conflicts that produced changes in the organization of power, and the consequences of power distribution within and among societies, led me to pursue a PhD in sociology at McGill University in Montreal. My training in political sociology and economic sociology at McGill helped me understand the interplay of ideas, interests, and institutions in political economy. In the meantime, I was still mesmerized by the unfolding EMU experiment and decided to continue working on it. I chose to focus on what Andy Martin and George Ross (whom I first knew as leading scholars on the euro and fortunately as role models after that) saw as "the single most important area still reserved to national politics" – the welfare state (Martin and Ross 2004, 17).

Even before the euro went into circulation, we were all convinced that the EMU would institutionalize austerity across Europe. With respect to its effects on Europe's welfare states, expectations on the political left, right, and centre were more or less the same. Given its neoliberal origins, the supranational EMU straitjacket would corner member states into downsizing their social security programs. Facing material cost-cutting pressures, politicians, particularly those on the left, would feel obliged to introduce welfare state cutbacks to secure entry in the EMU. Others, especially on the right, would be able to use the EMU card in pursuing slash-and-burn strategies to "rightsize" their welfare states. Thus, virtually everyone who pondered on the euro's social consequences agreed on the impact of Euro-austerity on Europe's welfare states. It was this curiously widespread agreement, not only in academic and policy circles but also among the public, that prompted my PhD project. And I was intent on showing, with all the evidence I could find, the ways and means through which Euro-austerity would spontaneously retrench the welfare states in Europe.

As a first step, I set out to show how the EMU institutionalized an austerity regime at the EU level and how this regime constrained fiscal policy decisions at the national level. I found that, among the member states, the higher the need for austerity to qualify for the EMU, the stronger the reversals in fiscal policies and the more significant the changes in fiscal politics. All governments that aimed for EMU entry slashed government deficits and public debt in line with the requirements of the Maastricht Treaty.

Then came the second step: did Euro-austerity translate into welfare state retrenchment in the 1990s? For this, I mustered key evidence that comparative welfare state specialists commonly used to detect changes in all the EU member states of the time. I constructed a variety of indicators on the basis of public social expenditures and analyzed changes in them. I then traced the development of legislated social rights by focusing on the replacement rates used in social security programs. Finally, I traced the changes in the key social security programs in Belgium, Greece, and Italy, the member states that needed to introduce the most radical fiscal changes. I followed, using in-depth case studies, all the key welfare state reforms introduced by every government that had come to power in these countries.

As I confronted the evidence I obtained at every step, I was struck by how off the mark those earlier expectations – including my own – had been. The evidence showed no systematic welfare state cutbacks in the countries in which we had expected to see radical retrenchment as a result of Euro-austerity. Europe's welfare states had proved resilient because the beneficiaries of mature welfare programs – labour unions, political parties, and even coalition partners in ruling governments – had defended social rights against frontal attacks.

The fact that we could not have predicted this was understandable. No one in the early 1990s who had been theorizing the euro's effects had had access to the detailed statistical data on social expenditures and social rights that I had obtained for my research. Moreover, scholars who expected dire scenarios back then had not fully received the insights of new theoretical perspectives. The "new politics of the welfare state," which could help explain its resilience, became influential only in the 2000s. In addition, the evidence showed that the political economy of welfare reform was also shaped by forces depicted in the "old politics of the welfare state." Labour unions and their allies, organized under union leadership, played key roles even at the peak of Euro-austerity in virtually all reform processes in Belgium, Greece, and Italy.

In the end, I learned that the extent to which pressures may be modified, muted, or even fully mitigated by counter-pressures has been, and will continue to be, contingent on the very political economy of reform. At the time I was writing, I benefited from hindsight as new data became available. Thus, I was able to develop a new perspective on all these events, which I share in this book.

In its first incarnation, this book told the story of how these extraordinary events occurred in what we later learned to be only the *first episode* of Euro-austerity. Just as I was completing this work, the Great Recession hit. Europe began to struggle with yet another wave of austerity – Euro-austerity Episode II. Strikingly, just as in Episode I, doom-and-gloom scenarios ran through the popular press as well as scholarly work. Europe's welfare states may have outlasted the first episode of Euro-austerity. But this time, almost everyone concurred, it was different: welfare states would not be able to survive the second episode.

Just as in Episode I, commentators and scholars making predictions about the impact of the current episode of Euro-austerity on welfare states did not have enough data. But we now know much more than ever about the link between Euro-austerity and welfare states. We have come to learn that partisan politics structure all decisions about who gets what, when, and how, even under the direst circumstances. We have also learned that institutions, and the coalitions that support them, are shaping and reshaping partisan choices. We know, therefore, that welfare states will not disappear, no matter how structural the austerity constraints are or how powerful the Euro-austerity card is.

We talked about tightening our belts back in the 1970s; little did I know that we would still be talking about it decades later. But what this book shows, or so I hope, is that governments and progressive forces should beware writing off democratic politics even when taking on Goliaths. I tried to illustrate how Euro-austerity was largely what governments made of it: when there was political will, there was a (in fact, more than one) way. I also tried to show how Euro-austerity was what organized societal actors made of it. I hope these messages in the book will shed some light as we explore democratic alternatives in the current and future episodes of austerity.

Acknowledgments

Like many first books, this one grew out of a doctoral project that I completed while doing a PhD at McGill University. It took a community to produce that earlier work. I have many individuals and institutions to thank, and it is my great pleasure to mention some of them here. I cannot thank enough my professors, peers, friends, and extended family. I had the greatest fortune of drawing on the advice of Axel van den Berg, who not only supervised my research but also guided my childlike sense of wonder when I was trying to learn everything all at once. Being an outspoken defender of McGill University Sociology Department's "Ho, ho, not so fast" approach to social change, Axel taught me how institutions never, ever change overnight. My training-through-research with Axel also taught me, among zillions of other things, how I could develop my passionate persona in writing. At McGill, I also benefited immensely from long conversations with Donald von Eschen, Kari Polanyi Levitt, and Michael Smith on economic sociology and political economy. When it came to European studies, it was Barbara Haskel who served as the *pôle*. I was very fortunate to carry out fieldwork at the Institut d'études européennes at the Université Libre de Bruxelles (ULB), on Barbara's initiative, as part of the EU-Canada Transatlantic Exchange Partnerships Programme.

My continued interest in the political economy of the euro was only possible thanks to two institutional entrepreneurs who were extraordinarily generous to graduate students in ways more than one: Amy Verdun, who created the European Studies Program and everything to do with it at the University of Victoria, and Jane Jenson, who not only built the Université de Montreal/McGill University Institute for European Studies but was also the centre of gravity for European studies in Canada. Amy and Jane, being their resourceful selves, did everything to help my research be not only possible but also less austere at the ULB's

Institut d'études européennes, the Max Planck Institute for the Study of Societies in Cologne, and the Zentrum für Sozialpolitik at the Universität Bremen. My earlier work would not have been possible without their exceptional generosity and constant encouragement.

Philippe Pochet was another institutional entrepreneur, one who had built the Observatoire social européen in Brussels, a Mecca for anyone working on the social dimension of the euro. Philippe was extraordinarily generous with all kinds of resources when he hosted me at the Observatoire during multiple stages of my earlier work. He has been a role model with his open-mindedness to being proved wrong as new evidence contradicts one's research.

While it took a community to complete my doctoral project, it took another to revise it for this book. My interest in the political economy of the euro had peaked when I stumbled on Kenneth Dyson's *Elusive Union* (1994). Kenneth's work was truly an inspiration for an economics master's student interested in the political construction of the euro. The only downside about my conversations with Kenneth was that I met him only after having completed my research at McGill. I never stopped learning from reading and re-reading his work. Kevin Featherstone was probably one of the kindest, alongside being one of the most insightful, discussants I could have ever dreamt of having on my conference panels. I could not have learned more from observing how gentlemanly and genuinely Kevin engages with the individuals around him.

I do not think I would have invested so much time and energy on the impact of monetary integration on Europe's welfare states had Andrew Martin and George Ross not produced the inviting exemplary work on it. I remember, while at McGill, savouring every tiny little research note on the euro that these pioneering Europeanists had written, collectively and individually. The power of their work inspired my research and this book. I was very fortunate to meet George Ross at the Université de Montreal/McGill University Institute for European Studies events just before I completed my PhD. I met Andy only later, while I was a visiting scholar at the Minda de Gunzburg Center for European Studies at Harvard University. I learned so much from their work and my conversations with them. My debt to Andy and George for all this is immeasurable.

The formative ideas in my research had been significantly shaped by the work of Peter Hall. I had read *Governing the Economy* (Hall 1986) for the first time when I was taking a graduate course in economics at METU, and it showed me that there was an entirely different world out there on the comparative political economy of economic policy choice beyond my usual reading lists. It was through Peter's work that I finally put my mind to studying ideas, interests, and institutions in a wider social science perspective. I felt blessed to have conversations about my work with him at Harvard's Center for European Studies after being influenced by his work for so many years.

I also had the good fortune to have conversations with many scholars and policy practitioners: Caner Bakır, Iain Begg, Mark Blyth, Tanja Börzel, Marco Buti, Caroline de la Porte, Bernhard Ebbinghaus, Henrik Enderlein, Ebru Ertugal, Martin Heipertz, David Howarth, Stephan Leibfried, David Natali, Işık Özel, George Pagoulatos, Claudio Radaelli, Thomas Risse, James Savage, Alberta Sbragia, Fritz Scharpf, Waltraud Schelkle, Vivien Schmidt, Ben Ross Schneider, Lyle Scruggs, Peter Martin Smith, Dimitri Sotiropoulos, Wolfgang Streeck, and Kathleen Thelen, among others. These individuals had been very influential on the way I saw the political economy of reform in the run-up to the EMU.

My graduate students at Bilkent University in Ankara were exposed to almost all the ideas in this book. Their not only endless curiosity and research assistantship but, more importantly, critical engagement heartened me in the countless rounds of revisions. I am grateful to Sena Dicle Günay, Emina Hasanagic, Ali Berk İdil, Timur Kaymaz, Kerem Gabriel Öktem, Efe Savaş, Ozan Taşdemir, and Deniz Yıldırım for all these reasons.

Finally, I would like to thank Amy Verdun once again for her constant support in turning this project into reality. The book's message is much clearer thanks to Amy's editorial guidance and the three rounds of refereeing. I cannot express how grateful I am to all the anonymous reviewers involved in each of these rounds. They helped me rethink my argument every time I revised the manuscript. The University of Toronto Press's acquisitions editor Daniel Quinlan has been extraordinarily kind and patient with me. He was also one of the sources of encouragement in the final stages of the project, and I thank him for all this. I am also grateful to Stephanie Stone, my extraordinarily adept copy editor. Stephanie's close reading of the text inspired me to develop my arguments in clearer ways. Moreover, her attention to detail added so much to how I communicated my ideas.

I dedicate this book to my son, Can Doğa. I am blessed with his presence in good times as well as tough times. I get an endless kick out of watching him learn, and letting him teach me. I truly hope he will learn, as smoothly as possible, that crises are a part of life and will hit home from time to time. I want him to remember that it is, however, *not* crises themselves that define us; what defines us, instead, is what we make of them.

EURO-AUSTERITY AND WELFARE STATES

Comparative Political Economy of Reform during the Maastricht Decade

1 Euro-Austerity and Europe's Welfare States

This book analyses the political economy of welfare state reform in the first episode of Euro-austerity, spanning the 1990s. It explores the effects of *Euro-austerity*, understood as the constraints imposed on government budgets by the Economic and Monetary Union (EMU), laid out in the Maastricht Treaty of 1992, on welfare states in Europe. In doing so, it defines a *welfare state* as the sum of all the benefits provided through different public programs in all social policy areas measured in three ways: social expenditures, social rights, and program development. The book shows how the welfare states survived in spite of the unremitting fiscal constraints stemming from the EMU. Based on this analysis, it provides lessons for scholars as well as policy practitioners for Euro-austerity's second episode, which began with the Great Recession in 2008 and continues into the present.

The 1980s saw one European government after another convert to macroeconomic discipline. Euro-austerity was gradually written into the macroeconomic rulebooks across the European Union (EU). Yet it was not until the Maastricht Treaty was signed that Euro-austerity was fully institutionalized for those EU member states that aspired to join the single currency, the euro. The treaty marked the beginning of the first episode of Euro-austerity, known as the "Maastricht decade." More than fifteen years after the treaty came into effect, the dominant policy response of European governments to the Great Recession was, again, austerity. After an initial impulse of fiscal stimulus, governments engineered policies to cut the mounting budget deficits that the recession had produced. Europe has come full circle, and Euro-austerity has set in once again.

In the short history of European economic and monetary integration, we have had, therefore, not one, but two episodes of Euro-austerity. In each episode, scholars, policymakers, and citizens from all walks of life expected Euro-austerity to erode Europe's welfare states. They perceived the EMU as threatening the welfare states in two ways. One was evidently direct: the conditions for EMU membership, known as the Maastricht convergence criteria, would constrain government expenditures, through which welfare state programs were largely financed. These criteria included benchmarks on inflation, interest rates, exchange rates, and budgetary requirements. The most relevant to the welfare states were those that set budgetary limits – namely, maximum deficit positions of 3 per cent and public debt ratios of 60 per cent of gross domestic product (GDP), respectively. These limits were widely expected to force cuts in expenditures, resulting in sizeable retrenchment. The impact would be most severe in those states aspiring to enter the EMU whose fiscal imbalances in 1991 exceeded the criteria the most. It was these states that would find it most difficult to meet them. Indeed, some governments, notably the German government, counted on the criteria to keep out of the EMU certain states that it regarded as ill suited for membership. First and foremost Italy, but also Greece, were deemed unable to deliver the policies consistent with membership because of their weak capacity for economic governance.

The other way the EMU would threaten the welfare states was indirect. The EMU had a design flaw, one that would institutionalize a deflationary regime in members of the euro area. Once it was in operation, the EMU's contractionary effect on economic activity would erode the tax base. This would severely constrain the financing of Europe's welfare states since their programs were largely financed through tax revenues. The contractionary spells would also lead to higher demand for welfare state benefits, such as unemployment insurance. While facing ever diminishing financial resources due to declining tax revenues, policymakers would have to square the circle of financing ever tighter budgetary burdens.

These widespread expectations of the effects of Euro-austerity were undoubtedly plausible back then. They are plausible now, too. Anxieties are high today, just as they were in the 1990s. In fact, today, daily newspapers, Twitter feeds, circulating emails, policy briefs, and scholarly papers are filled with these deep, strong, heartfelt concerns, just like those we read about back in the 1990s. It is these big, real-world concerns that prompted this book.

Did these overwhelming concerns ultimately turn out to be true? The book shows that as far as the first Euro-austerity episode is concerned, the answer is, partly yes and partly no. It is partly yes because Euro-austerity *did* have a severely constraining effect on government budgets. Detailed analysis of the empirical evidence about government expenditures and budgetary politics points unambiguously to the constraints imposed by the EMU. The in-depth comparative case studies on the political economy of reform in countries where the EMU's impact was expected to be greatest (Belgium, Greece, and Italy) show that all governments – whether on the left, on the right, or in the centre – felt the acute need to retrench their budget deficits and public debt.

The answer is partly no because the EMU's constraints did not automatically result in the erosion of Europe's welfare states. The detailed case studies on Belgium, Greece, and Italy show that the ruling governments had greater room to manoeuvre than we originally thought. When push came to shove, they rediscovered good, old ways of raising revenues and reducing expenditures in areas other than their welfare state programs. Whenever these governments were intent on welfare state reform, their reform capacity was constrained by a rather cohesive bloc composed of labour unions, interest groups, traditionally protected groups, professional groups, opposition parties in Parliament, and even coalition partners sharing Cabinet seats. These case studies on reform politics, therefore, point to how cohesive coalitions devised ways to shield their welfare states from the constraining impact of Euro-austerity.

As far as the second, present episode of Euro-austerity is concerned, the jury is still out. The findings on the first episode suggest that popular concerns may not always be grounded in reality, and this may prove to be the case for the second. Comparable empirical evidence is not yet available for this second episode, and, therefore, it is too soon to be certain whether the same popular expectations meet reality. The fact that the welfare states were shielded from the otherwise devastating impact of austerity in the first episode cautions us against jumping to conclusions about its presumed impact on the welfare states now.

Yet heightened popular concerns are far from subsiding. When the Great Recession began, commentators all across Europe concurred: "This time it's different!" Euro-austerity had nipped at Europe's heels ever since the Maastricht Treaty was signed, but it did not quite bite. For many, the cascading crises meant that Euro-austerity would finally take hold. In fact, after only an ephemeral Keynesian response, proponents of Euro-austerity quickly hijacked the political agenda. The dominant tone in European political and public debates on Euro-austerity's effects is now pessimistic, and apprehensive citizens are bracing for the final blow to their welfare. Their assessments of the "social climate," as reflected in Eurobarometer polls, have been lower year after year since the Great Recession began (European Commission 2009, 2010, 2011, 2012, 2013, 2014). For the last two years for which we have data, citizens believe that "there is worse to come" (European Commission 2013, 92) and that this pessimism is not likely to be dispelled anytime in the foreseeable future (European Commission 2014, 99; Ferrera 2017).

It comes as no surprise, then, that these worries have given way to electoral volatility across Europe. One election after another has led to the removal of incumbents and the reversal of governments, especially in austerity-ridden eurozone members like Greece, Portugal, Ireland, Spain, and Italy (G. Ross 2012, 185). No wonder a leading volume on comparative welfare states opens, "The welfare state," to say the least, "has people worried in the aftermath of the deepest economic crisis since the Great Depression" (Hemerijck 2013, 1).

These reactions are, in many ways, no different than those that Europeans had at the height of Euro-austerity – Episode I. Europeans were gravely concerned about what two leading scholars of the EMU called the "effects of the single most important and supranational step in European integration on the single most important area still reserved to national politics" (Martin and Ross 2004, 17). Anyone who followed the headlines in the 1990s will distinctly recall the popular apprehensions concerning severe austerity in the run-up to the EMU. As this chapter will show, for both advocates and opponents of the EMU, meeting its draconian requirements with their strict deadlines required a Herculean effort. Euro-austerity, then, was sanctioned not only by powerful sticks – exclusion from the EMU, downgrading to second-class citizenship, naming and shaming by EU partners, and existential threats from financial markets – but also by very attractive carrots: first-class citizenship, generous EU funding, and financial market rewards. These sticks and carrots are no strangers in Euro-austerity – Episode II of the 2010s.

Euro-Austerity – Episode I and the Welfare States: The Debate[1]

In everyday political and public debates back in the 1990s, Europeans expected that Euro-austerity would erode the welfare states. Perhaps a few were ready to bite the austerity bullet for their dream of a prosperous federal Europe, but for many, EMU-*cum*-austerity meant sacrificing their cherished European social model. These concerns were so deeply rooted that they flowed naturally into the early 2000s. In fact, uneasy Europeans rejected the euro on different occasions, largely for fear that it would bring an end to the European social model. In both the Danish and the Swedish referenda on the euro in 2000 and 2003, respectively, although the Maastricht decade was over, the victorious No camps capitalized on the prevailing negative sentiment that the EMU would endanger their welfare state. In 2005, during the referendum on the European Constitution in France, the No camp mobilized the still apprehensive citizens, who believed that the Constitution, based on a "too liberal" economic model, would compromise the French model of society.

These political debates of the 1990s and early 2000s on Euro-austerity – Episode I resonated across the comparative political economy literature of the time on the EMU's impact on Europe's welfare states.[2] In this relatively self-contained but very intense literature, eminent political economists as well as international organizations debated the impact of what they saw was the single most powerful source of reform during the Maastricht decade. This group was divided into two diametrically opposed camps on the basis of their beliefs in the value of the welfare state. While those on the left were incensed by the EMU's constraints on the welfare state, others on the right were delighted. Whether with anxiety or exultation, this otherwise diverse research community was surprisingly in agreement on its expectation of the impact of the euro on the welfare state: both sides predicted that the EMU would lead to across-the-board downsizing of the welfare states by enforcing fiscal austerity.

These reactions in academia were only natural given the EMU-*cum*-austerity's overwhelming strictures. Scholars were mesmerized by conservatives' fiery rhetoric on austerity, which dominated the headlines. When the Maastricht decade came to a close, these reactions gradually dissipated as new evidence on actual reform paths became much clearer in the 2000s. Let us now take a closer look at how comparative political economists in both camps reacted to Euro-austerity – Episode I.

The first camp emphasized a set of mechanisms through which EMU-*cum*-austerity would result in welfare state *downsizing*. A first group of political economists in this camp emphasized that the Maastricht convergence criteria had caught the EMU candidate countries (which were already going through a deep recession) off guard while they were experiencing extraordinarily high levels of budget deficits and public debt. They argued that the strict fiscal limitations of the convergence process would impose a fiscal straitjacket on their publicly funded programs. Given the fact that welfare state programs constitute big-ticket items in budgets, restrictions on budget deficits (as well as on public debt levels) would require reducing the resources allocated to such programs. The EMU's fiscal criteria would necessarily "foreclose the deficit option" for most of the European welfare states (Scharpf 2000, 200). This would, many expected, severely constrain the financing of welfare state programs. Through these constraints, therefore, the EMU would dictate sizeable cutbacks to existing welfare state programs (Teague

1998). In fact, the only way to make it to the single currency, many concurred, was through "cuts and rationalization in social welfare provision" (Rhodes 1996, 322).

A second group of comparativists argued that, in addition to constraining social expenditures, the EMU imposed "a strict deflationary
bias" (Hay, Watson, and Wincott 1999, 11). Such bias hampered economic activity, total output, and employment. Falling incomes would
lead to reduced revenues and tighter budget constraints, which would
leave less room for manoeuvring in the financing of social expenditures (Begg and Nectoux 1995; Burkitt and Baimbridge 1995; Grahl and
Teague 1997; Leibfried 2000). By imposing a new "macroeconomic policy regime," influential comparativists observed, the EMU "imposed
austerity and deflationary policies on all countries." The common
expectation was, again, "pressures for lowering of social expenditures"
(Huber and Stephens 2001, 224).

Finally, a third group of scholars saw the EMU as nothing but a cun-
ning plan for imposing "neoliberal marketization" (Martin and Ross
1999), "default neoliberalism" (Hay 2000), "subversive liberalism"
(Rhodes 1998), and "disciplinary neoliberalism" (Gill 1998). These
scholars were united in expecting a scenario of slash-and-burn: the
EMU would render transparent all non-wage costs (*read:* social security
contributions) across the eurozone. It would, thus, reveal the cost dis-
advantages of producers in generous welfare states, which had higher
non-wage costs, vis-à-vis their competitors in less generous welfare
states, which had lower non-wage costs. To remain internationally
competitive and retain and/or attract investment, governments would
be compelled to engage in a dog-eat-dog competition to reduce these
non-wage costs. As a result, an inescapable "race to the bottom" would
force dramatic cutbacks in generous welfare state programs (Leander
and Guzzini 1997; Martin and Ross 1999; Rhodes 1997).

By effectively locking in Euro-austerity at the supranational level,
these influential political economists expected, the EMU would "spell
the death-knell" of the European social model (Martin and Ross 1999,
171). Many saw the project as "the most serious attack mounted on the
welfare state during the post-war period" (Burkitt and Baimbridge
1995, 110). In time, many others added, the EMU would become "the
altar upon which the European social model [would] ultimately [be]
sacrificed" (Hay 2000, 521). All this would result in "the end of the
national welfare state as we know it" (Leibfried 2000, 49).

The second camp's expectations were in surprising unison with
those of the first camp. This time in a positive tone, scholars expected
the EMU to bring "corrective" austerity "compelling" governments to

introduce rigorous reforms. The end result, in this scenario, would be *rightsizing* the "overburdened" welfare states. Mainly voiced by international organizations such as the International Monetary Fund (IMF) and the Organisation for Economic Co-operation and Development (OECD), this scenario was premised on an assumed causal link between the EMU and welfare state reform: fiscal austerity requirements for the EMU would prove ineffective in correcting macroeconomic imbalances unless it was accompanied by welfare reform. The OECD warned that the EMU, to remain viable, "require[d] serious social security system reforms" (OECD 2000, 20; see also OECD 1999, 165–6). The IMF's chief economist was louder and clearer: for the EMU to be successful, "national authorities whose policies have generated the social welfare problem need to step forward to take full responsibility for the necessary reform" (Mussa 1997, 220). In fact, "the only viable option for most EU members," another senior IMF official warned, "is to avert these [fiscal] imbalances with a large-scale social security reform" (Kopits 1997, 22).

Comparative political economists writing during the Maastricht decade identified two key mechanisms linking EMU-*cum*-austerity to welfare state cutbacks: (1) the material constraints imposed by the EMU on the welfare states and (2) the discursive opportunities that the EMU afforded to ruling governments (Dyson 2002, 24).

The first mechanism concerned the EMU's material fiscal constraints, which would force the welfare states to become "leaner" (according to the second camp) or "meaner" (according to the first camp). To meet these fiscal targets, governments, which were "strapped to the mast," would have to adopt draconian cost-containment strategies (Dyson, Featherstone, and Michalapoulos 1998). This mechanism was the centrepiece of most of the studies on the EMU's impact on the welfare state. Interestingly, the comparative welfare state literature rarely considered exogenous factors as primary independent variables driving welfare state change. Instead of *causing* change, globalization and European integration were typically seen as contextual variables that could only make the situation worse. Many political economists, however, saw the EMU as a "far more immediate and pressing" force of change in the welfare states than any other exogenous pressure (Hay, Watson, and Wincott 1999, 6; see also Grahl and Teague 1997; Gill 1998; Hay 2000; Rhodes 1998).

The second mechanism through which Euro-austerity would impact Europe's welfare states was the discursive opportunities afforded by the EMU. Political economists pointed out how the EMU could be exploited when governments needed a pretext for justifying unpopular policies of welfare downsizing or rightsizing. Many believed that the EMU would provide a *"vincolo esterno,"* an externally imposed constraint necessitating fiscal discipline in launching welfare state cutbacks that would prove otherwise unpalatable (Dyson and Featherstone 1996, 1999).

This view of the EMU as a politically convenient excuse was rather widespread in the literature of the 1990s. Many sceptics of the EMU viewed it as a rhetorical tool conveniently used by conservative governments having retrenchment agendas. In parallel, advocates of the EMU saw the Maastricht rules as a trump card that would allow ruling governments to prune their welfare states. Scholars believed that welfare reforms were "inevitable," even "in a world without EMU" across Europe (Pierson 2001, 92). They emphasized, however, how governments discursively constructed a seemingly causal link between EMU-*cum*-austerity and welfare reform. Although the Maastricht criteria did not require spending cuts or, hence, retrenchment of social expenditures per se, they were seen to have "considerably strengthen[ed] the hand of those seeking such cuts" (Leibfried and Pierson 2000, 285). Thus, governments introducing welfare reforms during the 1990s could typically argue that "we have to change because Europe and the coming of the euro obliges us to – we are all in this boat together and if we don't get into EMU we will suffer" (G. Ross 2000, 107–8). Scholars also argued that policymakers in the 1980s had decided to reform the welfare states, but since doing so would prove politically treacherous, they devised the EMU as an instrument for "legitimation" of welfare state reform (Verdun 2002, 204).

This debate, which heated up towards the end of the Maastricht decade, essentially hinged on a shared expectation: the EMU had led or would lead to welfare state cutbacks by imposing material constraints (i.e., the overwhelming budgetary austerity felt by everyone at the time) and by affording governments fresh discursive opportunities (i.e., powerful political capital helping them deflect blame for unpopular reforms). This expectation is summed up as what I call the *Euro-austerity hypothesis*, which I present in the next section. This working hypothesis represents the popular concerns we often heard during Euro-austerity – Episode I, concerns that continue to resonate during Euro-austerity – Episode II.

Research Questions, the Euro-Austerity Hypothesis, and Research Design

Despite the draconian austerity strategies implemented in the name of the euro during the 1990s, new evidence that became available during the 2000s on welfare state restructuring showed that Europe's welfare states had largely averted across-the-board downsizing. The fact that this decade saw no radical retrenchment came as a surprise for many from at least three angles. First, austerity during the Maastricht decade was seen as an inexorable, tangible force that every EMU candidate was exposed to. Second, European citizens as well as scholars were convinced that EMU-*cum*-austerity would rule the day and that this would bear down on the welfare state. Third, the opportunity for EMU membership gave governments (especially those in the conservative ranks) a prime opportunity to justify even the most draconian measures.

The gap between the apprehensions in the 1990s and the more recently revealed facts on welfare reforms evokes a set of research questions that I address in this book: (1) What does the empirical evidence on comparative welfare reform reveal about the domestic reform outcomes in the EMU candidates? (2) If there was no radical retrenchment during the Maastricht decade, was there no welfare reform at all? (3) How was radical retrenchment averted in spite of not only the EMU's material pressures but also the discursive opportunities it afforded to ruling governments? (4) What were the intervening factors that cushioned the otherwise intense impact of the EMU on welfare reform paths? (5) If EMU entry did not bring about sizeable savings from welfare reforms, then what alternative strategies did governments rely on to meet the fiscal targets? (6) Under what conditions were incisive reforms possible, and what role did the EMU play in these processes? And finally, (7) What insights do the first episode of Euro-austerity offer us for assessing the consequences of the second episode? The answers to these questions are vital to the future of not only the EMU and welfare states but also the European integration project.

To address these questions, I engage with the literature to derive deductively what I call the Euro-austerity hypothesis: the greater the need for austerity to qualify for EMU entry, the more incisive and far-reaching the welfare state reforms. According to this hypothesis, first, the further an EMU candidate is from meeting the Maastricht fiscal criteria, the larger the budgetary cutbacks it faces to qualify for the euro. Second, the larger the required budgetary cutbacks, the more austere their effects on its welfare state. Thus, if there were any welfare state retrenchment in Europe, it would necessarily take place in the EMU candidates that faced the largest fiscal cutbacks. Countries needing to go through radical fiscal cutbacks, therefore, constitute ideal test cases because one would expect to see the greatest amount of welfare state downsizing in these cases.

The book identifies Belgium, Greece, and Italy as the "most likely" "crucial cases" on the basis of the Euro-austerity hypothesis. It is these cases, under this working hypothesis, that would have been "predicted to achieve a certain outcome" – the largest welfare state cutbacks (Gerring 2007, 232). I use the empirical evidence from these carefully selected cases to unpack the relationship between Euro-austerity and welfare state outcomes.

From a research design perspective, the book addresses a set of *effects-of-causes* questions informed by the Euro-austerity hypothesis. In this research design, we start with "a *potential cause*" and then explore "its impact on *Y*" (Goertz and Mahoney 2012, 41; emphasis added). I ask whether and, if so, to what extent the potential cause (EMU-*cum*-austerity) has the effects (downsizing of these welfare states) that a distinct body of research in comparative political economy is centred on. The book, therefore, focuses on any exclusive impact Euro-austerity may have had on welfare states during the Maastricht decade. It does *not* address the *causes-of-effects* question on *all* drivers of welfare state change in Europe.[3]

The Argument in Brief

This book argues that the Euro-austerity hypothesis proved to be essentially incorrect. The reform outcomes in the EMU candidates are characterized less by radical retrenchment than by ordinary recasting, recalibration, restructuring, and reorganization. The argument is developed in two ways. One is by providing evidence in the form of statistical data on public social expenditures from 1991 to 2001; the other is by explaining, through three case studies, how governments managed to achieve budgetary positions that qualified them to enter the EMU without engaging in significant welfare state retrenchment.

The logic of the statistical analysis rests on a simple comparison: data on the variation in *welfare effort* in terms of social expenditures (consisting of nine key welfare state programs included in the OECD and other databases) are compared with data on the variation in total public expenditures. The comparison shows that, in the EMU candidates, social expenditures remained generally stable, even when total public expenditures declined. Instead of cutting welfare state expenditures, they concentrated their cuts in other policy areas. Making these cuts enabled them to minimize the changes to their welfare states and leave welfare state expenditures as a percentage of GDP virtually unchanged. In other words, Euro-austerity exerted significant pressure on budgets, but it was deflected from the welfare state programs.

However, this does not necessarily mean that governments did *not* implement cuts in welfare state programs in response to Euro-austerity.

There are various ways in which welfare effort might be misleading because it might hide actual cuts. One way is, for example, if there were an increase in the proportion of those parts of a population (such as retirees and unemployed workers) that was eligible for benefits – the dependent population – even when total social spending was stable. When changes in the dependent population are controlled for, however, the data the book is presenting show that there was generally no reduction in social spending. This book carefully avoids these misleading inferences by drawing on the "dependent variable problem debate" in the comparative welfare state literature. In doing so, it relies on the substantial accumulation of statistical data addressing the problem, which were not available during the Maastricht decade or the early years of the EMU.

The book also presents and examines data on benefit replacement rates, an alternative conventional measure, for three key welfare state programs: unemployment insurance, sick pay insurance, and public pensions. The replacement rates presented in the book also show that, even under intense Euro-austerity, entitlements in the three welfare state programs remained stable across the EU. Trends in replacement rates corroborate the book's overall finding that the EMU candidates managed to keep their social standards and that the impact of Euro-austerity was deflected to budget components other than welfare state programs. Moreover, the book shows that social spending behaviour was in no way systematically different in the EMU candidates than in member states not seeking EMU membership. This implies that monetary integration does not seem to have led to any more retrenchment in the EMU candidates than in other countries that had opted out of, or chose to remain outside, the EMU.

Although the statistical evidence suggests that the widely anticipated worst-case scenario was averted, it does not explain how and why the EMU candidates managed to avoid across-the-board welfare state retrenchment. The book presents in-depth, qualitative, comparative case study material on welfare reform in the 1990s in Belgium, Greece, and Italy. With skyrocketing fiscal imbalances, these three underdogs were required to brave the largest budgetary cutbacks in all of the EMU candidates. These case studies show conclusively how the doom-and-gloom Euro-austerity scenario did not materialize. They explain how these governments passed the Maastricht test without having to sacrifice their welfare states. True, all governments that came to power announced that they were resolutely committed to meeting the Maastricht criteria – for most of them, at all costs. Their intentions were reflected in their election manifestos, party programs, and official declarations. By imposing severe constraints on budgets and providing discursive opportunities, the EMU *did* foster dramatic fiscal turnarounds. These turnarounds were possible for all governments that came to power that introduced across-the-board austerity for Maastricht. When it came to introducing incisive welfare reform, however, they were effectively pushed back by a rather cohesive bloc composed of labour unions, interest groups, traditionally protected groups, professional groups, opposition parties in parliament, and even coalition partners sharing Cabinet seats with ruling parties.

The fate of these reform initiatives varied greatly. In some cases, draft bills were quietly shelved. In others, reforms were possible only after governments' ambitions were seriously scaled down. When reforms were passed, they ended up introducing changes in the program parameters, such as new entitlement, indexation, or calculation rules. They generally resulted in some minor, incremental changes. Paradoxically, there were cases where governments felt the need to *expand* popular welfare programs under severe austerity. They were compelled to do so to appease social tensions that could potentially derail their entire fiscal consolidation efforts for EMU entry. Overall, therefore, virtually none of these reforms produced significant savings or contained costs to help governments qualify for eurozone membership.

Policymakers were successful in introducing welfare state reform when the EMU helped them deflect blame by externally empowering them. The EMU's empowerment impact was stronger under governments with technocratic leadership. It was also stronger when and where public opinion was supportive of European integration. When governments had to push for austerity under the Maastricht timetable, the EMU goal helped build cooperation among organized actors, leading to social pacts. Cooperation proved easier, especially when governments offered compensation – when cutting some programs was accompanied by introducing new programs or expanding existing ones. The reforms were passed only when all actors were convinced that the reforms would ensure the *long-term* sustainability of the welfare states or when they were concealed under the guise of "urgent requirements" for euro entry.

When successive attempts at welfare reform failed to generate savings, governments resorted to Plan B strategies to meet the Maastricht deadline. These alternative strategies included revenue-raising measures, such as raising fiscal revenues by introducing special taxes, launching tax reforms, improving tax compliance, broadening the tax base, and rationalizing tax administrations. Most EMU candidates also raised non-fiscal revenues by implementing one-off measures such as privatization programs, which grew rapidly in size as the Maastricht deadline approached and came to a halt as soon as it was met. Some EMU candidates received sizeable transfers from the EU, which gave them more room to manoeuvre in sustaining social expenditures. In addition to introducing revenue-raising measures, the governments also resorted to cutting public expenditures. When they did so, however, they often reduced *non-social* expenditures. These reductions were in funds allocated to, for example, industrial subsidies, defence budgets, and general public services. Finally, almost all governments that struggled to satisfy the Maastricht targets relied on creative accounting, which, in some cases, resulted in seriously underreporting deficit figures.

Based on the two sets of evidence on social expenditures and the political economy of reform, therefore, I show that Europe's welfare states went through a series of reforms during the first episode of Euro-austerity, only some of which resulted in some retrenchment. Even in the hardest-pressed EMU candidates like Belgium, Greece, and Italy, Euro-austerity shaped reform objectives, direction, and timing, but did not overdetermine the content of these reforms. Based on these findings, I conclude that a clear causal link between EMU-*cum*-austerity and welfare state downsizing cannot be established.

Structure of the Book

The book is organized in seven chapters. After this introductory chapter, chapter 2 traces the institutionalization of Euro-austerity at the EU level. It reviews the institutional arrangements for coordinating budgetary policy and the fiscal criteria that operationalized austerity across the EU. After having reviewed the post-Maastricht quandaries, it traces how austerity was reinforced through the over-ambitious Stability and Growth Pact (SGP). The chapter then discusses the impact of the Maastricht rules and financial markets on the EMU candidates' fiscal retrenchment strategies.

Chapter 2 also identifies the period of Euro-austerity under study – which I call the extended Maastricht decade – which starts immediately after the announcement of the convergence criteria and ends with countries securing entry to the eurozone. This was the decade when the "Maastricht effect" crystallized. The chapter also identifies Belgium, Greece, and Italy as three countries that had not only deficit levels at some multiples of the reference values on budgetary position but also public debt that exceeded their entire national income. It shows in what ways these EMU candidates are the ideal test cases for evaluating the impact of Euro-austerity on Europe's welfare states.

Chapter 3 provides a first stab at evaluating the Euro-austerity hypothesis by examining it against statistical data on social expenditures. It shows that there was virtually no systematic or significant social expenditure retreat anywhere on the road to the EMU. In fact, despite the budgetary austerity that the EMU imposed, which was reflected in ever-declining total public outlays, social spending among the EMU candidates remained relatively stable. The figures show that the share of the welfare state in government budgets grew dramatically vis-à-vis other expenditure items. During this period, therefore, there was a remarkable prioritization of social goals at the expense of non-social goals. Even levels of social spending per dependent remained stable in real terms, a fact that points to the stability of social standards on the road to EMU membership.

Chapter 3 also presents welfare state program-level data that are at odds with the widespread expectations for program overhaul. Several summary measures that were constructed on the basis of program-level spending indicate that there was more upsizing in welfare state programs than downsizing. The chapter presents data, in addition to those on social expenditures, on the development of social rights. It shows that trends in benefit replacement rates were largely in parallel with those observed in social expenditures. Therefore, the findings of this chapter demonstrate that the EMU convergence process was characterized much less by retrenchment than by the stability of European welfare states.

Chapters 4, 5, and 6 unpack the relationship between the EMU and welfare state change through detailed case studies. Relying on comparative historical methods, these case studies test the Euro-austerity hypothesis on the causal link between the EMU and welfare state reform. The case studies illustrate how Belgium, Greece, and Italy managed to avoid across-the-board downsizing despite the EMU-induced budgetary pressure. Each case study, first, explores how the EMU candidate qualified for entry to the eurozone despite its extraordinarily large fiscal imbalances. It presents the budgetary strategies adopted by successive governments and outlines how the Maastricht targets were met. Second, each case study explores the reforms in key welfare state programs to demonstrate the extent to which each government that came to power was successful in reforming its welfare state. It presents the goals of the policymakers in each reform initiative and emphasizes the striking gaps between the initial reform plans and actual reform outcomes. Each case study shows how the political capacities of successive governments were effectively constrained by forces opposing welfare reform, eventually leaving these welfare states at the end of the Maastricht decade largely intact.

Chapter 7 revisits the comparative findings on the political economy of welfare state reform in Belgium, Greece, and Italy. It highlights key variables that shaped the politics of reform on the road to the EMU. In so doing, the chapter reassesses the validity of the Euro-austerity hypothesis in light of cross-national statistical data and the evidence from the three comparative qualitative case studies. It discusses the relevance of these findings to the "new politics" of the welfare state literature that has come to dominate much of contemporary welfare state research.

Chapter 8 draws lessons from the first episode of Euro-austerity at a time when Europe is embroiled in yet another wave of austerity. At this time of cascading crises and heightened uncertainty, Europeans are concerned about their welfare states. To evaluate the impact of the current episode of Euro-austerity on European welfare states, we need comprehensive, systematic evidence. We have very little of it, however. And not enough time has passed to scientifically evaluate its impact. In the absence of such evidence, the chapter draws a set of insights from what we have learned about the impact of Euro-austerity – Episode I and applies them to Euro-austerity – Episode II.

2 The Institutionalization of Euro-Austerity

The establishment of a monetary union in Europe is perhaps the boldest and most far-reaching project in the history of European integration. It came to full fruition in January 2002, when the euro became the exclusive currency in circulation in the twelve EU member states that made up the original eurozone. This chapter shows how Euro-austerity was institutionalized in the rules governing macroeconomic policy in the run-up to the EMU through the establishment and operation of the convergence criteria and the SGP. It describes how these rules, and their monitoring by the EU institutions, effectively constrained the EMU candidates' macroeconomic policy choices. In the end, the budget deficits of these countries were remarkably reduced. This was especially true in the EMU candidates that were furthest from compliance when the Maastricht decade began. The chapter singles out these EMU candidates as the critical cases, those where the greatest impact on the welfare state should have been found if Euro-austerity had had the expected impact.

The chapter is organized as follows. It first traces the history of economic and monetary integration to the signing of the Maastricht Treaty, which laid out the EMU's structure and the path to its introduction. It then outlines the institutional framework of macroeconomic austerity prescribed in the treaty. After laying out the European-level governance arrangements for the member states' budgetary policies, the chapter describes how Euro-austerity was operationalized through the deficit and debt limits for membership in the EMU. It goes on to review the ratification hurdles that the treaty had to overcome and the 1992 currency crisis, which almost derailed the drive to the euro. After detailing how the overly restrictive SGP reinforced the Euro-austerity framework, the chapter describes how the states aspiring to EMU membership complied with the fiscal convergence criteria by imposing remarkable fiscal retrenchment. It then reviews the evidence demonstrating the role of the Maastricht rules and the financial markets in bringing about that retrenchment. The chapter closes by identifying three EMU candidates – Belgium, Greece, and Italy – whose budget deficits and debt-to-GDP ratios at the outset of the Maastricht decade exceeded the convergence criteria limits much more than those of any other EMU candidates. This makes them ideal test cases for evaluating the impact of Euro-austerity on domestic budgets and national welfare states.

The Road to Maastricht

The aim of forming a single currency did not appear in the Treaty of Rome (1957), which created the European Economic Community. A first initiative in that direction emerged as early as 1969, when the leaders of the original six member states commissioned the Werner Report. That report, delivered in 1970, set out the details of the first plan for establishing the EMU, according to which member states would complete full monetary union as early as 1980. The economic turmoil of the 1970s derailed the implementation of this plan. In a subsequent effort to stabilize the turbulent exchange rates in Europe during this period, French and German initiatives resulted in the creation of the European Monetary System (EMS) in 1979. The EMS was based on the Exchange Rate Mechanism (ERM), whereby fluctuations in the currencies of the member states were controlled and kept within pre-announced bands. In 1986, EU member governments relaunched the European integration project by adopting the Single European Act, which set the objective of completing the single market by 1992.

Although the EMS temporarily restored exchange rate stability, it enabled the Bundesbank, Germany's central bank, to continue to dominate European economic policy. The expectation that its dominance could be overcome in a monetary union led to French and Italian efforts to revive the long-standing goal of a single European currency. While German Chancellor Helmut Kohl supported this goal as a means of strengthening European integration, Germany could not agree to it if the Bundesbank opposed the single currency. The Bundesbank agreed to it only if the currency would be managed by a central bank as independent and committed to price stability as it was. This condition was met by a committee of European leaders formed to draw up a plan for establishing the EMU. The committee was chaired by the then president of the European Commission, Jacques Delors. The Delors Report (1989) served as the blueprint for the treaty negotiations at the Intergovernmental Conference that produced the Maastricht Treaty of 1992.

The treaty's objective was to crown market integration with the creation of a single currency. It aimed to do this by establishing a single monetary policy alongside strengthened coordination of the economic policies of the member states. Thus, although the single currency structure is referred to as the Economic and Monetary Union, the roles assigned to economic and monetary policies by the treaty were asymmetrical. The treaty focused mainly on the monetary aspects of the EMU. It confined economic union to restricting the levels of budget deficit and public debt of the member countries. In this way, the macroeconomic regime was premised on a centralized monetary policy, carried out by a European-level central bank, alongside a decentralized fiscal policy, carried out by the member states and subject to the constraints imposed by the single monetary policy. In this sense, *monetary union* represents positive integration because it implies transferring sovereignty over monetary policy to the European Central Bank (ECB). *Economic union* represents negative integration because it imposes binding rules on the budgetary policies of the member states. These rules were designed to support the ECB's prime objective of maintaining price stability (Verdun 2013).

The most central feature of the EMU was the ECB, established as the only central institution for managing the European economy. The treaty also established the European System of Central Banks (ESCB), composed of the national central banks and the ECB, to conduct the single monetary policy. The treaty thereby extended the primary objective of the ECB – maintaining price stability – to the entire ESCB. According to Article 105 para. 1, "The primary objective of the ESCB shall be to maintain price stability. Without prejudice to the objective of price stability, the ESCB shall support the general economic policies in the Community with a view to contributing to the achievement of the objectives of the Community."

In conducting the single monetary policy, the ECB is politically independent not only in exercising its mandate but also in unilaterally deciding what maintaining price stability entails. Article 107 of the treaty states, "Neither the ECB, nor a national central bank, nor any member of their decision-making bodies shall seek or take instructions from Community institutions or bodies, from any government of a Member State or from any other body." Through Article 108, member states were obliged to grant independence to their central banks before the ESCB was established.

The treaty set out the establishment of the EMU in three stages. The first was scheduled to begin by 1 July 1990, while the treaty was still being negotiated. In this stage, capital movements were liberalized, and all currencies were to remain within the narrow band of the ERM. The second stage, known as the transition stage, was scheduled to begin on 1 January 1994, when the economic convergence of the member countries was to be secured in preparation for full monetary union. Most importantly, member states were obliged to avoid excessive deficits. Moreover, any form of central bank lending to public institutions and privileged access to financial institutions would be prohibited. Member states would grant independence to their central banks. The forerunner of the ECB, the European Monetary Institute (EMI), would be set up with a mandate to strengthen cooperation among the central banks, coordinate the monetary policies of the member states, and monitor the functioning of the EMS. In the third stage, as of 1 January 1999, the ECB would become the sole issuing authority for the currency in circulation, and the ESCB would come into effect. Member states granted EMU membership would be assigned irrevocably fixed exchange rates, and the euro would replace the national currencies.

Convergence towards Euro-Austerity[1]

Even before the intergovernmental negotiations for the Maastricht Treaty began, the Economic and Financial Affairs (ECOFIN) Council had decided that the EMU would be achieved through convergence on a set of benchmarks. As early as March 1990, during the first stage of the EMU, the Council adopted a resolution on the convergence of economic policies. For this purpose, it introduced multilateral surveillance.[2] A year later, in June 1991, the Luxembourg European Council emphasized the "need to make satisfactory and lasting progress with economic and monetary convergence" to ensure "price stability and sound public finance" – the lynchpins of Euro-austerity (Council of the European Union 1991). The European Council called upon member states to submit multi-annual programs detailing their plans for securing these goals.[3] Although the member states could not agree on how to measure convergence at that time, the Council had already begun the process of multilateral surveillance, aimed at ensuring Euro-austerity.

The treaty laid out a detailed plan for institutionalizing convergence towards Euro-austerity that included three instruments. The first of these, better known as the *convergence criteria*, set down the requirements for participation in the final stage of the EMU (Article 109j and Protocol No. 5). The treaty stipulated that:

1. "The achievement of a high degree of price stability ... will be apparent from a rate of inflation which is close to that of, at most,

the three best performing Member States in terms of price stability." In practice, the inflation rate of a given candidate could not exceed by more than 1.5 percentage points that of the three best-performing member states in terms of price stability during the year preceding the examination of the situation in that member state.

2. "The sustainability of the government financial position … will be apparent from having achieved a government budgetary position without a deficit that is excessive." The Commission would examine compliance with budgetary discipline on the basis of the following two criteria:

   a government deficit: the (actual or planned) budget deficit of each country must be no more than 3 per cent of GDP unless the ratio has been declining and is close to the reference value or unless any excess is exceptional and temporary.

   b government debt: gross general government debt must not exceed 60 per cent of GDP unless the ratio is declining towards this reference value at a satisfactory rate.

3. "The observance of the normal fluctuation margins provided for by the exchange-rate mechanism of the European Monetary System, for at least two years, [must occur] without devaluing against the currency of any other Member State." The member state must have participated in the ERM of the EMS without any interruption during the two years preceding the examination of the situation and without severe tensions. At the same time, it must not have devalued its currency on its own initiative during the same period.

4. "The durability of convergence achieved by the Member State … [must be] reflected in the long-term interest-rate levels." In practice, the nominal long-term interest rate must not exceed by more than 2 percentage points that of, at most, the three best-performing member states in terms of price stability. The period taken into consideration is the year preceding the examination of the situation in the member state concerned.

These requirements would be examined before the end of 1996 to identify the member states that qualified to participate in the final stage of the EMU. The Commission and the EMI would report to the Council on the progress that the EMU candidates had made towards meeting these criteria. These reports would also examine the compatibility between each member state's national legislation and the relevant articles of the treaty and the Statute of the ESCB and of the ECB.

The second instrument that the treaty introduced for monitoring the member states' compliance with Euro-austerity was the excessive deficit procedure (EDP). The treaty required that "Member States shall endeavour to avoid excessive government deficits" (Article 109e (4)). The EDP would begin with the Commission reporting on the budgetary deficits and debt in all EMU candidates. Having taken the opinion of the Monetary Committee, the Commission had the option of recommending to the Council a decision that an excessive deficit existed. If the Council decided that an excessive deficit existed, the Council had to make a confidential recommendation to the member state concerned to reduce its deficit within a certain period of time. The Council, however, had the option of making its recommendation public, giving notice to bring the situation to an end within a specified period, and issuing sanctions against the member state. The Council would abrogate its decision or the measures it had taken if it deemed that the excessive deficit in that country had been corrected. The EDP would be implemented with the launch of the second stage on 1 January 1994. Unlike the assessment of the convergence criteria (which would take place only at the end of the second stage), the EDP would be carried out every subsequent year throughout the transition phase. Thus, among all the criteria defined in the treaty, only the fiscal criteria were to be monitored throughout the second stage.

The third instrument the treaty used to institutionalize Euro-austerity was the Broad Economic Policy Guidelines (BEPGs) (Article 103 (2)). The EMU candidates were required to conduct their economic policies to achieve "objectives of the Community" (Article 102a). They would "regard their economic policies as a matter of common concern and shall coordinate them within the Council" (Article 103 (1)). The treaty called on the Council to formulate a draft BEPGs for the member states and for the Community. The BEPGs would provide the framework for more effective multilateral surveillance throughout the second stage of the EMU. The Council would discuss "a conclusion on the broad guidelines" and, on the basis of this conclusion, would adopt a recommendation. To ensure closer coordination and convergence of policies, the Council would monitor and regularly assess economic developments in the member states and the consistency of their economic policies with the BEPGs. The multilateral surveillance procedure was reinforced because member states would forward information to the Commission about any important economic policy measures. When the economic policies of a member state were deemed to be inconsistent with the BEPGs, the Council had the option of making its recommendations public.

Operationalizing Euro-Austerity: The Fiscal Criteria

The central pillar of the Maastricht path to Euro-austerity was the fiscal criteria. The treaty emphasized "sound public finances," which member states had already committed themselves to at the ECOFIN Council meeting of March 1990 and Luxembourg European Council of June 1991. The reference values and other details had not yet been elaborated, however. It was these issues that dominated all high-level meetings after the Delors Report was published (Gros and Thygesen 1992, 388; Bini-Smaghi, Padoa-Schioppa, and Papadia 1994, 27; Walsh 2000, 97–8). During the intergovernmental negotiations on the treaty, the responsibility for defining the convergence criteria and the details of the EDP had been delegated to the Monetary Committee, a technical body largely insulated from the politics of treaty negotiations (Dyson and Featherstone 1999, 430). After intense negotiations, a "near consensus" emerged on the reference values at the committee's meetings in June and October 1991 (Dyson 1994, 148, 156; Dyson and Featherstone 1999, 432).

The treaty negotiations broadly followed the decisions of the Monetary Committee. The committee first determined the reference value for the debt criterion, which it set at the Community average of around 60 per cent of GDP (Bini-Smaghi, Padoa-Schioppa, and Papadia 1994, 29; see also Verdun 2001, 93; Savage 2001, 46; 2005, 32–3; Walsh 2000, 98). The big issue left on the table was the reference value for the budget deficit criterion. The committee proposed 3 per cent of GDP (Agence Europe, 9 October 1991). It assumed an estimated growth rate of 4 to 8 per cent; thus, the 60 per cent debt level would be consistent with a reference value of between 2.3 and 4.4 per cent (Dyson and Featherstone 1999, 735).

The Germans, supported by the Danes and the Dutch, insisted that the reference value should remain on the lower end (3 per cent), as the committee had proposed. The French delegation thought that such a tough criterion would send a strong signal to Germany about how committed France was to the EMU, and it endorsed the 3 per cent benchmark (Dyson and Featherstone 1999, 241). The delegations from Italy, Belgium, Greece, Spain, Ireland, and Portugal objected on the grounds that it was excessively "restrictive," but to no avail. In the end, the Germans insisted on the tough benchmark because they believed that allowing fiscally profligate countries into the EMU would put political pressure on the future ECB to relax monetary policy and that this would result in expensive bail-outs (Walsh 2000, 98; G. Ross 1995, 204).

Observers noted that, during the negotiations, Germany made an intense effort to force the other states to demonstrate their commitment to the EMU by agreeing to these strict entry criteria. Many interpreted this as an attempt to prevent particular states, above all Italy, from entering the third stage of the EMU (Moravcsik 1998, 443; Dinan 1999, 174–5; Sbragia 2001, 80).[4] "For most Germans," Heisenberg (1999, 164) observed, "the thought of Italy joining the EMU in the first wave of countries was ludicrous and dangerous." Likewise, Buiter, Corsetti, and Rubini (1993, 88) argued that the budgetary criteria "reflect not economic logic, but a mixture of German horror at the Italian national debt, and Dutch Puritanism." Dyson and Featherstone (1999, 9) added that "the German preoccupation with 3.0 per cent seemed to many theological and artificial." The Italian government, Dyson (1994, 149) observed, "suspected, quite rightly, that the adoption of tough criteria … was proposed in order to reduce the prospects for Italian eligibility in the absence of radical domestic action."

Although the final version of the reference value in the treaty reflected the German insistence on the 3 per cent rule, France and Italy (after securing the support of the United Kingdom) proposed a "dynamic interpretation" by inserting a clause whereby a member state's deficit would not be judged excessive if it "has declined substantially and continuously and reached a level that comes close to the reference value … or the excess is only exceptional and temporary." Likewise, if the debt level were to diminish enough to approach the 60 per cent target, it was also not to be judged excessive (Dyson and Featherstone 1999, 524). The negotiators also agreed to a flexible interpretation of the criteria by appointing the intergovernmental ECOFIN Council to vote by qualified majority when deciding whether a member state's budget was excessive.

Although it took some time before member states could agree on the exact reference values, at high-level meetings they signed on to convergence towards Euro-austerity. Thus, by the time the fiscal criteria were announced, they were already effectively shaping the context in which national budgetary policies were being designed and implemented. Once austerity had been written into the treaty, the next step to was to put it into effect.

Post-Maastricht Difficulties and Currency Crises

For the Maastricht Treaty to take effect, it had to be ratified by the member states. The target date for completing the national ratification processes was initially set as the end of 1992, but the process took much longer than expected. The Danes rejected the treaty in a referendum in June of that year by a very narrow margin, and this derailed the entire implementation timetable. Coming two weeks later, the Irish referendum endorsed the treaty. In the United Kingdom, the government suspended passage of the legislation enabling ratification, pending the treaty's approval by all the other member states. The French referendum in September 1992 resulted in a *petit oui*. Emboldened by the ratification problems, opponents of the treaty in Germany challenged its legality in that country's Constitutional Court. The court ruled in October 1993 that the treaty was not unconstitutional but that the Bundestag could not be denied the opportunity to hold a vote on whether the convergence criteria had, in fact, been satisfied. In the meantime, a second referendum in Denmark in May 1993 produced a narrow approval. The ratification process had come to a conclusion, and the treaty came into force on 1 November 1993 – after almost a year's delay (Dinan 1994, 183–7; Verdun 2000, 94–6).

Uncertainties surrounding the treaty's ratification were accompanied by growing tensions in the ERM due to insufficient convergence by the member states, the incompatibility of their fiscal and monetary policies, and the weakness of the US dollar. As a result, after a series of currency crises that took place between September 1992 and August 1993, the ERM collapsed. The ECOFIN Council of August 1993 finally announced the de facto suspension of the narrow ERM by widening the margins of fluctuation in the currencies of the member states to ± 15 per cent. At first, member states believed that the wider ERM bands would be temporary and that currencies would return to the normal ERM bands of ± 2.25 per cent.

During the early months of 1995, a new wave of currency attacks revealed that the ERM zone was not insulated from shocks. The treaty, however, required that currencies stay within the normal margins of fluctuation without severe tensions for at least two years before entering the third stage of the EMU. This raised the question of what constituted normal bands at this stage. The Commission and the EMI refrained from issuing a clarification, with the result that the evaluation of the exchange rate performance criterion would be implemented with more flexibility than had been set out in the treaty (Crowley 1996, 45; Eichengreen and Wyplosz 1993; Padoa-Schioppa 1994).[5] The exchange rate criterion was redefined so as to be evaluated in relative terms, like the criteria on inflation and long-term interest rates. Candidates would pass the test as long as there was nominal convergence on these variables across the EU. As a result, from 1992 on, all attention turned to the budgetary criteria (Verdun 2000, 94).

Reinforcing Euro-Austerity: The Stability and Growth Pact

All these difficulties were symptoms of the deepening economic recession. The member states responded to the recession with accommodating fiscal policies. This policy response contributed to soaring budget deficits, as table 1 shows. In 1991, a year before the treaty was signed,

Table 1. EMU Convergence Criteria: General Government Net Lending (−) / Net Borrowing (+) (% of GDP)

Country	1991	1992	1993	1994	1995	1996	1997	1998	1999	−3.0% – peak
Austria	−3.0	−2.1	−4.2	−5.0	−5.2*	−4.0*	−2.5*	−2.4	−2.3	−2.2
Belgium	**−7.4**	**−8.1**	**−7.1**	**−4.9***	**−3.9***	**−3.2***	**−2.1***	**−0.9**	**−0.6**	**−5.1**
Denmark	−3.0	−2.6	−2.8	−2.4*	−2.4*	−0.7	0.7	0.0	1.3	0.0
Finland	−1.0	−5.5	−8.0	−6.4	−4.7*	−3.3*	−0.9	1.7	1.7	−5.0
France	−3.0	−4.6	−5.8	−5.8*	−4.9*	−4.1*	−3.0*	−2.6	−1.8	−2.8
Germany	−2.9	−2.4	−3.2	−2.4*	−3.3	−3.4*	−2.7*	−2.3	−1.6	−0.3
Greece	**−9.9**	**−11.0**	**−13.8**	**−10.0***	**−10.3***	**−7.5***	**−4.0***	**−3.9***	**−3.1**	**−10.8**
Ireland	−2.8	−2.8	−2.7	−1.7	−2.2	−0.4	0.9	2.2	2.6	0.2
Italy	**−11.3**	**−10.3**	**−9.5**	**−9.2***	**−7.7***	**−6.7***	**−2.7***	**−2.7**	**−1.9**	**−8.3**
Luxembourg	0.7	−0.2	1.7	2.8	1.9	2.5	1.7	3.4	3.4	2.8
Netherlands	−2.7	−4.2	−3.2	−3.8*	−4.0*	−2.3*	−1.4	−0.9	0.4	−1.2
Portugal	−6.9	−4.4	−6.1	−6.0*	−5.7*	−3.2*	−2.5*	−3.9	−3.1	−3.9
Spain	−4.3	−4.0	−6.9	−6.3*	−7.3*	−4.6*	−2.6*	−3.0	−1.3	−4.3
Sweden	−1.1	−7.3	−12.2	−10.3	−6.9*	−3.5*	−0.8*	0.7	0.9	−9.2
UK	−3.1	−6.4	−7.9	−6.8*	−5.5*	−4.8*	−1.9*	−0.1	0.9	−4.9
EU-15	**−4.1**	**−5.1**	**−6.1**	**−5.2**	**−4.8**	**−3.3**	**−1.6**	**−1.1**	**−0.3**	**−3.7**

Source: For 1993–7: European Commission (1998); for 1991–2 and 1998–9 (except for Spain and Sweden): European Commission (2013); for Spain and Sweden: 1991–2 and 1998–9: European Commission (2004).[6]

Note: The last column represents the greatest discrepancy between −3.0% and a country's fiscal performance during this period.

*Denotes a year in which there was a Council decision on the existence of an excessive deficit.

nine member states had a budget surplus or deficit ratio below 3.0 per cent of GDP. However, by the end of 1993, when the second stage of the EMU was to begin, only three member states (Denmark, Ireland, and Luxembourg) had kept their previous position. For the EU as a whole, whereas average fiscal deficits had remained around 4.1 per cent of GDP during the treaty negotiations, by 1993 they had risen to a historical high of 6.1 per cent, the highest level recorded since the establishment of the Community in 1957. This figure was considerably higher than those during the economic downturns following the oil-induced shocks of the 1970s (EMI 1995, 20).

The economic recession that produced surging government deficits led to a rise in public-debt-to-GDP ratios all across the EU. As table 2 shows, although initial levels of public debt varied markedly when stage 1 began in 1991, nine EU members had debt levels comfortably below the 60 per cent reference value. From the early 1990s, however, all member states, save Luxembourg, saw their debt surge. Rising debt ratios were even more worrying in member states where public-debt-to-GDP ratios were significantly higher than the 60 per cent benchmark. In Italy, Greece, and Belgium, the debt ratios were higher than their entire national income.

Member states were racking up worsening public balances against their coordination efforts as part of their preparations for the EMU. In spite of ambitious national convergence programs, budgetary positions across the Union deviated from the Maastricht benchmarks. There was some variation in fiscal positions in the EMU candidates with respect to the goodness of fit between their current ratios and the targets, but worsening budgetary imbalances and debt ratios in most member states meant that EMU membership required sizeable and urgent corrections. Thus, the pressure to impose fiscal austerity had begun to be applied even before the second stage of the EMU began in 1994.

Referring to these large imbalances, Germany's Finance Minister Theo Waigel insisted that they would undermine the future currency's "stability," and in November 1995, he tabled a memorandum for a treaty, the Stability Pact for Europe. In this memorandum, the German government demanded tightened rules for budgetary policy and automatic sanctions in cases of breach. Initially, member states welcomed the German initiative for clearer rules. However, they opposed renegotiating the Maastricht Treaty or concluding an intergovernmental agreement outside the EU treaty framework: the solution had to remain within the framework (Heipertz and Verdun 2010). But Waigel did not budge, and in December 1996, the European Council in Dublin agreed on the main elements of the rebranded Stability and Growth Pact (SGP). The

Table 2. EMU Convergence Criteria: Gross General Government Debt (% of GDP)

Country	1991	1992	1993	1994	1995	1996	1997	1998	1999	60% – peak
Austria	56.4	56.3	62.7	65.4	69.2	69.5	66.1	64.4	66.8	9.5
Belgium	**126.9**	**128.5**	**135.2**	**133.5**	**131.3**	**126.9**	**122.2**	**117.2**	**113.6**	**75.2**
Denmark	62.8	68.0	81.6	78.1	73.3	70.6	65.1	61.4	58.1	21.6
Finland	22.3	40.1	58.0	59.6	58.1	57.6	55.8	48.4	45.7	–
France	36.0	39.7	45.3	48.5	52.7	55.7	58.0	59.6	59.0	–
Germany	39.5	42.0	48.0	50.2	58.0	60.4	61.3	60.5	61.3	1.3
Greece	**74.0**	**79.1**	**111.6**	**109.3**	**110.1**	**111.6**	**108.7**	**95.4**	**94.9**	**51.6**
Ireland	93.3	90.4	96.3	89.1	82.3	72.7	66.3	53.0	47.0	36.3
Italy	**97.6**	**104.7**	**119.1**	**124.9**	**124.2**	**124.0**	**121.6**	**114.3**	**113.1**	**64.9**
Luxembourg	4.1	4.8	6.1	5.7	5.9	6.6	6.7	7.1	6.4	–
Netherlands	76.6	77.3	81.2	77.9	79.1	77.2	72.1	65.7	61.1	21.2
Portugal	55.6	50.1	63.1	63.8	65.9	65.0	62.0	51.8	51.4	5.9
Spain	43.4	45.9	60.0	62.6	65.5	70.1	68.8	64.2	62.4	10.1
Sweden	48.8	61.6	75.8	79.0	77.6	76.7	76.6	69.9	64.3	19.0
UK	33.0	37.5	48.5	50.5	53.9	54.7	53.4	46.0	43.2	–
EU-15	**58.0**	**61.7**	**72.8**	**73.2**	**73.8**	**73.3**	**71.0**	**65.3**	**63.2**	**13.0**

Source: For 1993–7: European Commission (1998); for 1991–2 and 1998–9: European Commission (2013).
Note: The last column represents the greatest discrepancy between the Maastricht benchmark (60%) and a country's fiscal performance during this period.

pact was formally adopted in Amsterdam in June 1997 with a European Council resolution on its implementation. The SGP would take effect once the third stage of the EMU began on 1 January 1999.

The SGP required each member state to commit itself to running close to a balanced budget or a surplus in the medium term. It also introduced a surveillance process based on peer pressure. For this purpose, the EMU members would be required to present stability programs, while non-participants were obliged to submit convergence programs. The SGP would thus further strengthen the multilateral surveillance procedure. The stability and convergence programs would also serve as "early warnings" for the ECOFIN Council in case of significant deterioration in budgetary positions.

The SGP also fleshed out the definition of *excessive deficits*, as laid out by the Maastricht Treaty.[7] In addition to specifying the deficit limits, the SGP introduced two pillars: (1) multilateral budgetary surveillance (a preventive arm) to ensure better coordination of national budget plans and (2) a strengthened EDP (a corrective arm), which would also govern the third stage of the EMU and which would introduce sanctions if excessive deficits had not been corrected by an imposed deadline.

The strengthened EDP provided for quasi-automatic sanctions and exemptions under certain conditions. A member state could request "exemption" from the 3 per cent requirement if its deficit resulted from an unusual event that was outside its control and that had a major impact on the government's financial position, or if it resulted from a severe economic downturn.[8] In these cases, the deficit would be considered "exceptional and temporary," and the Council would normally decide not to impose sanctions. Should a member state fail to correct the excessive deficit within certain deadlines, however, sanctions could be applied. These sanctions included a non-interest-bearing deposit, which would be converted into a fine after two years if the deficit remained "excessive." The Amsterdam European Council of June 1997 adopted the resolutions on the SGP and on the new (wider) ERM. The Luxembourg European Council of December 1997 spelled out the principles and procedures for closer economic coordination during the third stage of the EMU.

Fiscal Consolidation under Euro-Austerity

Despite the unfavourable economic conditions of the early 1990s, member states still attempted to keep their budgetary policies in line with the multilateral surveillance procedure adopted by the ECOFIN Council of March 1990. One member state after another began to submit convergence programs to prove their commitment to the EMU. In fact, the

Figure 1. Fiscal Balances in 1993

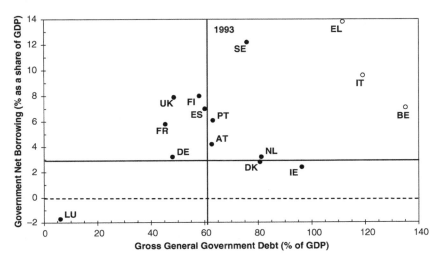

Council had already reviewed the convergence programs of Italy, Portugal, Ireland, and Germany, submitted as early as October 1991, even before the treaty was signed.

In all the convergence programs, the main emphasis was on achieving fiscal discipline. Efforts to meet all the other criteria remained of secondary importance. Such emphasis on the fiscal criteria was duly acknowledged in the Commission's first *Convergence Report* (European Commission 1993a, 53). Despite showing their countries' political commitment to the EMU, however, these convergence programs were overly optimistic about achieving fiscal targets in a timely manner. Although all governments attempted to push through austerity packages, the recession and rising interest rates derailed these ambitious plans (ibid., 59). By 1993, as figure 1 shows, *none* of the member states, save Luxembourg, was meeting both fiscal requirements: all countries except Ireland, Denmark, and Luxembourg had deficit ratios above the 3 per cent benchmark. This was a contrast from the year in which the treaty was negotiated, when only the "fiscally profligate" "Club Med" countries (Italy, Greece, Spain, and Portugal), along with Belgium, had deficits exceeding 3 per cent. During the same period, all member states were also experiencing rising debt ratios.

Although the majority of EU member states had debt-to-GDP ratios lower than the Maastricht benchmark of 60 per cent in 1991–2, only five of them (Germany, France, Luxembourg, Finland, and the United Kingdom) were within the limits by the end of the first stage of the EMU. In the "fiscally irresponsible" member states (Italy, Belgium, and Greece), the governments' total public debt exceeded their entire GDP. When seen from the early 1990s, therefore, fulfilling the fiscal criteria seemed virtually impossible for many of the EMU candidates. As a result, in its first *Convergence Report* (European Commission 1993a, 60), the Commission sounded a dire warning to all the member states. Since the fiscal criteria (unlike others) were defined in absolute terms (3 per cent and 60 per cent), there was no possibility of a flexible interpretation.

The warning was even more threatening for Italy, Greece, and Belgium. Observers writing at the time agreed that the austerity that these countries were facing was of epic proportion (Eichengreen 1993, 1349; Garrett 1994, 50–1; Fratianni and von Hagen 1992, 9; Gros and Thygesen 1992, 467–73; Crowley 1996, 47). Some influential scholars of the time warned that the austerity effort would be nothing less than "dangerous fiscal overkill" (Buiter, Corsetti, and Rubini 1993b, 72). These difficulties were so intensely felt that the Madrid European Council of December 1995 had to postpone the launch of the EMU to 1 January 1999.

Fiscal performance across the EU deteriorated even further as the second stage of the EMU began. Deficit and debt levels were recording all-time highs. Throughout the second stage, as tables 1 and 2 show, only two member states – Luxembourg and Ireland – had never been the subject of a Council decision on the existence of an excessive deficit. The other thirteen members had failed to meet the fiscal criteria at least once for one year or, in most cases, for longer periods. The last columns of tables 1 and 2 represent the discrepancy between the Maastricht benchmarks (3.0 per cent and 60 per cent) and the fiscal performance in the year in which fiscal balances deviated the most. For budget deficits, the size of the austerity effort required was the highest in Greece (10.8 percentage points), Sweden (9.2 percentage points), Italy (8.3 percentage points), and Belgium (5.1 percentage points). For public debt, the fiscally profligate three stood out with enormous deviations: Belgium (75.2 percentage points), Italy (64.9 percentage points), and Greece (51.6 percentage points).

By the mid-1990s, the best-laid plans for the surveillance mechanism and all the sanctions appeared to have failed. Shortly after, however, the economic upturn, lower inflation rates, and exchange rate stability during 1996 and 1997 helped member states make the planned transition to the third stage of the EMU. In May 1998, the ECOFIN Council decided that eleven candidates (Belgium, Germany, Spain, France, Ireland, Italy, Luxembourg, the Netherlands, Austria, Portugal, and Finland) fulfilled the convergence criteria and the other necessary conditions for adopting the single currency on 1 January 1999. The United Kingdom and Denmark had already opted out of the EMU's third stage at Maastricht, and Sweden had decided to remain outside. Greece, which did not qualify for membership during the 1998 assessment, did so in 2000.

The ensuing fiscal retrenchment across the EU during the 1990s was remarkable. All member states, except Greece, had brought their budget deficits below the Maastricht benchmarks by 1997. With the exception of Belgium, Greece, and Italy, all had curtailed their debt levels substantially. The Commission, in its *Convergence Report* (European Commission 1998, 89), declared that member states had realized a "genuine budgetary adjustment process"; their "genuine break with past behaviour," the Commission emphasized, constituted "a major step toward budgetary discipline."[9] In its 1998 assessment of the EMU candidates, the Council made its decision on EMU entry based largely on their fiscal performance since the other convergence criteria had been satisfied during (and in most cases even before) the Maastricht process. In its report "Statistics on Convergence Criteria," Eurostat (1998) disproportionately emphasized developments in the fiscal balances, among other criteria. In fact, 59 out of 84 pages of the report were devoted to budgetary conditions. This extra emphasis is but one reflection of how the deficit criterion counted much more than others.

The first day of January 1999 marked the effective starting date of the EMU – a project that had been on Europe's political agenda for decades. From this date forward, the EMU meant, first, in economic terms, increased convergence of policies, with reinforced multilateral surveillance and an obligation on the members of the eurozone to avoid excessive deficits; second, in monetary terms, a single monetary policy managed by the ESCB, which consisted of the ECB and the national central banks; and third, the introduction of the euro as the single currency of the participating countries. The euro had been launched as book money on 1 January 1999 in eleven member states. After Greece was admitted on 1 January 2001, actual euros went into circulation on 1 January 2002. The end of February 2002 saw the former national currencies lose their status as legal tender. Transition to the euro was now complete.

As perhaps the boldest and most far-reaching project in more than half a century of European integration, the EMU had a turbulent start. In the decade the Maastricht Treaty was signed, political commitment to the project was tested time and again. The treaty's ratification hurdles – the economic recession, the currency crisis that rocked the ERM, and mounting fiscal imbalances – were only the most notable ones.

Political commitment to the EMU continued to be tested once the third stage began, when the Commission played a more proactive role in coordinating economic policy. For example, in February 2001, it initiated an ECOFIN Council decision to issue a formal recommendation to Ireland within the framework of the BEPGs. Fiscal balances in Portugal, France, Italy, and Germany were also deteriorating, and in response, the Commission initiated the early warning mechanism of the SGP for these member states. In 2002, the budget deficits of Portugal, France, and Germany exceeded the prescribed limit. While Portugal corrected its excessive deficit, France and Germany failed to do so.

The next step according to SGP rules was for the ECOFIN Council to issue a resolution on these countries, warning that it would impose financial sanctions. But this did not occur. The SGP rules were effectively suspended at the ECOFIN Council of November 2003, when the French and German finance ministers managed to dominate the Council to vote down the Commission's proposal to instigate disciplinary procedures against them. The Commission took the Council decision to the European Court of Justice. In a ruling in July 2004, the Court found the Council decision illegal. The Court added, however, that the Council had the right *not* to follow the Commission's recommendations. After its de facto suspension, the SGP was revised to provide greater flexibility about the circumstances in which member states would be allowed to incur excessive deficits.

The EMU survived despite all odds, but further tests kept cropping up. The global financial crisis of 2008 led to a sovereign debt crisis in Europe. In response, some of the SGP rules were strengthened to bolster fiscal austerity. A new institutional structure, the European Stability Mechanism, became operational in 2012. In addition, the Treaty on Stability, Coordination and Governance in the Economic and Monetary Union (known as the Fiscal Compact), which was signed in March 2012, aimed to enshrine a binding commitment to fiscal discipline in national law, along with closer cooperation on economic policy. Despite weaknesses in the EMU's institutional infrastructure, the political commitment to it remains strong. It continues to effectively shape the macroeconomic policies of all member states of the eurozone.

Mechanisms of Euro-Austerity: The "Maastricht Effect"

What was the role of the EMU in the remarkable turnarounds in fiscal performance of the eurozone countries? In fact, some studies emphasized that there were no such real turnarounds in the first place and that EMU membership was possible only through creative accounting

(Baskaran 2009; Blavoukos and Pagoulatos 2008; Dafflon and Rossi 1999; Milesi-Ferretti and Moriyama 2006; Savage 2001).[10] A larger literature, however, found that there were significant reversals in fiscal performance and that it was the Maastricht rules that accounted for them. Scholars emphasized that some states resorted to accounting tricks and one-off measures to improve their fiscal balances under false pretences. They argued further, however, that tricks and one-off measures could not themselves account for the remarkable deficit reductions in most EMU candidates. The fudging might have eased the pressure on the candidates, but, they added, it could not explain the overall extraordinary turnaround in the member states' budgetary performance (Hallerberg 2004; Hallerberg, Strauch, and von Hagen 2009).

How did the EMU impose austerity on the member states? The literature identified two mechanisms through which the Maastricht fiscal criteria impacted fiscal policy and performance. The first mechanism was the more direct, political–legal "Maastricht effect" on governments in the run-up to the third stage of the EMU. Scholars who identified this effect demonstrated that the process of fiscal consolidation in the 1990s in Europe owed its success mainly to the member states' convergence efforts to meet the fiscal criteria (Rotte 1998; Rotte and Zimmerman 1998; Freitag and Sciarini 2001; Buti and Giudice 2002; Hughes Hallett and Lewis 2008). For example, in their econometric analysis of the probabilities of initiating fiscal consolidation, von Hagen, Hughes Hallett, and Strauch (2001) found that fiscal consolidation in the 1990s could not have been predicted by a model of budgetary behaviour estimated using past data. They concluded that the EDP and the convergence programs prepared within the multilateral surveillance procedure "constituted an important institutional change of the budget process for all EU member states" (ibid., 50). This finding, the authors showed, was corroborated by detailed case studies of fiscal consolidation as well as a survey conducted among leading journalists covering economic affairs in the EMU candidates.

Other scholars proposed a more nuanced Maastricht-effect argument. Hallerberg (2004, 8), for example, found that whereas the fiscal policy framework largely explained policy changes in Southern Europe (which had a history of fiscal profligacy), it had virtually no impact on the Scandinavian member states. Likewise, Busemeyer (2004) found that the Maastricht effect was stronger on smaller member states than larger ones because the former were more constrained by the rules and procedures of the Maastricht process than the latter. Still others argued that while the Maastricht effect was clearly identifiable for the 1990s until the decision for eurozone membership was taken, it vanished afterwards. This literature shows that Euro-austerity was most intense during the 1990s, when governments were politically committed to making it into the EMU.

The second mechanism through which the Maastricht fiscal criteria affected fiscal policy and performance was the more indirect Maastricht effect of financial markets on governments' fiscal policies. This literature suggested that if there were any financial market constraints on policy choices in the EMU candidates, they would be "strong but narrow": financial market participants take into consideration only a "few market signals" regarding government policy when making cross-border asset allocations (Mosley 2000, 766). These actors, these studies showed, watched "a limited number of well-defined areas – chiefly big deficit spending funded by big borrowing" (Weiss 2003, 12). The fiscal criteria (especially the budget deficit criterion) served as quantifiable benchmarks, and governments' compliance with these criteria could easily be monitored (Sbragia 2001, 83).

In this way, the Maastricht criteria provided "a common language for market actors" (Weiss 2003, 66; see also Sbragia 2001, 83). In particular, the deficit rule became a "key decision-making criterion." Investors took compliance with the criteria as a "signal for resolve" since they believed that if a government was firmly committed to joining the eurozone, it would find a way to meet the deficit criterion (Mosley 2004, 185). Conversely, if a government failed to meet the criterion, there was no reason to expect any commitment on its part to the EMU and, by implication, its future fiscal performance. The literature suggested that the Maastricht fiscal criteria took on a political dynamic of its own as well as acting as a political–legal constraint on fiscal policy choices. Thus, financial market actors perceived the fiscal targets as a measuring stick against which they tested governments' willingness to pursue EMU membership.

The EMU Candidates that Faced Extreme Euro-Austerity

As the previous sections showed, the EMU candidates that were furthest from meeting the fiscal criteria by the early 1990s were Belgium, Italy, and Greece. It was these member states, under the Euro-austerity hypothesis, that needed to take the greatest austerity measures in the Maastricht decade. Their deficit levels were some multiples of the Maastricht deficit criterion. Moreover, their public debt ratios, which exceeded their national incomes almost every year, were much higher than those of other EMU candidates.

These three countries not only violated the criteria at the onset of the transition period; they also systematically continued to do so until

1998, the year of final assessment for EMU eligibility. Accordingly, if there were to be *any* EMU-austerity pressure to meet the deficit criterion, it would be applied to them the most. Moreover, it was mainly these three countries (due to their massive fiscal imbalances) that were repeatedly named and shamed in ECOFIN Council meetings. For example, in fall 1994, the Council explicitly singled out these three member states as "deficit delinquents" (*Dow Jones International News*, 9 September 1994). In the scholarly literature, too, this notorious trio was consistently referred to as "laggards" (Dyson 2000, 114–17). They were also identified as the basket cases in which the pressure to comply with the Maastricht budgetary criteria would be the strongest of all the EMU candidates (e.g., Hallerberg 2004; Strauch, Hallerberg, and von Hagen 2004). Therefore, according to the Euro-austerity hypothesis, the scale and urgency of the need to slash budget deficits in these countries made them prime candidates for downsizing their welfare states.

3 From Euro-Austerity to Welfare State Retrenchment?

During the Damoclean decade in the run-up to the EMU, member states aspiring to join the eurozone underwent unprecedented and massive fiscal austerity. It is no wonder that many scholars, writing at a time when fiscal consolidation meant nothing less than slash-and-burn budgets, were seriously concerned about "fiscal overkill." This was a time when memories of frontal attacks on the welfare state of the 1980s were still fresh. Not surprisingly, governments' austerity efforts, which were intensifying in the 1990s, were read as their true intentions on retrenchment. This chapter explores the extent to which Euro-austerity resulted in the widely expected retrenchment scenario. This analysis is a first stab at testing the Euro-austerity hypothesis. Whether the EMU can be causally linked to welfare state retrenchment will be examined in the case studies on welfare state reform in chapters 4 to 6.

This chapter reviews the methodological discussion on conceptualizing and operationalizing the welfare state as a key variable. It presents the rationale for focusing on social expenditures in measuring welfare state change under Euro-austerity. It then explores patterns of continuity and change in the most frequently used indicator in comparative research: welfare effort. It traces government expenditures to contextualize the changes in social spending, and it shows the contractionary impact of Euro-austerity on domestic budgets. After revealing the unanticipated sources of this contraction – non-social expenditures – it emphasizes the surprising salience of welfare goals in budgets. It goes on to trace social spending in real terms per beneficiary and show the surprising stability in welfare standards. It then discusses the relatively limited change in the programmatic structure and individual programs of European welfare states, then verifies these findings by analysing an alternative measure: replacement rates in three key programs. As another conventional measure of the welfare state, replacement rates corroborate the findings based on social expenditures. After summarizing all these findings, the chapter concludes by focusing on expenditure and replacement rate trends in the three "basket cases" of Belgium, Greece, and Italy.

The "Dependent Variable Problem" in Comparative Welfare State Research

In comparative welfare state research, *welfare state* is defined as an institution committed to providing basic economic security for its citizens by protecting them from a number of risks, including those associated with old age, unemployment, sickness, and disability. It provides protection by instituting programs that typically include old age pensions, health care, and family, housing, disability, unemployment, and social assistance. Although there exists a consensus on "what [is] to be explained" (Amenta 2003, 114–16) in the comparative research, scholars disagree on the direction, magnitude, and nature of recent changes in the welfare state. The debate is even more polarized about the period of austerity. Even the "single most pressing question" of "how much change has there been" has no single, conclusive answer (Pierson 2011, 11).

Such disagreement has been an overarching theme in the "dependent variable problem" debate in comparative research (Green-Pedersen 2004; Clasen and Siegel 2007; Bolukbasi and Oektem 2018). This debate stems from the fact that different ways of conceptualization, operationalization, and measurement lead to different conclusions about welfare state change. This debate concluded that "no definition of the welfare state is a priori better or worse than others" (Green-Pedersen 2004, 6). It is the *research question* guiding a study, the literature concluded, that should determine the conceptual and operational definitions in that study.

This book relies on the conceptualization of the welfare state as a "policy definition," one that centres on the benefits provided by the state in different social policy areas (Green-Pedersen 2004, 6). This "narrow definition" has come to serve as the "conventional" conceptualization of most comparative studies in the welfare state research (Clasen and Siegel 2007, 6). It is also becoming the new standard in comparative public policy research (Steinebach, Knill, and Jordana 2019; Steinebach and Knill 2017). This chapter measures changes in policies as outputs by tracing the path of *welfare effort*, the percentage of GDP that a nation devotes to social expenditure. It also relies on other indicators constructed on the basis of social expenditures in the OECD's Social Expenditure Database (SOCX). SOCX categorizes social expenditures in terms of nine social policy programs: old age, survivors, incapacity-related benefits, health, family, active labour market programs, unemployment, housing, and other social policy areas.

Despite their wide use in recent studies, analyses based on social expenditures have often been criticized. Some argued that expenditures are atheoretical and, hence, "misleading" measures of the welfare state (Esping-Andersen 1990, 19). Others thought that spending levels are irrelevant for welfare state goals (and hence outcomes) such as combating inequality, poverty (Clayton and Pontusson 1998), "decommodification" (Esping-Andersen 1990), and unemployment (Korpi 2003; Korpi and Palme 2003). By adopting the policy definition of the welfare state, however, this book relies on measuring changes in the programmatic structure of the welfare state. It does not concern itself, therefore, with the intended outcomes such as inequality, poverty, unemployment, or decommodification. In this way, it conceptualizes the welfare state as the sum of all the benefits provided through different public programs in all social policy areas. Here, any change at the program level is registered in the relevant component of social spending. To triangulate these findings, the chapter analyses social rights as an alternative measure relying on different conceptual and operational definitions. This measure registers programmatic changes in the three core welfare state programs (unemployment insurance, sick pay insurance, and public pensions) and gauges their "generosity" (Scruggs, Jahn, and Kuitto 2013).

In the comparative literature, measures based on social expenditures, such as those used in this chapter, are widely seen as highly *valid* and *reliable* indicators of welfare state change. There are many reasons for this methodological choice. First, the classic works in the comparative literature relied on social expenditures to the extent that they are considered the "gold standard" in operationalizing the dependent variable (Amenta 2003, 118). They have been the "best proxy" for what comparativists have been interested in (Stephens 2010, 515). "If one had to pick a single metric," comments one comparativist, social expenditures "would almost surely be the one" (Levy 2010, 559). Moreover, when it comes to measuring welfare state change, social expenditures are still seen as "the most obvious and direct way" (Hay and Wincott 2012, 99). In addition to being a "convenient" and "common" "yardstick," another comparativist adds, social spending stands as an "entirely valid measure" of "welfare stateness" (Jensen 2011, 338, 328).

Second, we have come a long way since Esping-Andersen (1990) criticized using aggregate expenditure figures. We now have detailed, fine-grained, cross-national, and longitudinal data whose reliability has improved significantly. The comparative literature has been making use of this disaggregated data in addressing big, real-world questions (Castles 2004; Obinger and Wagschal 2010).

Third, and most important, the methodological decision to operationalize the welfare state in terms of social expenditures is directly informed by the research question. For any study on austerity and cost containment, the literature concludes, there are "good theoretical reasons" to operationalize the welfare state based on social expenditures (Vis 2013, 275; see also Castles 2004, 8; Levy 2010, 559; Siegel 2007, 49). As chapter 1 showed, most of us working on the impact of the EMU expected severe austerity to directly translate into across-the-board cuts in social expenditures. We all expected policymakers to see such cuts as *immediate aims in themselves*, as part and parcel of their push for cost containment to meet Maastricht's impending targets. Since welfare states are largely publicly financed and constitute the biggest-ticket item in public budgets across the EMU candidates, social spending can directly reflect retrenchment strategies. These are the reasons why social spending is *the* ideal conceptual and operational definition of the welfare state and, thus, the one that should be most directly affected by Euro-austerity.

Welfare Effort: Stable Total Public Social Spending[1]

This section explores the patterns of continuity and change in total public social spending, known as welfare effort, during the Maastricht decade. The decade begins with the year 1991, which was effectively the first year of the EMU's first stage. In terms of the business cycle, 1991, as the base year, was a "normal" period, with no extreme fluctuations. There was no particular economic downturn overinflating social expenditures, nor were there any particular booms underestimating welfare effort. Thus, 1991 serves as an unbiased, base year for longitudinal comparison.

European economies plunged into a deep recession shortly after the signing of the Maastricht Treaty in early 1992. The recession led to severe fiscal pressure, and, in 1993, average budget deficits jumped to a record high of 6.1 per cent of GDP across the EU. At the same time, the recession pushed up social expenditure as a result of increased demand for social protection at a time when GDP was expanding slowly, if at all.

As table 3 shows, over the Maastricht decade, average levels of social expenditure in the EU-15 remained virtually unchanged. With a minor

Table 3. Total Public Social Expenditures in the EU (% of GDP)

Country	1991	1992	1993	1994	1995	1996	1997	1998	1999	2000	2001	1991–2001
Austria	23.5	24.2	25.5	26.4	26.0	26.1	25.6	25.4	25.8	25.5	25.6	2.1
Belgium	**25.2**	**24.2**	**25.2**	**24.7**	**25.2**	**25.7**	**24.7**	**24.7**	**24.6**	**23.5**	**24.0**	**-1.2**
Denmark	22.4	22.6	23.8	25.4	25.5	24.9	24.2	23.7	24.5	23.8	24.3	1.8
Finland	28.2	32.2	32.3	31.6	28.9	28.7	26.6	24.5	23.8	22.6	22.5	-5.8
France	24.9	25.6	27.0	27.1	28.3	28.6	28.5	28.6	28.6	27.5	27.5	2.6
Germany	22.4	24.1	24.8	24.9	25.2	25.8	25.4	25.4	25.5	25.4	25.4	3.0
Greece	**15.2**	**15.4**	**16.2**	**16.3**	**16.6**	**17.0**	**16.9**	**17.5**	**18.0**	**18.4**	**19.7**	**4.5**
Ireland	17.7	18.5	18.5	18.1	17.5	16.6	15.5	14.6	13.7	12.6	13.4	-4.4
Italy	**21.0**	**21.7**	**22.0**	**21.9**	**21.0**	**21.4**	**22.2**	**22.3**	**22.8**	**22.6**	**22.9**	**1.9**
Luxembourg	18.4	18.8	19.1	18.9	19.7	19.8	20.1	20.0	19.4	18.6	19.9	1.4
Netherlands	23.9	24.4	24.5	23.1	22.3	21.2	20.5	19.9	19.1	18.4	18.5	-5.5
Portugal	13.1	13.8	15.1	15.2	16.0	16.6	16.4	16.8	17.2	18.5	19.0	5.9
Spain	19.9	21.1	22.3	21.3	20.7	20.6	20.0	19.9	19.8	19.5	19.1	-0.8
Sweden	29.1	32.7	34.2	32.9	30.6	30.1	28.9	28.6	28.0	26.8	26.9	-2.2
UK	16.5	18.1	18.7	18.4	18.3	18.1	17.6	17.9	17.7	17.7	18.5	2.0
EU-15	**21.4**	**22.5**	**23.3**	**23.1**	**22.8**	**22.8**	**22.2**	**22.0**	**21.9**	**21.4**	**21.8**	**0.4**
EMU-12	**21.1**	**22.0**	**22.7**	**22.5**	**22.3**	**22.4**	**21.9**	**21.6**	**21.5**	**21.1**	**21.5**	**0.4**

Source: OECD (2016a).

(0.4 percentage point) increase, social expenditure reached, on average, 21.8 per cent by 2001. After a decade of intense fiscal austerity, expenditure levels in the EMU-12 remained stable, reaching 21.5 per cent, after a marginal increase of 0.4 percentage points.

In terms of fluctuations in spending within the period, table 3 shows that social spending did not follow a uniform, secular trajectory. Expenditure ratios increased markedly until 1993, peaking at 23.3 per cent across the EU-15. In eleven of the fifteen member states (Austria, Denmark, Finland, France, Germany, Greece, Italy, Portugal, Spain, Sweden, and the United Kingdom), spending as a share of GDP increased by more than 1 percentage point between 1991 and 1993. From 1994 on (the year marking the end of the recession), social spending in the EU-15 continued to increase, yet at a rate lower than that of GDP. After the recession, spending as a proportion of GDP in the EMU-12 dropped, on average, by about 0.2 percentage points per year between 1994 and 2000. The declining trend was reversed in 2001, which saw a slight increase in expenditures again to 21.5 per cent of GDP.

Social spending patterns in the individual member states were rather diverse in this decade. Between 1991 and 2001, ten member states saw their social expenditures grow, with Portugal and Greece experiencing massive expansions (5.9 and 4.5 percentage points, respectively). In other member states, spending increases ranged from 3.0 percentage points (Germany) to 1.4 percentage points (Luxembourg). Some member states registered reductions in social spending: sizeable reductions were recorded in Finland, the Netherlands, and Ireland (5.8, 5.5, and 4.4 percentage points, respectively). Others experienced less marked reductions, ranging from 2.2 percentage points (Sweden) to 0.8 percentage points (Spain).

All these changes point to the diversity of social spending patterns across the EMU-12. Suffice it to note here that such a diverse pattern is simply *not* compatible with the Euro-austerity hypothesis, which would lead us to expect draconian welfare cuts across all the EMU candidates. Although the Maastricht decade saw some reductions in social spending, in the majority of the EU-15, social expenditures increased. While their end-of-period average social expenditure levels remained stable (in fact, recording mostly slightly higher levels than their base levels), a general movement towards the EU-15 mean emerged. It is also interesting to note that social spending did not behave differently across the EMU candidates (with an increase of 0.3 percentage points) or the EU-15 (with an increase of 0.4 percentage points).[2]

Euro-Austerity as Context: Declining Total
Public Outlays

To contextualize welfare effort within general patterns of public spending, table 4 presents data on a second measure for the Maastricht decade – total disbursements of general government as a share of national income. As foreshadowed by the story of the institutionalization of Euro-austerity, the 1990s represented a decade of "successful convergence" towards Maastricht's fiscal strictures. Convergence was achieved after a period of turbulent recessions in the early 1990s, when budgetary balances were furthest away from the fiscal criteria. These severe imbalances meant that governments had to undertake massive budget cuts. In the end, the Maastricht template forced a remarkable fiscal convergence across the EU-15. Intuitively, one would expect a move towards lower public spending across the EMU candidates as part and parcel of their fiscal consolidation strategies.

As the European economies were beginning to climb out of recession in 1993, all member states found themselves off course with respect to their budgetary plans. In fact, for some, as chapter 2 showed, the prospect of meeting the Maastricht fiscal targets seemed virtually nil. Yet, after 1993, the treaty, with its coercive fiscal instruments, triggered an unprecedented fiscal consolidation that, by the end of the decade, made the EMU possible. As a result, average total spending in the EU declined from 52.3 per cent of national income in 1993 to 45.4 per cent in 2001. This was a level much lower than that for 1991. This decade of austerity saw draconian cutbacks in total outlays in Finland (16.8 percentage points) and Sweden (15.6 percentage points) from their peak in 1993. Other countries that cut public outlays at a rate higher than the EU-15 average included Ireland (11.3 percentage points), Spain (10.4 percentage points), and the Netherlands (10.2 percentage points). Over the decade, however, cutbacks in total public outlays were highest in Ireland (11.1 percentage points), the Netherlands (9.3 percentage points), Finland (9.3 percentage points), Sweden (6.1 percentage points), Spain (6.1 percentage points), Italy (5.5 percentage points), and Belgium (4.7 percentage points). For the EMU candidates, these drastic cutbacks obviously reflected their governments' efforts to contain costs in the run-up to the EMU.

Most significantly, there is an unambiguous contrast between patterns of social spending (table 3) and those of total outlays during the Maastricht decade (table 4). Public outlays across the EU-15 decreased significantly in most member states, and the EU average fell from

Table 4. Total General Government Disbursements in the EU (% of GDP)

Country	1991	1992	1993	1994	1995	1996	1997	1998	1999	2000	2001	1991–2001
Austria	52.5	53.2	56.2	55.9	56.1	55.9	52.4	52.4	52.3	50.7	51.4	–1.0
Belgium	**53.9**	**54.1**	**55.3**	**52.9**	**52.4**	**52.7**	**51.2**	**50.6**	**50.1**	**49.0**	**49.2**	**–4.7**
Denmark	55.0	56.1	59.2	59.3	58.5	58.0	55.9	55.4	54.5	52.7	52.8	–2.1
Finland	56.6	61.7	64.1	62.5	61.1	59.5	56.1	52.4	51.0	48.0	47.3	–9.3
France	50.7	52.0	54.6	54.0	54.2	54.3	53.9	52.3	52.1	51.1	51.2	0.4
Germany	46.2	47.2	48.0	47.9	54.6	48.9	48.0	47.7	47.8	44.7	46.8	0.6
Greece	**46.7**	**49.4**	**52.0**	**49.9**	**51.0**	**49.2**	**47.8**	**47.8**	**47.6**	**49.9**	**47.8**	**1.1**
Ireland	43.6	44.0	43.8	43.2	40.9	39.1	36.5	34.6	33.9	30.9	32.5	–11.1
Italy	**53.0**	**54.5**	**55.4**	**52.7**	**51.7**	**51.7**	**49.6**	**48.3**	**47.4**	**45.4**	**47.5**	**–5.5**
Luxembourg	39.1	40.7	40.6	39.7	40.7	41.1	41.2	41.8	39.4	37.8	38.3	–0.9
Netherlands	52.4	53.3	53.3	51.2	53.7	46.9	45.3	44.1	43.5	41.8	43.1	–9.3
Portugal	42.4	43.5	45.1	43.5	42.6	43.1	42.4	42.7	42.6	42.6	44.1	1.8
Spain	44.5	45.4	48.9	46.7	44.3	43.0	41.6	41.0	39.9	39.1	38.5	–6.1
Sweden	59.1	66.9	68.6	66.1	63.6	61.5	59.2	57.3	56.7	53.6	53.0	–6.1
UK	37.7	39.7	39.7	39.2	39.2	37.3	36.3	36.0	36.0	35.9	37.2	–0.5
EU-15	**48.9**	**50.8**	**52.3**	**51.0**	**50.6**	**49.5**	**47.8**	**47.0**	**46.3**	**44.9**	**45.4**	**–3.5**
EMU-12	**48.5**	**49.9**	**51.4**	**50.0**	**49.9**	**48.8**	**47.2**	**46.3**	**45.6**	**44.3**	**44.8**	**–3.7**

Source: For all countries except Greece: OECD (2016a); for Greece: reference series to OECD (2004).

48.9 per cent to 45.4 per cent of GDP. Social expenditures (which remained remarkably stable at around 21.8 per cent of GDP) stood out against the draconian cutbacks in total spending.

Sources of Cutbacks: Non-social Spending

The reasons behind such a discrepancy between aggregate social spending and total outlays are worth exploring. If total outlays are declining while social expenditures remain stable, there has to be some decline in the components of total outlays that fall *outside* the social expenditure categories. To reveal the extent of the changes in the expenditure categories other than welfare effort, table 5 presents data on a third measure – nonsocial spending. This indicator is calculated by deducting total public social expenditures (reported in table 3) from total general government outlays (reported in table 4) and expressing them as a percentage of GDP.[3]

Although total government spending came under severe austerity pressure during the Maastricht decade, table 5 shows that it did not translate into outright retrenchment of social expenditures. In fact, if there were across-the-board retrenchment in any of the spending categories, it was non-social items. The decline in non-social expenditures was more pronounced in Italy (7.4 percentage points), Ireland (6.7 percentage points), Spain (5.2 percentage points), Portugal (4.1 percentage points), and Belgium (3.5 percentage points). According to the Maastricht rules, it did not matter which spending category savings came from; it was *total* spending that was subject to cost-containment strategies. Contrary to expectations, the overwhelming majority of the EMU candidates that faced severe fiscal austerity preferred to sacrifice *non-social* policy priorities.[4]

Social Expenditures in the Budget: The Continued Salience of Welfare Goals

Tables 3 and 4 show that while average social expenditures in the EU remained largely stable, total government expenditures declined markedly under Euro-austerity. These tables suggest that the political salience of welfare goals (even when facing intense austerity) must have only increased. To obtain a clearer and more detailed picture of the relative importance of spending on social purposes within the overall budgetary priorities, table 6 presents data on the share of social expenditures within total public outlays.

Table 6 shows that, during the Maastricht decade, most member state governments increased social expenditures within their budgets.

Table 5. Total Non-social Expenditures in the EU (% of GDP)

Country	1991	1992	1993	1994	1995	1996	1997	1998	1999	2000	2001	1991–2001
Austria	28.9	29.0	30.7	29.5	30.1	29.8	26.8	27.0	26.5	25.2	25.8	-3.1
Belgium	**28.7**	**29.9**	**30.0**	**28.2**	**27.2**	**26.9**	**26.5**	**25.8**	**25.5**	**25.5**	**25.2**	**-3.5**
Denmark	32.5	33.5	35.4	33.9	33.0	33.1	31.8	31.7	30.0	28.9	28.5	-4.0
Finland	28.4	29.6	31.9	31.0	32.2	30.8	29.5	27.8	27.1	25.4	24.9	-3.5
France	25.8	26.4	27.6	27.0	25.8	25.6	25.4	23.7	23.5	23.6	23.7	-2.2
Germany	23.8	23.1	23.2	23.0	29.4	23.1	22.6	22.4	22.3	19.3	21.4	-2.4
Greece	**26.6**	**29.2**	**30.8**	**28.8**	**29.7**	**27.1**	**25.7**	**25.0**	**24.0**	**26.3**	**23.4**	**-3.2**
Ireland	25.9	25.5	25.3	25.1	23.3	22.5	21.0	20.0	20.2	18.3	19.1	-6.7
Italy	**32.0**	**32.7**	**33.4**	**30.8**	**30.8**	**30.2**	**27.4**	**26.0**	**24.7**	**22.8**	**24.6**	**-7.4**
Luxembourg	20.7	22.0	21.5	20.8	21.0	21.3	21.1	21.9	20.0	19.2	18.4	-2.3
Netherlands	28.5	28.9	28.8	28.1	31.4	25.7	24.8	24.2	24.4	23.4	24.7	-3.8
Portugal	29.3	29.7	30.0	28.3	26.6	26.6	26.0	25.9	25.3	24.1	25.1	-4.1
Spain	24.6	24.3	26.6	25.4	23.6	22.4	21.6	21.1	20.2	19.6	19.4	-5.2
Sweden	30.0	34.2	34.4	33.2	33.0	31.4	30.3	28.7	28.7	26.9	26.2	-3.9
UK	21.2	21.6	21.0	20.8	20.8	19.2	18.8	18.1	18.2	18.2	18.7	-2.5
EU-15	**27.1**	**28.0**	**28.7**	**27.6**	**27.9**	**26.4**	**25.3**	**24.6**	**24.0**	**23.1**	**23.3**	**-3.9**
EMU-12	**26.9**	**27.5**	**28.3**	**27.2**	**27.6**	**26.0**	**24.9**	**24.2**	**23.6**	**22.7**	**23.0**	**-4.0**

Source: OECD (2016a, 2017a); table 4.

Table 6. Total Public Social Expenditures as Share of Total General Government Disbursements in the EU (% of GDP)

Country	1991	1992	1993	1994	1995	1996	1997	1998	1999	2000	2001	1991–2001
Austria	44.8	45.5	45.4	47.2	46.4	46.7	48.9	48.5	49.3	50.3	49.8	5.0
Belgium	**46.7**	**44.7**	**45.7**	**46.6**	**48.0**	**48.9**	**48.3**	**48.9**	**49.0**	**47.9**	**48.8**	**2.1**
Denmark	40.8	40.3	40.2	42.8	43.6	43.0	43.2	42.9	45.0	45.1	46.0	5.1
Finland	49.8	52.1	50.3	50.5	47.3	48.3	47.5	46.8	46.8	47.2	47.5	-2.4
France	49.1	49.3	49.5	50.1	52.3	52.7	52.8	54.7	54.9	53.8	53.8	4.7
Germany	48.5	51.1	51.6	52.0	46.2	52.8	52.9	53.2	53.3	56.8	54.3	5.8
Greece	**32.5**	**31.2**	**31.2**	**32.6**	**32.5**	**34.6**	**35.4**	**36.5**	**37.8**	**36.8**	**41.2**	**8.7**
Ireland	40.7	42.0	42.2	41.9	42.9	42.4	42.5	42.1	40.4	40.7	41.1	0.4
Italy	**39.6**	**39.9**	**39.7**	**41.5**	**40.5**	**41.5**	**44.7**	**46.2**	**48.0**	**49.8**	**48.2**	**8.5**
Luxembourg	47.2	46.1	47.0	47.6	48.4	48.2	48.7	47.7	49.3	49.2	52.0	4.8
Netherlands	45.7	45.8	45.9	45.2	41.6	45.2	45.2	45.2	43.8	44.1	42.8	-2.8
Portugal	30.9	31.7	33.5	35.0	37.6	38.5	38.7	39.4	40.5	43.4	43.1	12.1
Spain	44.8	46.4	45.7	45.7	46.7	47.9	48.1	48.5	49.5	49.8	49.7	4.9
Sweden	49.2	48.8	49.8	49.8	48.1	49.0	48.8	49.9	49.4	49.9	50.6	1.5
UK	43.8	45.6	47.2	47.0	46.8	48.5	48.3	49.7	49.3	49.3	49.8	5.9
EU-15	**43.6**	**44.0**	**44.3**	**45.0**	**44.6**	**45.9**	**46.3**	**46.7**	**47.1**	**47.6**	**47.9**	**4.3**
EMU-12	**43.4**	**43.8**	**44.0**	**44.7**	**44.2**	**45.6**	**46.1**	**46.5**	**46.9**	**47.5**	**47.7**	**4.3**

Source: For all countries except Greece: OECD (2016b); for Greece: reference series to OECD (2004); OECD (2017a).

The share of social spending in total outlays (*read*: the salience of welfare goals) increased dramatically in Portugal (by 12.1 percentage points), Greece (by 8.7 percentage points), and Italy (by 8.5 percentage points). Other countries that saw sizeable expansions were the United Kingdom (by 5.9 percentage points), Germany (by 5.8 percentage points), Denmark (by 5.1 percentage points), Austria (by 5.0 percentage points), Spain (by 4.9 percentage points), Luxembourg (by 4.8 percentage points), and France (by 4.7 percentage points). The relative salience of the welfare state declined only in the Netherlands (by 2.8 percentage points) and Finland (by 2.4 percentage points). Therefore, the table shows significant increases in the salience of the welfare state within government budgets across the EU – a finding squarely at odds with the Euro-austerity hypothesis.

Stability in Welfare Standards: Real Social Expenditure by Dependent

One caution that we need to keep in mind when using welfare effort is that it does not take into account changes in the size of dependent populations. An expansion of a dependent population, *ceteris paribus*, automatically increases overall demand for social provision, and this, in turn, can result in higher levels of social spending. Under such circumstances, the resulting increase in spending should not be interpreted as a sign of expanding entitlements. Even when social spending expands, an adverse demographic shift could cause spending per dependent to decline. Such a shift may stem from, for example, an increase in the aging population; this would affect the size of this core demographic category, which depends on social provision. An increase in the number of unemployed, too, would have the same effect (Clayton and Pontusson 1998; Hicks and Swank 1992; Huber, Ragin, and Stephens 1993; Huber and Stephens 2001; Swank 2002; Korpi and Palme 2003).

A second caution when using welfare effort concerns the impact of changing price levels on nominal expenditures. An expansion in nominal social spending in national currency may conceal reductions in real social spending if these changes are recorded in an inflationary environment. Therefore, we need to follow what happens in real social expenditures.

A third caution is the possibility that changes reported by welfare effort (which, as mentioned earlier, is social spending as a share of GDP) may not reflect actual changes in welfare standards due to the "denominator effect." For example, while welfare effort may seem to be reporting expansion, this does not necessarily stem from expanding social spending (the numerator); it may just as well be the outcome of shrinking GDP (the denominator) or a combination of the two. Therefore, to capture the actual changes in welfare standards in real terms, we need to isolate the impact of changes in the size of the population that depends on social provision, changes in the price level, and the denominator effect.

Following best practices in the literature (Huber and Stephens 2001, 204; Swank 2002, 81; Castles 2004, 26–8), table 7 presents social spending figures that are independent of (1) the price level (adjusted by the GDP deflator), (2) the denominator effect, and (3) the size of the beneficiary population (operationalized as the sum of the total number of unemployed persons and persons aged sixty-five and over). Thus, the table presents welfare standards in real terms in standardized form (where the reference base year is 1991 = 100).

Table 7 shows that average real welfare standards in the EU increased by more than one-quarter during the Maastricht decade. There were remarkable expansions. While real spending by dependent almost doubled in Ireland (which recorded a 90.8 per cent increase), the figure increased sizeably in Denmark (by 64.2 per cent), the United Kingdom (by 58.9 per cent), Portugal (by 54.8 per cent), and Luxembourg (by 37.5 per cent).

Three cases of expansion in the EMU candidates are noteworthy. First, the Irish case is particularly interesting because the phenomenal increase in real welfare standards (shown in table 7) is at odds with the declining trend in total public social expenditures (shown in table 3). Although the latter indicator reported a decline, this was largely due to the denominator effect (since Ireland experienced tremendously high growth rates during the 1990s) alongside a smaller dependent population – no wonder the "Celtic Tiger" of the 1990s *could* expand real welfare standards per dependent. Second, the Portuguese case is also striking, but for entirely different reasons. Welfare standards rose dramatically in that country (by 54.8 per cent) from the lowest level in the EU. But they rose *despite* a marked increase in the aging beneficiary population. Third, another member state that faced an adverse demographic shock was Greece. Although this EMU candidate saw the largest rise in the EU in the number of dependent persons (by more than 35 per cent between 1991 and 2000), table 7 reports that social provision standards increased (by 21.2 per cent). Although this increase is slightly lower than the EU average, it is still remarkable.

There is one exception to the general trend of rising welfare standards shown in table 7. Although Finland was among the highest spenders

Table 7. Standardized Real Social Expenditures by Dependent (unemployed and population aged 65+; adjusted by GDP deflator)

Country	1991	1992	1993	1994	1995	1996	1997	1998	1999	2000	2001
Austria	100.0	103.5	106.9	114.1	114.0	115.0	114.2	116.7	123.9	127.0	128.4
Belgium	**100.0**	**94.1**	**92.7**	**90.5**	**93.4**	**96.2**	**94.9**	**97.4**	**105.5**	**107.3**	**110.8**
Denmark	100.0	103.0	103.9	127.2	135.4	137.0	143.1	145.5	154.2	158.1	164.2
Finland	100.0	95.2	84.1	84.4	81.5	84.5	86.2	85.4	88.2	88.4	90.5
France	100.0	100.7	101.3	100.9	107.6	107.2	107.4	111.4	114.4	116.2	119.0
Germany	100.0	102.1	98.0	98.6	100.4	100.7	97.6	100.0	103.5	105.8	105.2
Greece	**100.0**	**96.7**	**97.0**	**96.0**	**97.6**	**99.2**	**101.1**	**103.2**	**105.0**	**110.9**	**121.2**
Ireland	100.0	105.8	105.8	111.0	124.3	127.4	136.6	146.6	159.8	167.3	190.8
Italy	**100.0**	**103.4**	**104.1**	**102.1**	**97.8**	**99.4**	**102.9**	**103.4**	**106.3**	**109.6**	**113.3**
Luxembourg	100.0	100.9	103.2	101.9	105.3	104.3	109.4	114.8	119.7	125.4	137.5
Netherlands	100.0	107.6	105.9	99.1	97.4	96.6	98.5	102.5	104.3	106.2	110.1
Portugal	100.0	105.1	106.8	102.8	109.7	115.2	118.3	129.5	137.4	151.7	154.8
Spain	100.0	100.6	95.7	89.5	89.2	90.4	91.4	96.1	103.0	108.1	115.8
Sweden	100.0	103.8	97.8	97.5	94.9	93.2	91.7	98.7	104.1	107.8	111.8
UK	100.0	107.0	112.2	116.3	121.1	123.9	127.0	136.7	140.1	146.0	158.9
EU-15	**100.0**	**102.0**	**101.0**	**102.1**	**104.6**	**106.0**	**108.0**	**112.5**	**118.0**	**122.4**	**128.8**
EMU-12	**100.0**	**101.3**	**100.1**	**99.2**	**101.5**	**103.0**	**104.9**	**108.9**	**114.3**	**118.7**	**124.8**

Source: OECD (2016b, 2017b); author's calculations.

in real terms, its welfare standards declined by 9.5 per cent during the Maastricht decade. Interestingly, they did so against a marked expansion in the beneficiary population (by about 20 per cent). Nevertheless, it seems that Finland embarked on a serious cost-containment strategy, and this is reflected in several indicators.

Limited Structural Transformation, Downsizing, and Upsizing: Program-Level Changes

The comparative welfare state literature also cautions us that aggregate spending may hide underlying changes in the structural, program-level characteristics of welfare states. Thus, it may be impossible to follow trends and counter-trends at the program level. This can be especially difficult if there are compensatory movements: where one program is expanding while another is being retrenched. In an extreme case where the changes are of equal size, this expansion and retrenchment may not be affecting the overall aggregate figures. For example, unemployment benefits may grow, but if family benefits are cut back by the same amount, aggregate social spending levels would remain unchanged.[5] Although Euro-austerity did not discriminate among programs as long as there were savings, it is still worthwhile to detect any changes in the structure of welfare states by drilling down into spending patterns in individual programs.

Table 8 provides information on two sets of summary measures, both of which gauge changes in the shape and direction of social spending over time. The first summary measure (column 2) reports on the degree of *structural transformation*: the degree of statistical association among the distributions of the nine spending components at base (1991) and end-of-period (2001) levels. Following Castles (2004, 33–4), I rely on the adjusted R^2 to measure the statistical association among these distributions. This statistic is especially suitable for detecting changes over time in the *relative* size of particular spending components (i.e., individual welfare state programs) in a given distribution of components (aggregate welfare state programs). The measure of structural transformation is calculated by multiplying the adjusted R^2 obtained by regressing the values of the social expenditure components for a given country in 2001 (measured as a percentage of GDP) on the values for that country in 1991, then subtracting this figure from 100.

The evidence reported by this first summary measure suggests that the degree of structural transformation (summarizing changes at the program level) in welfare states during the Maastricht decade is no more

Table 8. Degree of Structural Transformation, 1991–2001, and Indices of Upsizing and Downsizing

Structural transformation		Extent of downsizing (%)		Extent of upsizing (%)	
Country	9-component	9-component	8-component	9-component	8-component
Austria	0.86	2.7	2.3	4.8	4.5
Belgium*	**2.57**	**5.4**	**4.8**	**4.2**	**3.8**
Denmark	3.07	3.8	3.8	5.7	5.6
Finland	6.02	12.2	9.6	6.5	3.9
France	1.44	2.3	1.8	4.9	4.7
Germany	1.47	2.5	1.9	5.5	4.8
Greece	**1.62**	**1.4**	**1.3**	**5.9**	**5.9**
Ireland	24.96	6.8	4.9	2.5	2.2
Italy	**1.74**	**3.1**	**2.7**	**5.0**	**4.8**
Luxembourg	24.56	4.9	4.7	6.4	5.9
Netherlands	9.32	7.7	6.1	2.2	1.8
Portugal	5.11	1.3	1.0	7.2	6.6
Spain	10.74	6.7	3.8	5.9	4.7
Sweden	3.98	10.3	8.7	8.1	7.0
UK	2.41	2.5	1.7	4.5	4.2
EU-15	**6.66**	**4.9**	**3.9**	**5.3**	**4.7**
EMU-12	**7.53**	**4.8**	**3.7**	**5.1**	**4.5**

Source: OECD (2016b); author's calculations.
*Calculations were carried out using eight components rather than nine, and seven components rather than eight, due to missing data on the country's housing program.

than those modest changes indicated by the other measures of welfare state change analysed above. The low levels of the structural-change measure show that the relative size of the spending components (each representing a different social policy program) in the EU-15 remained virtually intact during the run-up to the EMU.

When the shares of different programs in 2001 are compared with those in 1991, we see that Austria (0.86), France (1.44), Germany (1.47), Greece (1.62), Italy (1.74), and Belgium (2.57) saw virtually no shift in spending priorities with respect to their social policy programs. Programmatic structures in the United Kingdom (2.41), Denmark (3.07), Sweden (3.98), Portugal (5.11), and Finland (6.02) changed only marginally. Thus, this measure shows that the programmatic structures of eight EMU candidates (along with three non-EMU candidates) remained rather stable under intense Euro-austerity conditions. Welfare states in Ireland (24.96), Luxembourg (24.56), Spain (10.74), and the Netherlands (9.32), however, seem to have undergone higher degrees of structural transformation. These findings show that only in these countries can we expect governments to realign their programmatic priorities.

One major shortcoming of this statistic is that if all components of social spending change proportionately, the structural transformation measure will not report any change. To control for this potential problem, table 8 provides a second set of summary measures: a downsizing index (columns 3 and 4) and an upsizing index (columns 5 and 6). These measures aim to capture independent, positive (upsizing) and negative (downsizing) changes in program components separately. Focusing on unidirectional changes, these indices reveal aggregated expansions (upsizing) and cutbacks (downsizing) in individual program spending.

The *downsizing index* measures the direction of change in a welfare state by reporting the sum of only annual decreases in expenditures in individual program components. To calculate this index, I take the difference between the sum of all annual negative changes (i.e., spending reductions) in expenditure components in 1991 and the sum of all those in 2001. I then divide the difference by the social expenditure share of GDP in 1991 and multiply it by 100. According to Castles (2002, 627), who constructed it, the downsizing index measures "the extent to which policymakers have been willing or have been forced to downsize existing welfare provision either to reduce overall aggregates of taxing and spending or to make way for other, higher priority, items of social spending." Since many expected that Euro-austerity would bring about an overall downsizing of European welfare states, this measure helps us further assess whether, and the extent to which, cost-containment pressure in the run-up to the EMU translated into retrenchment of individual programs.

The *upsizing index* is constructed by adding only annual incremental increases in expenditures on individual program components.[6] To do so, I take the difference between the sum of all annual positive changes (i.e., spending increases) in expenditure components in 1991 and the sum of all those in 2001. I then divide this difference by the social expenditure share of GDP in 1991 and multiply it by 100. Once again, the rationale for constructing both these indices is to go beyond the Euro-austerity hypothesis (which expects declining *overall* spending levels) to reveal possible changes in policy priorities.

The downsizing and upsizing indices reported in table 8 are constructed from two sets of program components following Castles (2002, 621; 2004, 32). First, the OECD's all-encompassing, nine-component measure is constructed on the basis of all the expenditures under the nine social policy programs (old age, survivor, incapacity-related benefits, health, family, active labour market programs, unemployment, housing, and spending on other social policy areas) (columns 3 and 4). Second, the eight-component measure is based on the same spending items included in the nine-component measure except for unemployment insurance programs (columns 4 and 6). It isolates the impact of changes in unemployment levels (and hence the demand for social provision) on welfare effort trajectories.[7] By excluding this item from aggregate expenditures, we can analyse the changes in social spending *net* of the cyclical effect of unemployment.[8]

The indices based on the nine social spending components (columns 3 and 5) show that, in the EU-15, the downsizing trends in some individual programs (4.9 per cent) were accompanied by slightly stronger counter-trends of upsizing in other programs (5.3 per cent). In fact, when the extent of programmatic change in individual programs in the EMU-12 is analysed, the upsizing index again shows, on average, a higher-percentage figure (5.1 per cent) than the downsizing index (4.8 per cent). Although the Euro-austerity hypothesis does not discriminate among changes in program-level spending, the fact that there was even more upsizing than downsizing taking place at the program level during the Maastricht decade further weakens its validity.

When individual member states are examined, the nine-component indices show some significant downsizing trends in some of the EMU-12 countries. The cutbacks in program components in Finland (12.2 per cent), Sweden (10.3 per cent), the Netherlands (7.7 per cent), Ireland (6.8 per cent), and Spain (6.7 per cent) are noteworthy. At the same time, however, there are some noteworthy trends in upsizing; these include Sweden (8.1 per cent), Portugal (7.2 per cent), Finland (6.5 per cent), Luxembourg (6.4 per cent), Spain (5.9 per cent), and Greece (5.9 per cent).

The eight-component downsizing index (column 4) indicates that downsizing trends in the eight program areas in almost all EU-15 members were less powerful than the nine-program index (column 3). Therefore, a large proportion of the downsizing was due to cutbacks in unemployment insurance spending. When we isolate this cyclical component, the eight-component index shows lower downsizing for all countries (except Denmark, where it remained the same) compared with that reported in the nine-component downsizing index. In particular, there are some discrepancies between the nine- and eight-component indices in Finland (12.2 and 9.6 per cent), Spain (6.7 and 3.8 per cent), Ireland (6.8 and 4.9 per cent), Sweden (10.3 and 8.7 per cent), and the Netherlands (7.7 and 6.1 per cent). These discrepancies suggest that the actual extent of downsizing (net of cyclical effects) in the eight-component downsizing index is lower than in the nine-component downsizing index. With respect to upsizing (compare columns 5 and 6), the eight-component upsizing index reports almost invariably greater upsizing than the nine-component upsizing index.

In terms of downsizing (columns 3 and 4), when the difference between the eight-component and nine-component indices is analysed, the former (3.9 per cent for the EU-15 and 3.7 per cent for the EMU-12) reports smaller downsizing in both the EU-15 and the EMU-12 than the latter (4.9 per cent for the EU-15 and 4.8 per cent for the EMU-12). In terms of upsizing (columns 5 and 6), the nine-component index (5.3 per cent for the EU-15 and 5.1 per cent for EMU-12) reports larger upsizing than the eight-component index (4.7 per cent for the EU-15 and 4.5 per cent for the EMU-12). When the EU-15 members and the EMU candidates are compared on the basis of the eight-component measures, EU-15 members score higher than the EMU-12 on both the downsizing (3.9 per cent in the EU-15 compared with 3.7 per cent in the EMU-12) and the upsizing indices (4.7 per cent in the EU-15 compared to 4.5 per cent in the EMU-12).

In conclusion, this section summarized information that we obtained from the indices of upsizing and downsizing presented in table 8. These indices indicate the extent to which existing individual social programs were cut or expanded. It is clear that, in most cases, cutbacks in some programs were outweighed by increases in spending in others. Such coexistence of trends (downsizing) and counter-trends (upsizing) suggests that, during the Maastricht decade, there were some compensatory movements among social expenditure components. All in all, however, whatever retrenchment there was of this kind at the individual program level did not result in massive cutbacks across programs. Some unidirectional changes may have taken place at the program level, but the extent of those changes remained, in most cases, marginal.

Social Rights: Stability in Entitlements

In the past decades, comparative welfare state researchers criticized the overwhelming reliance on conceptualizations of welfare stateness in terms of "spending-only" measures. The main line of criticism against using social expenditures was that this measure failed to measure welfare state generosity *directly*. In response, critics developed alternative conceptualizations and operationalization based on social rights. Based on this new way of looking at the welfare state, researchers have constructed alternative data sets on the institutional features of welfare state programs. Walter Korpi and Gosta Esping-Andersen were pioneers in developing a data set under the Social Citizenship

Indicators Program (SCIP). SCIP focuses on the institutional structures of five main social insurance programs: old age, illness, unemployment, work accidents, and family change. Since this data set was not publicly available, Lyle Scruggs developed the Comparative Welfare Entitlements Dataset (CWED) to replicate SCIP. CWED covers the three core welfare state programs: unemployment insurance, sick pay insurance, and public pensions.

The most commonly analysed institutional feature of the core programs in both these data sets is replacement rates. Table 9 presents replacement rates in the three core programs, reported in the most recent version of CWED, CWED 2. I rely on CWED 2 (instead of SCIP) for two reasons. First, while it covers fourteen of the EU-15 member states (excluding Luxembourg), SCIP covers only eleven member states. Second, SCIP aims to capture program-level changes and the resultant changes in entitlements in these programs "in isolation from all other social rights." In contrast, CWED 2 takes a more holistic approach to capturing changes by focusing on the total change in *all* cash-transfer programs as well as changes in the three core programs (Danforth and Stephens 2013, 1286; Ferrarini et al. 2013, 1254–5; Scruggs 2013, 1269).

Since this study focuses on the impact of Euro-austerity on the European welfare states, it relies on data obtained from CWED 2 that measure how a welfare state responds overall to the materialization of risks. Moreover, CWED 2 is designed to complement expenditure data. In fact, the codebook defines the purpose of CWED 2 as providing "an essential complement to program spending data that is available from international sources like the OECD's Social Expenditure Database" (Scruggs, Jahn, and Kuitto 2013, 2). The figures in CWED 2 are the net benefits that an "average production worker" would receive in case of unemployment, sickness, and retirement, all of which are measured as a percentage of the average wage of a production worker (9).

Table 9 shows that when the base level (1991) and end-of-period level (2001) of replacement rates are compared, average levels of entitlements across Europe remained more or less stable for all core programs. In particular, while there were minor cuts in entitlements in unemployment and sick pay insurance programs, entitlements in standard public pensions remained unchanged. Strikingly, even under intense Euro-austerity, entitlements in the three programs remained much more stable in the EMU candidates than in the non-EMU candidates. If we look at these programs at the aggregate level (overall changes in entitlements), the averages mask some significant changes: while nine member states (Spain, Sweden, Ireland, Denmark, France, Finland, Germany, the United Kingdom, and Belgium) underwent cutbacks of

Table 9. Replacement Rates in Unemployment, Sickness, and Pensions Programs, 1991–2001

Country	Unemployment			Sickness			Standard pensions		
	1991	2001	Change	1991	2001	Change	1991	2001	Change
Austria	65	60	–5	84	89	5	73	77	3
Belgium	**62**	**59**	**–3**	**89**	**86**	**–2**	**65**	**67**	**2**
Denmark	70	63	–7	60	58	–2	60	58	–2
Finland	67	63	–4	85	75	–10	65	69	5
France	72	69	–3	64	62	–1	64	57	–7
Germany	66	66	–1	93	90	–3	70	64	–5
Greece	**55**	**56**	**1**	**64**	**65**	**1**	**n/a**	**n/a**	**n/a**
Ireland	47	41	–6	47	41	–6	50	45	–5
Italy	**24**	**45**	**21**	**77**	**79**	**1**	**73**	**88**	**14**
Netherlands	78	80	2	78	80	2	53	55	3
Portugal	88	88	0	74	74	0	n/a	n/a	n/a
Spain	92	73	–20	78	77	–1	106	95	–11
Sweden	88	70	–19	86	82	–4	74	70	–4
UK	28	28	–1	31	24	–6	53	55	2
EU-14	**64**	**61**	**–3**	**72**	**70**	**–2**	**58**	**57**	**0**
EMU-12	**65**	**63**	**–2**	**74**	**73**	**–1**	**57**	**56**	**0**

Source: Scruggs, Jahn, and Kuitto (2017).
Notes: The table presents mean values for single (100%) and family (100% or 0%) household types. Luxembourg is excluded since CWED 2 does not cover this country. Index values for standard pensions for Greece and Portugal are not available.

varying degrees, five member states (Italy, Netherlands, Greece, Austria, and Portugal) saw expansions.

Euro-Austerity Hypothesis and Europe's Welfare States

Inspired by Castles (2004, 45), our measuring rod for the "half-empty/half-full question" (Pierson 1994, 5) in this study should be this: for the austerity hypothesis to have any validity, above and beyond the fact that only a few EMU candidates seem to have undergone some retrenchment suggested by some indicator, it should indicate a *general trend* towards sizeable cutbacks under severe Euro-austerity (Castles 2004, 45). This chapter, however, showed that even when an indicator points to some retrenchment in a country, some alternative measure suggests either an absence of cutbacks or some form of expansion. For example, in the case of the Netherlands, table 3 shows that social spending as a share of national income *declined substantially* during the 1990s, by 5.5 percentage points – one of the largest declines registered among all EMU candidates for this indicator. Such decline is also corroborated by the declining share of Dutch social spending within total public outlays (2.8 percentage points, shown in table 6). In contrast with these figures, however, table 7 shows that the Netherlands, in fact, saw an *expansion* (10.1 per cent) in terms of real spending per dependent during the same period.

Another striking example of coexisting contradictory trends is Ireland. Table 3 shows that social spending as a share of national income *declined* markedly, by 4.4 percentage points. However, table 7 reports that real spending per dependent almost *doubled* during the same period (90.8 per cent). This discrepancy could be the result of the phenomenal growth of the Irish economy during the 1990s, resulting in larger denominators in the spending share when expenditure figures are measured against GDP. Therefore, taken together, tables 3 and 7 show contradictory trends: while Ireland's spending levels declined relative to national income, social standards increased remarkably under the adverse circumstances of Euro-austerity.

Among the EMU candidates, Finland stands out as an exception: the largest *decline* in social expenditures as a share of GDP (table 3) coexisted with a *declining* salience of social goals in the budget (table 6) and a noticeable *reduction* in welfare standards (table 7). However, attributing these trends to Euro-austerity would be, in a way, a non sequitur. Finland (along with Sweden) was hit by a series of endogenous and exogenous shocks during the early 1990s, which led to a severe recession.[9] The recession pushed up social expenditure ratios from 23.3 per cent in 1990 to 28.2 per cent in 1991 and 32.3 per cent in 1993 (about 31 per cent in a matter of just three years) (OECD 2016b). Such a steep rise overinflated the base level for all comparisons. Moreover, because the increases in social spending ratios were taking place against a backdrop of a severe recession, they made the ratios look doubly overinflated in 1991 due to abrupt and severe reductions in the denominator. Finally, Finland joined the EU only in 1995, by which time the fiscal imbalances that had mounted during the recession had been almost corrected. Therefore, any retrenchment incorporated into the Finnish budget could not have resulted from Euro-austerity. All these factors strongly suggest that welfare state trajectories in Finland were largely independent of the Maastricht timetable.

This chapter has shown that, for almost all countries, evidence points to an *absence* of systematic, radical cutbacks at either the aggregate or the individual program level. The evidence *against* the Euro-austerity hypothesis is just too overwhelming to ignore. Additionally, across-the-board expansions in social spending items relative to government outlays attest to the still overwhelming (and, in fact, increasing) importance of social goals, even under Euro-austerity conditions. In the face of the severest cost-containment pressure, European governments managed to maintain their social provision standards. In conclusion, the Maastricht decade was characterized much *less* by welfare state retrenchment than by stability.

Additionally, the data show that there is no evidence that the EMU candidates behaved any differently than the non-EMU candidates. Table 3 shows the high degree of stability, in both the EMU candidates and the EU-15 members, with respect to patterns of total public social expenditures as a percentage of GDP. Total public outlays, non-social expenditures, and total public social spending as a share of total outlays (tables 4, 5, and 6) show no systematic difference in trends among the EMU and non-EMU countries. In table 8, the second column points to only a marginal difference between the EMU candidates and the EU-15 in terms of structural transformation. The nine- and eight-component downsizing indices (columns 3 and 4) indicate slightly lower levels of downsizing in the EMU candidates than in the non-EMU candidates. Both upsizing indices (columns 5 and 6), however, report that program-level expansions in the EMU candidates were, again, marginally higher than those in the non-EMU candidates. The clear conclusion is that Euro-austerity did not lead to any more retrenchment in the EMU candidates than in other countries that opted out of or chose to remain outside the eurozone.

Euro-Austerity and Welfare State Change in "Crucial Cases"

As the previous chapter showed, Greece, Italy, and Belgium were the cases that were *furthest* from meeting the EMU criteria on public balances – the criteria that de facto determined whether an EMU candidate would enter the final stage of the EMU. Accordingly, one would expect to find that they experienced the most intense fiscal pressure – they had been in serious violation of the criteria, not only at the outset of the transition period but also throughout the Maastricht decade. The Euro-austerity hypothesis requires that, had *any* EMU-induced pressure been placed on the welfare states, they would have been borne by these three candidates. If, on the other hand, we do not observe the predicted patterns of Euro-austerity-driven welfare state retrenchment in these cases, we should not look for them elsewhere.

Let us drill down into the figures for Greece, Italy, and Belgium, starting with table 3. While in Belgium, total social spending ratios decreased marginally, by 1.2 percentage points, Greece's spending jumped by about 30 per cent, reaching 19.7 per cent. Italy's spending ratios saw an increase of 1.9 percentage points. These changes were taking place against a backdrop of a general decline in the share of total public outlays in national income, as shown in table 4. While the total outlays in Belgium and Italy declined by a hefty 4.7 percentage points and 5.5 percentage points, respectively, those in Greece saw a modest expansion of 1.1 percentage points.

With respect to the sources of cutbacks in public spending, table 5 clearly shows that non-social expenditure items bore the major brunt of Euro-austerity: while Italian non-social expenditure figures declined drastically (by 7.4 percentage points), the cutbacks in Belgian and Greek non-social spending items (3.5 and 3.2 percentage points, respectively) remained slightly less than the average for the EMU candidates (4.0 percentage points). Underlying these processes were remarkable increases in the share of social spending within total public outlays in these three cases, implying a striking shift away from non-social towards social priorities. Table 6 shows that Greece and Italy recorded the highest levels of increases in total social spending as a share of total outlays, with increases of 8.7 and 8.5 percentage points, respectively – much higher than the EMU average (4.3 percentage points). With an expansion of 2.1 percentage points, Belgium, too, recorded increases during this period.

When we analyse welfare standards in real terms, we observe that real social spending per dependent in Greece, Italy, and Belgium increased throughout the 1990s. They did so at a time when these governments were not only facing immense fiscal difficulties but also experiencing adverse demographic and labour market developments. This pressure inflated total real spending due to growing dependency rates and increasing unemployment. However, when real spending patterns per dependent are analysed (controlling for size of dependent population), the rise can be explained only by increasing levels of generosity.

The data on real social spending per dependent presented in table 7 provide further evidence for this generosity. Although social provision standards did not increase as dramatically as in other EMU candidates, real social spending per dependent in Greece expanded significantly (by 21.2 per cent) despite the fact that the country had witnessed the greatest rise in the number of dependent persons (35.6 per cent for 2000) in the EU during the Maastricht decade.[10] (OECD 2017b).

Similarly, In Italy, the 13.3 per cent increase in real social spending by dependent was possible against a 12.8 per cent increase in the dependent population.[11] Belgium saw an increase in real welfare standards by 10.8 per cent under Euro-austerity. This was possible despite the dependent population expanding by 14.5 per cent during the 1990s.[12] Under such dire circumstances, merely maintaining welfare standards even in real terms would have amounted to squaring the welfare circle. However, the increasing levels of real social spending per dependent (albeit at a lower rate than most EU members and EMU candidates) attest to the lack of evidence to support the Euro-austerity hypothesis.

All these findings are further supported by the data on the changes in the structure of welfare states provided in table 8. Column 2 reports the degree of change in spending levels of nine welfare programs during the 1990s. This measure of structural transformation shows that the Belgian (2.57 per cent), Greek (1.62 per cent), and Italian (1.74 per cent) welfare states underwent either no, or very limited, structural transformation with respect to their spending priorities under Euro-austerity. Moreover, these figures are much lower than those recorded for most of the EMU candidates.

When the extent of unidirectional changes are analysed for the same period, columns 3 to 6 of table 8 report the following: in Greece, the extent of upsizing in all nine components (5.9 per cent) exceeds that of downsizing in all nine components (1.4 per cent) by a significant margin. Moreover, when unemployment spending is removed to isolate the impact of the cycle on the welfare programs, the picture does not change. Greece is also a striking case among the eurozone countries: both upsizing indices are slightly higher, and both downsizing indices are markedly lower, than the averages for the EMU-12.

Likewise, in Italy, both the nine-component (5.0 per cent) and the eight-component (4.8 per cent) upsizing indices exceed the nine-component

(3.1 per cent) and eight-component (2.7 per cent) downsizing indices. These figures suggest that downsizing trends were offset by upsizing trends in individual programs when the early 1990s and early 2000s are compared. In Belgium, however, the extent of downsizing in all nine components (5.4 per cent) was slightly higher than the upsizing of all nine components (4.2 per cent). When the impact of cyclical unemployment spending is taken out, the eight-component upsizing index (3.8 per cent) reports a slightly lower level than the downsizing index (4.8). Taken together, these indices suggest that the Belgian welfare state changed only marginally in its structure with respect to its spending priorities during the 1990s.

Finally, when alternative indicators of welfare state generosity are analysed, table 9 demonstrates that, despite acute Euro-austerity, Italy experienced a phenomenal expansion in entitlements in unemployment insurance and standard pensions programs compared with the rest of the EU. Although the data for standard pension replacement rates are not available, Greece saw some marginal expansions in unemployment insurance and sickness benefits. Finally, Belgium recorded a minor expansion in standard pensions along with some cutbacks in unemployment insurance and sickness programs.

This discussion suggests, therefore, that with respect to all the measures constructed and analysed in this chapter, the Belgian, Greek, and Italian welfare states did not follow the route mapped out suggested by the Euro-austerity hypothesis. The previous chapter showed that these three cases had undergone serious changes in fiscal behaviour that made it possible for them to pass the Maastricht test. In none of these cases, however, did the scale and urgency of the need to slash deficit and public debt translate into outright retrenchment.

4 Euro-Austerity and the Political Economy of Reform in Belgium

With the largest stock of public debt in the EU in the 1990s, Belgium was one of three EMU candidates destined to swallow the bitter pill. Every government that came to power was under intense structural pressure to put the fiscal house in order, and everyone expected that it would play the EMU card to push through austerity. For many, austerity would zero in on the social security system – the biggest-ticket item in government expenditures. Hence, Belgium stands out as a crucial case for evaluating the Euro-austerity hypothesis.

Although Belgium was a basket case in this respect, strong commitment and vigorous effort resulted in its timely entry to the EMU, along with ten other member states, on 1 January 1999. In this chapter, I show how economic and monetary integration led to significant changes in its fiscal policy and politics. I argue, however, that integration did not have the result that the Euro-austerity hypothesis expected. While the Belgian welfare state underwent some changes, these were largely confined to parametric adjustments.

I develop my argument in two steps. First, I show how Belgium qualified for EMU membership despite exceptionally large fiscal imbalances. I discuss the budgetary strategies adopted by successive governments on the road to the EMU and trace the institutional changes in fiscal policy and politics that resulted in increased government capacity to rein in runaway public expenditures. By analysing episodes of fiscal consolidation, I show how Euro-austerity was both a fundamental constraint on domestic budgets and a *vincolo esterno* for reforming the welfare state for policymakers who desperately wished to join the euro.

Second, I present each reform attempt, especially in the pensions program, which was perhaps *the* political hot potato of the Maastricht decade. I lay out the ambitious goals of policymakers at each round of reform, then show the large disparities between the original reform proposals and the reform outcomes. In tracing each reform initiative, I explain how the political capacity of successive governments was effectively constrained by societal groups opposing welfare reform. In the end, the unions and their allies effectively blocked politicians' reform attempts. While Belgian governments were successful in pushing through fiscal austerity to attain EMU membership, they largely failed to cut back social expenditures and restructure welfare programs despite the structural constraints stemming from, and the discursive opportunities provided by, the EMU.

The chapter is structured as follows. It begins by reviewing earlier attempts at fiscal and welfare state reform under the Martens governments of the late 1980s and early 1990s. It then traces the formation of the first Dehaene government in 1991 and its efforts to put Belgium on track for joining the euro. It emphasizes the preparation of the first Belgian convergence program and the increasing prominence of the High Council of Finance in preparing the budget. Belgian governments, as this section shows, often resorted to raising new taxes and privatization receipts to meet the convergence program targets. This section also traces the failure of the government's attempt to launch a pact with its social partners and the subsequent introduction of the Global Plan. It shows how the long-awaited pension reform had to be aborted in the face of strong opposition, saving the social security system from the axe. This section concludes by reviewing the political parties' election manifestos. It highlights the consensus reached by all the political parties on meeting the EMU targets and on the necessity for social security reform to achieve this overarching goal.

The next section presents the social security reform attempt by Dehaene's second government to meet the EMU budgetary targets. To qualify for the euro, the government obtained extraordinary powers from Parliament. While it met the EMU goals by exercising these powers, it failed to push through a large-scale social security reform. Strong opposition meant that the reform led to only modest parametric changes, thereby leaving the social security system almost intact. When the government intended to reform public-sector pensions and health care programs in a subsequent move, it faced popular resistance once again. Although social security reforms failed to increase budgetary savings, the government found a way to meet the Maastricht targets with its 1997–8 budgets. The chapter goes on to discuss the process of Belgium's eventual admission into the EMU despite its enormous public debt – a source of constant friction between the Belgians and the Germans. It concludes by providing an overview of the political economy of welfare state reform in Belgium and its implications for the Euro-austerity hypothesis.

A "Pace-Setter" with "No Hope" of Joining the EMU

Belgium had always been a "consistent *demandeur*" in monetary affairs, trying to keep the EMU project at the top of Europe's political agenda even in turbulent times (Maes and Verdun 2005, 333–4). At the time of the Maastricht Treaty negotiations, Belgium "always want[ed] to move ahead faster with European integration than most other member states" (Economist Intelligence Unit, 3rd Quarter 1991). Unlike the Greek and Italian delegates, the Belgians had agreed with the Germans about introducing stringent fiscal criteria. Behind the Belgian government's preferences, the literature shows, was the expectation that the government would be able to use the EMU as a pretext for implementing measures to correct the country's severe fiscal imbalances (Maes and Verdun 2005). Finance Minister Philippe Maystadt's appeal to the EMU at the negotiations foreshadowed the (future) use of the euro as a *vincolo esterno*: "Belgium will have to get tighter control over its vast budget deficit if it wants to join the European Community's economic and monetary union when it starts in 1996"; "if we do not apply more strict budget standards, Belgium may not be ready (to join the EMU) by 1996" (*Reuters News*, 31 October 1991).

However, the country's economic track record, especially with respect to its fiscal balances, did not match its bold ambitions. Although Belgian and EU authorities did not problematize Belgium's performance on price stability, interest rates, or exchange rates, they clearly diverged from the Maastricht criteria. In fact, its public imbalances were notoriously off the Maastricht benchmarks (EMI 1996). Thus, in the words of a keen observer, "The most difficult economic issue" for timely entry to the EMU was compliance with the "targets on the public sector deficit" (Fitzmaurice 1996, 77). Even when the treaty was signed and the macroeconomic fundamentals for almost all EU members were in line, Belgium's deficit ratio was more than double the Maastricht benchmark, and its public debt level exceeded the levels of all other advanced industrialized nations. Its public imbalances were comparable only with those fiscally profligate basket cases, Greece and Italy. In its 1991 survey of the Belgian economy, published soon after the treaty was signed, the OECD (1991) identified government finances as the "key problem" facing the Belgian economy. These exceptional imbalances persisted for years, leading the Economist Intelligence Unit (1995, 5), profiling Italy, to conclude, "There can be no hope whatsoever of Belgium's meeting the Maastricht Treaty's convergence criteria."

Scholars shared this sad opinion. During the early 1990s, Belgium, along with Italy and Greece, was singled out as an EMU candidate facing "acute problems" on the fiscal front (Buiter, Corsetti, and Rubini 1993b, 64), and any fiscal strategy aimed at EMU entry would lead to "the economics of the lunatic asylum." Getting even halfway to the Maastricht targets (and even later than planned), the literature concurred, would involve "fiscal overkill" (71–2). Reminding us that Belgium "had never managed to have less than 6% of budget deficit," Schelkle and Barta (2008, 3) argued that "no other state in Western Europe [was] in [as] desperate a position as Belgium" (see also Jones 1995, 168).

Belgians were repeatedly named and shamed by their EU neighbours for their fiscal performance. In a communication to the Council in July 1991, the European Commission noted that several member states were required to change their policies significantly. Its assessment of gaps in convergence gave Belgium the third-worst ratings, after Greece and Italy: one grey rating for the budget deficit (partially unsatisfactory situation), one grey for external accounts (partially unsatisfactory situation), and, most important, two black ratings for the official debt (negative situation) (*Agence Europe*, 4 July 1991). Based on its fiscal position vis-à-vis the Maastricht's benchmarks during the early 1990s, therefore, Belgium's chances for joining the euro seemed extremely low.

As a founding member of the EU, Belgium had everything to lose by missing the EMU train. Joining the first wave of the EMU was a high-stakes game for the government, for two reasons. First, because Belgium's trading partners were almost certain to enter, failure to do so would damage the credibility of the country's hard franc policy, pushing up the currency's interest rate differentials with the eventual euro. Along with Belgium's massive standing public debt, this would undermine any effort to reduce the budget deficit. It would also foreclose any chance of joining the EMU at a later stage. Pressure on the franc would push up interest rates and increase unemployment, all of which would have very high "political costs" (Pochet 2004, 201).

Second, the fate of Belgian unity hinged on the legitimacy of the European project. With a society divided along multiple fault lines, Belgian governments had traditionally relied on European integration to increase their capacity "to bargain domestically" (Jones 1995, 170). It was widely believed that qualifying for the euro would "[counterbalance] long-standing regional divisions" (Pochet 2004, 201), and, thus, failure to do so would threaten national cohesion. The euro project was "a matter of survival for the country" (*Financial Times*, 28 June 1995).

For one senior adviser to Finance Minister Maystadt, the EMU was "the cement holding the political consensus" together (Economist Intelligence Unit, 1st Quarter 1992). For all these political economic reasons, the Economist Intelligence Unit concluded, "Belgium cannot contemplate failure to enter the EMU" (ibid.).

When the time came for official assessment of Belgium's compliance with the Maastricht benchmarks in 1998, its huge debt, "some twice the level provided for in the Maastricht Treaty," was the cause for major concern for its European partners, especially Germany. In its own report on the state of convergence, the Bundesbank was "severe in its judgments on the Italian and Belgian preparedness" (Dyson and Featherstone 1999, 7). In time, however, Belgium managed to qualify for the single currency. It had adopted significant adjustment measures since the early 1990s in the framework of two convergence programs, alongside institutional changes in fiscal policy and politics. Its budgetary position had improved sharply after the launch of the first program. Moreover, the pace of improvement was faster than the EU average: the budgetary balance moved from a deficit of 8.1 per cent of GDP in 1992 to almost equilibrium by 2000. But despite acute Euro-austerity, developments in public debt remained less positive. Although the debt-to-GDP ratio had fallen rapidly from a peak of 135.2 per cent in 1993 to 113.6 per cent in 1999, Belgium was still an outlier in the eurozone.

During the Maastricht decade, Belgian commitment to the EMU was so strong that "the main priority" for all Belgian governments was "membership of the Eurozone" (Wessels, Maurer, and Mittag 2003, 71). In reviewing Belgian macroeconomic policies and performance during the 1990s, the OECD remarked that "Belgium succeeded in what had been its *overriding goal*, i.e. meeting the Maastricht criteria and participating in the Economic and Monetary Union ... from its inception" (OECD 2001, 37; emphasis added). The Commission's *Convergence Report* (European Commission 1998, 114) praised the efforts of the Belgian authorities for implementing "a substantial consolidation effort" and preparing the country for the third stage of the EMU. The OECD (1997, 38–40) added that "since the early 1990s, fiscal consolidation ha[d] been significantly more rapid [in Belgium] than in other EU countries." Observing the Belgian government's efforts at pushing for fiscal austerity in the name of the EMU, at times through even extraordinary legislative and executive powers, the *Financial Times* (19 November 1996) remarked that "few European Union countries have shown as much determination as Belgium to guarantee a place among the first countries to join a single European currency." This chapter shows how

Belgian policymakers successfully used the EMU to bring about budgetary reform on the road to joining the euro.

Belgium Enters the 1990s: The Dehaene I Government

Financing social security was perhaps the most divisive issue occupying Belgium's political agenda during the late 1980s. Ironically, despite its mounting public debt, the social security system had run surpluses in both 1989 and 1990,[1] but the government was confiscating this surplus to finance its growing budget deficit. When the 1991 budget was being drafted, the system was projected to produce another hefty surplus for the third year in a row. Facing pressure from the trade unions, the government pledged to record the surplus as a "special contribution to be kept in reserve" for future years of financial hardship. Facing dire fiscal conditions, the government decided to reduce its contribution to the system to 16 per cent of total social security revenues (Couttenier 1991, 362).

The explosive public debt put social security reform back on the government's agenda (Jones 2002). Despite the surplus in the social security system, Belgian policymakers blamed the debt on the state's bailing out the social security system (Jones 1995, 170). Referring to statements by Budget Minister Hugo Schiltz, who stated that significant savings had to be made in social security, the Economist Intelligence Unit's *Country Report* for Belgium predicted that social security would certainly be the "prime target" for future rounds of budget cuts (Economist Intelligence Unit, 3rd Quarter 1991). Policymakers were not alone, however. Whenever the OECD and the IMF warned the Belgian government about its debt, they recommended reducing government transfers to the social security system. The IMF expressly recommended urgent measures that included, first and foremost, "sharp cuts" to social security (ibid.). Likewise, the OECD blamed the debt problem on rapid increases in social spending and warned that "it seem[ed] inevitable that strict controls on social expenditure [would] have to be maintained and, in fact, strengthened" (OECD 1991, 81).

In September 1991, a conflict between the Wallonian and Flemish political parties escalated, causing the Flemish Volksunie party to leave the Martens VIII coalition government. Although Martens then formed the next government (Martens IX), it collapsed in October, and Belgians went to the polls. The November 1991 parliamentary election is known as "Black Sunday" because the traditional parties were routed in a protest vote. Coalition partners in Flanders (the Flemish Christian Democrats, who had been at the centre of every post-war government, and the Flemish Socialists) and in Wallonia (the Christian Social Party and the French-speaking Socialists) saw their votes melt away. There was a steep rise in votes for the extreme-right Vlaams Blok in Flanders and the Green Party (Ecolo) in Wallonia. The splintering of the vote and the swing to the extreme right in Flanders shocked the political establishment. After the acrimonious fall of the Martens IX government, attempts to form a new government were marred by communal rivalries. With parties in Flanders and Wallonia so directly opposed to one another, forming the next government proved very difficult (Couttenier 1992).

In the meantime, outgoing Prime Minister Martens was representing Belgium as a caretaker at the Maastricht summit. Facing pressing problems, especially budgetary reform, King Baudouin felt he had to intervene. After more than three months of negotiations, the outgoing parties finally reached an agreement on the new coalition in March 1992. Jean-Luc Dehaene formed a four-party, centre-left coalition formed by the two Christian Democrat and two Socialist parties. Prime Minister Dehaene announced that his team would constitute an "emergency cabinet" tackling "urgent problems" such as the ballooning budget deficit and the public debt (Couttenier 1993, 364; *Reuters News*, 5 March 1992).

The Emergency Program on the Road to
the EMU and the 1992 Budget

The new coalition's program was drafted "within the framework emergency program for 1992," which was presented as the government's declaration (*déclaration gouvernementale*).[2] The declaration rested on two main premises: first and foremost, preparing Belgium for the EMU by restoring public finances (which Dehaene later called his government's "framework of reference") and, second, continuing the process of devolution to develop the federal structure of the Belgian state. In it, emphasizing the "imperative" of Belgium's timely accession to the EMU, Dehaene insisted that Belgium "must belong to the group of leading countries embarking on the Monetary Union before the end of the decade." After proclaiming that Belgium had been complying with the Maastricht criteria regarding inflation, interest rates, and exchange rate stability, he remarked, "It is only in the budget deficit and public debt that Belgium does not fulfil the European criteria yet. This is why we need to continue with the restoration of public finances, so that we satisfy the criteria by the end of 1996." He added that his government would promptly determine "the main features of a convergence program requested by the European Community," which would be "submitted to the European authorities as soon as possible." This program, he claimed, "will make it possible for our public finances to meet the European criteria at the end of 1996" (Dehaene 1992; translation mine).

In his address, the prime minister referred to the urgency of social security reform and explicitly linked it to the EMU: "Structural measures for balancing social security" were needed for the "reduction of the deficit necessary to satisfy the requirements of European convergence." Yet he was careful to add that his government would respect the principles of social dialogue, while implementing both "the emergency framework program for 1992" and "the multi-annual [convergence] program" (Dehaene 1992; translation mine).

The Dehaene government started off ambitiously. Its first step was to revise the 1992 budget, which the outgoing Martens IX government had drawn up in 1991. Due to optimistic projections and the delay in implementing the budget, the deficit had spiralled out of control. Immediately after taking office, the government announced an additional package of spending cuts (BEF 60 billion) and new revenues (BEF 75 billion), with an estimated savings of BEF 95 billion (1.25 per cent of gross national product, or GNP). It raised revenues by redefining the value-added tax (VAT) on certain goods and services, suspending investment tax credits, and increasing social security contributions. On the expenditure side, cuts were particularly focused on defence spending, and stricter limits were applied to health care and unemployment benefits. Overall, the budget deficit was expected to decline to around 5.25 per cent of GDP (OECD 1994, 48; 1992, 33). The measures were approved in the Chamber of Representatives and the Senate.

Belgium's First Convergence Program (1992–6)

The Maastricht Treaty was to be ratified by the Chamber of Representatives in July 1992. Even before the ratification process began, the Dehaene government announced that it was drafting the first Belgian convergence program. The proposed measures focused on the country's ailing public finances because the other indicators in the Maastricht convergence criteria remained largely unproblematic. There were two scenarios in the draft program for achieving the Maastricht fiscal targets on time. First, the gradualist option, which had the broad agreement of the coalition partners, set transfers to Belgium's social security system at BEF 231 billion a year, ensured that fiscal receipts kept pace with output growth, and imposed zero growth on primary defence spending and on subsidies to state-owned companies. This soft approach would cut the deficit ratio to 5.2 per cent in 1993 and to 4.3 and 3.7 per cent in 1994 and 1995, respectively.

The second, strict option would impose stringent budget measures in 1993 (cutting the deficit-to-GDP ratio to 4.9 per cent) but ease up in 1994 and 1995 (4.3 and 3.7 per cent, respectively). These measures would allow fiscal receipts to grow faster than GDP and make real cuts in spending (*Reuters News*, 9 June, 11 June 1992). The government announced that it would opt for the strict option as the better way to prepare Belgium for the EMU: according to Finance Minister Maystadt, the government would "accelerate [its] budget cutting policy in 1993 so that the effort [would] be less arduous in the following years" (ibid., 19 June 1992).

Given the wide political support for the EMU project, the coalition partners agreed to the convergence program. The government submitted it to the EU in June 1992, and the Chamber of Representatives ratified the Maastricht Treaty in July with a large majority. This outcome reflected the wide consensus on, and commitment to, the EMU within the political establishment. Couttenier (1993, 375) remarked that "the Dehaene cabinet was the first Belgian government in history to restrict its freedom of action for the benefit of achieving integration into the European Monetary Union ..., a goal set by a supranational body."

The Maastricht Effect and the High Council of Finance[3]

In parallel with its preparations for the convergence program, the Dehaene government introduced a major innovation in fiscal policy with ramifications for fiscal politics. In June 1992, after having adopted the program, the government transferred responsibility for monitoring it to the High Council of Finance.[4] The government, in its coalition agreement, had pledged to meet all targets the council would recommend, and fiscal decisions were to be taken at the highest level to comply with the program targets. In its new role, the council became the "guarantor of the convergence process" (Schelkle and Barta 2008, 7). It could make recommendations on its own initiative to the Minister of Finance on the borrowing capacities of any level of government. It would also prepare a report every year, which would serve as the main document for budgetary review and would detail the extent to which budgetary targets were being met. In case of an overrun, it would issue an early warning so that the institution in breach of the target could pass a supplementary budget to reduce its excessive deficit. The government had effectively limited its own fiscal powers by delegating the monitoring and execution of fiscal-contract functions to the High Council.

The High Council began to implement its new monitoring tasks immediately. Every year, it specified the guidelines for the budget and set the deficit targets for all levels of government. Although, in principle, these targets were only recommendations, once they were announced, all levels of government adopted them with only minor changes. In fact, between 1992 and 1996, on the recommendation of the High Council, the federal government was forced to pass supplementary measures every single year to meet the Maastricht budgetary criteria.

The council's revised standard operating procedures led to institutional changes in Belgian budgetary politics. Unlike earlier periods, when fiscal targets were only a wish list, the rules of the fiscal game had changed. It was now imperative to eliminate the excessive deficits, and all actors were aware of it. All political parties and all levels of government believed that violating the targets would cost Belgium's timely entry to the EMU. No party or government wanted to be accused of being responsible for missing the EMU target. Since the Maastricht fiscal criteria were based on "general government" (rather than "central government"), the federal state as a whole was obliged to reverse course to meet the criteria.[5] In this way, the EMU was instrumental in defining the rigid parameters of fiscal politics in Belgium. After all, its life was at stake – failure to qualify for the euro could easily lead to the break-up of the country itself.

The 1993 Budget: Austerity Reinforced

In the meantime, Dehaene announced that, with the 1993 budget, the government would implement budgetary austerity to meet the deficit targets set out in the convergence program. He emphasized that he would opt for a strict fiscal consolidation strategy for reducing the deficit to the Maastricht benchmark by the end of 1996. The budget was drafted on the basis of three rules of austerity that had been written into the coalition agreement and the convergence program: no real increases in primary expenditure, revenue growth in line with GDP growth, and a balanced social security budget. The labour unions reacted to this strict consolidation strategy because they were concerned that reducing the budget in this way would be an attack on the Belgian welfare state. They pressed for spreading the austerity effort evenly over the entire period until the end of 1996. They added that politicians should be brave enough to announce that, to meet the EMU criteria, they had to levy new taxes. They warned the government not to burden the social security system any further (Couttenier 1993, 375).

The budget, drafted in the summer months of 1992, included corrective measures on the order of BEF 105 billion (1.25 per cent of GDP). The aim was to reduce the deficit to 5.2 per cent of GDP in 1993, in accordance with the convergence program. The budget proposed to raise BEF 38 billion by finding new fiscal revenue sources, while it would bring in non-fiscal revenues that included BEF 20.7 billion in receipts from the sale of state-owned assets as well as other real and financial assets. The government announced that that these sales constituted the first step in a four-year privatization program that would raise BEF 50 billion. It would find savings in non-interest expenditure items of BEF 50.5 billion and interest expenditure savings of BEF 31 billion. Social security measures (including increased contributions to holiday pay and cuts in unemployment benefits and health care) would save BEF 15.4 billion (Economist Intelligence Unit, 4th Quarter 1992).

The budget was attacked from all sides, and it soon became clear that implementing Dehaene's strict strategy was impossible. The Christian Social Party, a coalition partner, argued that the government had not gone far enough because the budget aimed solely to do the bare minimum to reach the EMU. Critics argued that the revenue-increasing measures were mainly one-offs and that the expenditure measures merely postponed expenditures into the future (Economist Intelligence Unit, 4th Quarter 1992; *Reuters News*, 28 August 1992). The centre-right press widely criticized the budget for failing to tackle the problem of "social security overspending." For example, the conservative–liberal *De Standaard* complained that "nothing had change[d] in the big money flows toward social security" and that, of the BEF 117.4 billion in austerity measures, only BEF 12.6 billion came from spending cuts in the social security sector (*Reuters News*, 7 August 1992). The budget row among the political parties quickly intertwined with tensions between the Flemish and Wallonian regions. The Flemish complained that Wallonia disproportionately benefited from the budget because there were large social security transfers from Flanders to Wallonia. In particular, Flemish nationalists called for the separation of the two communities (ibid.).

Finding these austerity measures inadequate, the ECOFIN Council announced in early September 1992 that it was postponing its review of Belgium's convergence program (*Reuters News*, 12 September 1992). Dehaene then admitted that the government could not adopt the strict strategy for fear it would antagonize the unions: "For social reasons we have opted for measures which will not reach their maximum effect until the end of the four-year period." He added that "the government should adopt without delay additional measures to safeguard [budgetary] targets" (ibid., 3 August 1992, 7 August 1992). Since the government was based on a fragile coalition divided along linguistic and political lines, it was reluctant to disappoint the unions.

Months of severe political tensions almost brought the government to collapse. Only by late September could the coalition parties agree on budget austerity. On the recommendation of the High Council of Finance, the government announced supplementary austerity amounting to BEF 21.8 billion; it needed to find BEF 16.6 billion to meet a revenue shortfall that had resulted from sluggish growth. Revenues in 1993 were estimated at BEF 1.324.1 trillion, down from BEF 1.340.7 trillion when the draft budget was drawn up in July. A further BEF 5.2 billion was needed in the social security budget to compensate for unemployment benefits, which had turned out to be higher than expected (*Reuters News*, 29 September 1992). The measures included plans to raise BEF 10 billion in privatization receipts (the largest item in the package), improve the collection of overdue taxes, close fiscal loopholes, and make further expenditure cuts. In terms of social security measures, additional income would be raised by cracking down on fraud and cuts in unemployment benefits.

The Chamber of Deputies approved the revised budget in early November. Soon after, the ECOFIN Council endorsed Belgium's convergence program by expressing its "positive appreciation of the program and the commitment to the process of convergence." The council warned, however, that "it will be necessary to continue to bear down vigorously on public debt levels for some time to come beyond the end of the period covered by the program, and that the government should take every opportunity to make maximum progress in reducing the debt burden" (*Reuters News*, 23 November 1992).

It became apparent towards the end of 1992 that the 1993 deficit target looked unattainable as the economy had weakened despite additional budgetary measures. Insisting that his government would meet the 3 per cent rule by January 1997 by "sticking to [its] 1993 budget deficit target of 5.2 per cent as set out in our EC Economic Convergence Plan" (*Reuters News*, 23 December 1992), Dehaene announced that the 1993 budget would have to be adjusted to cover a shortfall of BEF 21.8 billion. Privatization receipts worth around an extra BEF 10 billion would close half the conspicuous gap.

The government later announced that it had increased the privatization revenue targets from BEF 15 billion to BEF 25 billion. A further privatization of BEF 15 billion would be raised in 1994, and then BEF 10 billion in 1995 and 1996, until Belgium met the Maastricht fiscal criteria (*Financial Times*, 3 December 1992). Commenting on the government's massive privatization program, the *Financial Times* suggested that any discussion of the privatization issue, normally a taboo in Belgian politics, would not have been possible even a year before had it not been for trying to reach the EMU targets on time (ibid.). Responding to criticisms that the government was relying extensively on one-off measures, Finance Minister Maystadt hinted that these measures were the least politically unpopular: "If politicians had not liked the idea of privatization, then they might have to settle for unpopular cuts in social security," adding, "We really have no choice: we have to go on with the Convergence Program" (ibid.).

By early 1993, Dehaene was still unable to iron out the divisions among his coalition partners over the revisions to the 1993 budget. They had agreed that around BEF 110 billion (worth 1.6 per cent of GDP) would have to be cut to meet the EMU requirements. When it came to working out the details, however, opinions diverged. The Flemish Christian Democrats proposed suspending the indexation of wages and benefits, but after the unions threatened the government, the Wallonian Socialists opposed this move for fear that it would lead to protests and strikes from the unions and their supporters.

The stalemate led Dehaene to tender his resignation to the king, but he refused to accept it. None of the parties wanted to be seen as responsible for bringing down the government and delaying the preparations for the EMU; all supported the official bid to join the euro. The coalition partners eventually agreed on the adjustments that needed to be made to bring Belgian public finances back into line with the convergence program. They agreed to continue with the indexation of wages and benefits and decided that further savings would be made by raising social security contributions. The new package of BEF 105 billion (1.25 per cent of GDP) relied heavily on new revenues of BEF 75 billion. Of this, BEF 46 billion would come from new taxes and charges, BEF 15 billion from privatization and asset sales, and BEF 14 billion from improved revenue collection and cracking down on tax evasion. The government also introduced a new tax, called the "crisis tax," which would bring in a hefty BEF 33 billion by levying a 3 per cent surcharge on personal and corporate income taxes. Spending cuts were limited to BEF 30 billion, BEF 24 billion of which would come from planned savings in the social security account. The government also intended to limit rising health care expenditures and unemployment benefits (OECD 1994, 50–1).

The 1994 Budget, New Taxes, and Privatization

In June, the High Council of Finance announced that BEF 65 billion was required to meet the convergence program target for 1994. Cabinet began working on the budget in June and finalized it at the end of July. The main points had already been set out in the convergence program.

The budget predicted a deficit of BEF 315 billion (amounting to 4.3 per cent of GDP), which was fully in line with the target set by the program. Additional savings of about BEF 50 billion (nearly 0.75 per cent of GDP) were announced. While half would come from structural measures, the other half would be raised through one-off measures. Expenditure cuts of BEF 30 billion would come from changing the timing of subsidies to public enterprises and reorganizing the public sector. To raise revenues of BEF 20 billion, the government announced the privatization of Belgacom, the Belgian telecommunications company, and the Belgian National Lottery.[6]

In July, the Chamber of Deputies passed a series of bills on privatization and new taxes. The privatization bill would enable the state to surrender its controlling majority in public credit institutions.[7] The government planned to raise BEF 25 billion in 1993 from the sale of state assets and reach BEF 60 billion over the next four years. The bill implemented the above-mentioned 3 per cent crisis tax (*Reuters News*, 10 July 1993). In early August, still another tax was introduced, this time on domestic energy users, which was intended to generate some BEF 8.5 billion in revenue. This revenue would enable the government to reduce the social security contributions of employers in the export sector, which had been hit by the recession and the strong franc (Economist Intelligence Unit, 3rd Quarter 1993).

The National Bank of Belgium estimated that, by 1994, these new taxes would help bring the overall tax burden to about 49 per cent, up from 46 per cent in 1991. This was the highest tax burden of all EU member states (Economist Intelligence Unit, 3rd Quarter 1993). In contrast with these dramatic increases in taxes, the government did not take any further measure to offset the impact of the recession on the social security account. Budgetary measures in that area were thus postponed to the fall, when the government would discuss a new social pact with its social partners (OECD 1994, 51; Deschouwer and Deweerdt 1994, 275).

The Verplaetse Report, the Abortive Social Pact, and the Global Plan

Facing higher levels of unemployment and rising social security costs as a result of the 1992–3 recession, Dehaene announced that there was an urgent need for a debate on reforming social security. At the end of July 1993, the government revived the idea of a "social pact," which dated back to 1944 and to which employers, trade unions, and the government would subscribe (Vilrokx and van Leemput 1998, 337). Dehaene asked a committee of experts chaired by Alfons Verplaetse, Governor of the National Bank of Belgium, to prepare a report that would serve as the basis for negotiations with the social partners. One of the committee's main tasks was to find a way to eliminate the BEF 50 billion deficit in the 1994 social security budget, which, because of its thorny nature, had not been included in the talks on the 1994 budget (*Reuters News*, 5 August 1993). Dehaene was confident that if a social pact could be achieved, the government would be able to convince its EU partners that Belgium was eligible for the EMU (*Financial Times*, 7 October 1993).

In October, the Verplaetse Commission presented its report. It diagnosed the current economic problems and proposed a set of solutions in the areas of competitiveness, employment, and social security. On competitiveness, the report proposed that the principle of wage indexation should remain, but that the system should be revised to make salary increases less automatic when consumer prices rose. On employment, real wages should be frozen for three years (1994–6), thereby reducing nationwide wage costs by about BEF 100 billion, to 120 billion. On social security, the report had more radical suggestions. It proposed that employers' social security contributions be reduced. More importantly, it stressed that growth in social security spending had to be capped at a maximum 0.5 per cent of GDP per year over the next four years, until EMU entry could be secured.

The report expected these proposals to reduce the budget deficit by two-thirds throughout the convergence process by imposing limits on social spending. This meant that two-thirds of the entire burden of fiscal retrenchment would essentially fall on the social security budget. To achieve this objective, the report proposed massive social welfare cuts in the following program areas: health spending (40 per cent), family allowances (25 per cent), unemployment and early retirement benefits (20 per cent), and pensions (15 per cent). The report warned that even these savings would not suffice to meet the Maastricht target by 1997, and it set out alternative measures to finance the social security budget. These included introducing a new property tax, raising the withholding tax on interest income, and imposing a new tax on energy consumption and carbon dioxide emissions (*Reuters News*, 19 October, 20 October 1993).

When the report was introduced, talks on the social pact came to an impasse even before they started. Frustrated by the government's proposal for massive cuts in social security, the socialist unions announced that they were withdrawing from the negotiations. While they did not object to exploring alternative means of financing, they opposed any reduction in employers' contributions; instead, they demanded new taxes on interest income, real estate, and personal wealth (*EIRR* 1994, 245: 27–8). The Christian Democratic trade unions announced, however, that they were willing to continue the negotiations based on the report (*Reuters News*, 21 October 1993).

Facing a stalemate, Dehaene abandoned the idea of reforming social security. Instead, he announced that "the government itself [would] establish its own global plan" (*Reuters News*, 24 October 1993).[8] He then introduced the Global Plan on Employment, Competitiveness and Social Security in November. The plan closely followed the targets set out in the Verplaetse Commission's report and the budgetary priorities of the 1992 convergence program (OECD 1995, 2). It had five objectives: (1) make financing social security more favourable for employment, (2) redefine its basic principles, (3) reform its structure, (4) ensure the financial equilibrium of the system, and (5) revise certain spending mechanisms (*EIRR* 1994, 245: 28; see also Reman 1994, 132; Arcq and Chatelain 1994, 57–62; Marier 2008, 90).

It was evident that the government was determined to generate savings by reducing the deficit of the social security system to meet the Maastricht criteria (Marier 2008, 89).[9] To implement the plan, the government would cut social welfare spending by BEF 75 billion, impose a wage freeze in 1995 and 1996, and raise new taxes on capital and property. There were diverse responses to the plan: employers' organizations did not find it rigorous enough; the Christian unions immediately rejected it and called for a national strike; and the socialist unions joined them later.

Facing opposition, Dehaene defended the plan, which, he said, closely followed his government's convergence program. He stressed that Belgium would simply not be able to "gain a place in EMU" without this new austerity plan. Finance Minister Maystadt added that Belgium's EMU bid depended on the success of the social security reforms the government was proposing (*Reuters News*, 10 November 1993). Dehaene announced later that he was determined "to defend these measures" and confronted the unions by warning that "the reaction of the unions [was] their own affair" (ibid., 17 November 1993). The government decided to implement the plan without negotiating it with the unions. In response, the week of 22 November saw a series of general strikes break out at the national and provincial levels, organized by both the Christian and the socialist unions. The entire country almost came to a standstill. In particular, the national general strike, which took place on 26 November, completely paralyzed all Belgian public life for the first time since 1936 (ibid., 26 November 1993; *EIRR* 1994, 245: 29; Deschouwer and Dewerdt 1994, 277).

Despite the unrest, Parliament approved the plan. Belgium's first general strike in almost half a century, however, forced the government to agree to sit down with the unions. Dehaene noted that, although certain aspects of the plan were negotiable, its chief aim (to clean up public finances) simply had to be achieved. Bowing to pressure, he insisted that "the increase of indirect taxation is inevitable in order to guarantee an alternative financing for social security" and thereby minimize the cutbacks to the welfare state (*Reuters News*, 25 November 1993). He also signalled that certain measures on social security could be reviewed (ibid., 26 November 1993). He appealed repeatedly to the *vincolo esterno* during the talks, insisting that the new measures were absolutely essential for meeting the Maastricht targets. "The global plan requires an effort from everyone. ... This plan is necessary. There is no other solution" (ibid., 30 November 1993).

Unsatisfied with the negotiations, the unions continued to stage demonstrations and strikes during the European Council meeting in Brussels on 10 December to attract the EU leaders' attention during the Belgian presidency. The government, however, did not budge and approved the three-year wage freeze and cut in employers' social security contributions. In return for these two measures, however, it made concessions on social security. The planned cut in child allowances would be replaced with a new tax, levied as a general social security contribution. The revenue that it had planned to save from the aborted social security reform was to be raised from new taxes on alcohol, tobacco, and energy.

Although Dehaene repeated his government's intention to restructure the social security system, he could not pull it off given continued union opposition. Although the plan was successful in introducing changes in two areas (public finances and employment), the government could not implement many of its measures on social security (*Reuters News*, 24 December 1993; Marier 2008, 90). Dehaene had clearly miscalculated the power of union opposition when he announced earlier that he did not need the unions to pursue social security reforms. He later remarked that the Global Plan was "the most difficult operation" of his entire political life (Deschouwer and Deweerdt 1994, 277).

Willockx Pension Reform Shelved because of Opposition

Minister of Pensions Freddy Willockx had been pushing for wholesale pension reform since mid-1992. When discussions were taking place on the social pact, he had organized a roundtable on pensions that included social partners, pensioners' organizations, and experts to discuss various reform options put forward in a report released by the Federal Planning Bureau. The report called for raising the retirement age for women and adopting the same method of calculating benefits for men and women. Although there was some public discussion on the report, it had not received much attention due to the demonstrations. In January 1994, Willockx decided to push for a reform of the pensions of wage earners in the private sector and the self-employed. The reform, which was expected to bring in savings equivalent to BEF 20 billion, included the following measures: raising the retirement age for women and the duration of contributions for full pensions to align them with those for men by 2006, eliminating the revalorization of earlier pension contributions, and reforming the non-contributory elements of the pension system (Marier 2008, 90).

The negotiations for the reform plan proved very difficult because women's associations and the unions continuously opposed the plan in the first quarter of 1994. Even Cabinet members dissented, and Cabinet's discussion of the proposal was delayed. The project was effectively shelved in January 1995 following opposition within the government and a powerful wave of protest. Willockx left his post shortly afterwards (Anderson et al. 2007, 330–2; Marier 2008, 90–1).

The new minister, Marcel Colla, declared his intention to implement Willockx's plans for addressing the gender equality issue. The pension legislation was approved in the Chamber and reached the Senate, but it was blocked by massive opposition from both employers and unions. At the end of the day, Colla could implement only those measures that aimed to generate alternative means of financing, such as the solidarity contribution of 2 per cent for high-income pensioners, adopted earlier, and the tax on energy (Marier 2008, 93). He had to announce that all reform initiatives would be shelved until the upcoming federal election in 1995. Thus, in each attempt at reform, the Dehaene I government failed to bring about pension reform due to sustained opposition (Anderson et al. 2007, 332).

From the 1994 Budget Correction to the 1995 Budget

In February 1994, Budget Minister Herman Van Rompuy announced that the federal budget deficit for 1993 remained at 7.1 per cent of GDP – still more than double the Maastricht benchmark. The government, however, trod carefully by arguing that the higher-than-expected deficit was not due to lack of proper control over the central government budget; increases in both revenues and expenditures were in line with the convergence program. It was the social security budget that had deteriorated sharply due to the deep recession that had hit the European economies (Economist Intelligence Unit, 1st Quarter 1994).

At the March review for the 1994 budget, the High Council of Finance announced that Belgium had experienced a deficit slippage of BEF 17.2 billion (0.2 per cent of GDP). To increase savings, the government decided in March to speed up the privatization program that it had announced in 1993 and revised the amount forecast from privatization receipts from BEF 40 billion to BEF 60 billion. The difference of BEF 20 billion, Van Rompuy expected, would be covered by the privatization of Belgacom. At the same time, the sale of state-owned credit institutions, announced earlier, was bringing in much-needed revenue. Cabinet approved the necessary legislation for the sale of the most important of these assets, the National Investment Company (NIM/SNI) (*Reuters News*, 21 March 1994, 25 March 1994; Economist Intelligence Unit, 1st Quarter 1994).

In fact, although the Belgian authorities reported to Eurostat that these privatization receipts were *not* helping the country's deficit position, in actuality, they had been credited to the budget for not only 1993 but also 1994 (Savage 2005, 99, 107).[10] By the end of 1994, as a result of these measures, total government receipts had grown by 6.5 per cent. Most importantly, the 1994 budget relied more on "alternative financing" of the social security system: reductions in social security contributions were financed through increases in indirect taxes and additional funds raised from capital gains taxes. In terms of outlays, total expenditures continued to decelerate in 1994. The growth in public-sector wages slowed, and subsidies fell, reflecting the freeze on subsidies to public enterprises and a rescheduling of those payments. Public spending on goods and services, which had been falling over the previous few years, however, accelerated. More importantly, social expenditures increased by 1.3 per cent in real terms, while their rate of growth decelerated from the previous year (OECD 1995, 32–5).

Before preparations for the 1995 budget began, Dehaene warned in June 1994 that the talks would be tough because Belgium could not afford to diverge from its austerity strategy. The aim of the budget would be to meet the Maastricht criteria by reaching "the objectives of the Convergence Plan." He added, however, that stringent effort was needed to control the Belgian social security system (*Reuters News*, 25 June 1994). The High Council of Finance announced in late June that BEF 130 billion was needed if Belgium was to meet its convergence program targets. Part of this amount, BEF 25 billion, was needed to balance its social security sector (ibid., 30 June 1994). Shortly afterwards, the federal government and the three main regions collectively pledged to maintain budget discipline and declared that they would "do everything to meet the deficit objectives for 1996 that are contained in the convergence plan" (ibid., 19 July 1994).

The government hammered out the 1995 budget in July, the broad brushstrokes of which had, once again, already been set by the convergence program (OECD 1995, 35). Benefiting from higher-than-expected economic growth and increased privatization receipts, the budget explicitly aimed to keep Belgium on track for the EMU. In a statement, the government announced, "This budget is a new stage in the realization of the convergence plan" (*Reuters News*, 25 July 1994). The budget minister, however, warned that there was no room for complacency and that Belgium must continue with its austerity effort until it reached its goal of cutting the budget deficit to 3.0 per cent of GDP (ibid., 28 July 1994).

Social Security Escapes the Axe, More Privatization,
and the 1995 Budget

Despite the government's announcements, it was clear that the social security system, once again, had largely escaped the axe. In the 1995 budget, total spending on social security was set at BEF 1.275 trillion, representing an increase of 1.3 per cent in real terms. In contrast with the strict austerity applied to the federal government budget, the government refrained from imposing any substantial cuts to the social security budget[11] – even though a series of cuts was due, as laid out in the Global Plan.

Along with the plan, the government had announced structural measures to curb the growth of pension expenditures, including bringing in a new measure for calculating pensions with a longer base period and harmonizing pensions for men and women. Although the new calculation was altered by the introduction of a new index, harmonization was not possible. With respect to health care, the plan stated that annual growth in spending in 1995 would be capped at 1.5 per cent in real terms. Eligibility for the unemployment program had been tightened and linked more closely to employment. In fact, the Global Plan had introduced an overall cap on social expenditure growth in real terms for the period starting in 1996. The government had not provided specific details on the cap, however, saying only that the matter would have to wait until it introduced an overhaul of the social security system, which had been postponed until after the 1995 election. In response, the OECD (1995, 38) concluded, "Although progress has been recorded, no decisive measures have been taken to counter the expected impact of population ageing on social spending, and ... the structural reform of the social security system – notably its pension and health care components – will be one of the most urgent tasks of the new government."

It was the measures related to raising revenues that saw the most successful implementation of the plan. Cuts in spending in the family program had been replaced by new taxes. New revenues had been raised by alternative means of financing, such as increasing the withholding tax on interest income and the tax on property income.[12]

The main factor that explains the government's lax approach to the social security budget, according to the Economist Intelligence Unit, was the change in accounting practices to adopt those used in the EU. Using the new accounting practices would align the public accounts with the Maastricht Treaty's general government deficit criterion and would take effect beginning in 1995 (3rd Quarter 1994). They were, in fact, looser than those used in Belgium. In this way, these new practices "ha[d] given the government some temporary room for maneuver."(ibid).[13]

In September 1995, in his parliamentary address on his government's policy priorities for the coming year, Dehaene repeated his government's determination to finally achieve a budget deficit of 3.0 per cent of GDP by 1996, one year earlier than official screening, and that the austerity measures proposed in the Global Plan would be implemented in 1995. When the privatization of the government's most attractive asset, Belgacom, stalled, the government had to seek alternative sources of revenue because it had already budgeted BEF 57 billion in privatization receipts for 1994. It announced that, by the fall of 1994, it had raised only BEF 15 billion from the sale of the National Investment Company and that it was to receive another BEF 30 billion from that sale and from the sale of the National Lottery. Still another BEF 20 to 25 billion would come from the partial privatization of Belgacom. The government would not privatize the National Lottery by the end of 1994, but it would still have to pay an extra 15 billion francs to the Belgian state by then so that the amount could be included in the privatization receipts for 1994. This "corresponds to the concession a private operator would have to pay [the government] if the lottery were privatized" (*Reuters News*, 4 October 1994).

In October 1994, after the budget was presented, the ECOFIN Council warned the Belgian government that it should do everything in its power to cut its public deficit to 4.3 per cent of GDP in 1995, as laid down in its convergence program. Implicitly referring to the country's astronomical debt, the Council recommended that the government "put an end to the current situation of excessive deficit as soon as possible" (*Reuters News*, 10 October 1994). In response, Budget Minister Van Rompuy and Finance Minister Maystadt reiterated that the primary aim of Belgium's macroeconomic policy would remain ensuring the country's timely entry to the third stage of the EMU. When they announced that the government deficit had dropped to around 5.4 per cent of GDP compared with 6.7 per cent in the previous year, both ministers thought that this was the most appropriate response to the warnings from the ECOFIN Council. Moreover, the drop in the deficit demonstrated to the financial markets that the target of bringing down the deficit to the Maastricht benchmarks was "perhaps achievable after all" (Economist Intelligence Unit, 1st Quarter 1995). However, the High Council of Finance cautioned that the declining deficit figure had been attained essentially due to a recent statistical revision. It added that the growth in primary expenditures disbursed by the communities and regions, taken together (which constituted the basis for assessing the Maastricht fiscal criteria), had actually increased further in 1994.

The March review of the 1995 budget passed smoothly. Press reports stated that the exercise was "the easiest review for many a year" (Economist Intelligence Unit, 2nd Quarter 1995). Underlying these figures were positive assumptions about real economic growth, inflation, and unemployment. For 1994, the net financing requirement at the federal level remained at BEF 284 billion, equivalent to 3.6 per cent of GDP, while the general government deficit remained at 4.9 per cent.

1995 Election: All for Euro-Austerity, All for Social Security Reform

The government had managed to push through an austerity program that put Belgian finances on a firmer footing on the road to the EMU. It had also introduced a historic constitutional reform, transforming Belgium into a federal state. Because of political scandals, however, the Flemish and Walloon Socialist parties became unpopular, and the coalition weakened.[14] In the meantime, Dehaene was concerned that pushing through an austerity budget in 1996 to meet the Maastricht timetable while facing an immediate election was not a politically smart idea. The budget could tear the coalition apart, and this would have catastrophic ramifications for both the Christian Democrats and the Socialists. Seeking a renewed mandate for austerity and to facilitate the preparation of the difficult 1996 budget, Dehaene announced in February 1995 that the general election would be brought forward to May so that "the 1996 budget will allow us to meet the 3 percent (deficit) objective" (*Wall Street Journal Europe*, 20 February 1995; see also Downs 1996, 169).

Dehaene took every opportunity to play the Maastricht card and stress that the 1996 budget would have to contain more austerity measures for Belgium to qualify for the EMU in 1997. Emphasizing that reducing the budget deficit to meet the Maastricht criteria was a *sine qua non*, Dehaene stated, "I will not enter a government until I am sure and there is an agreement that we want to achieve three percent (of GDP for the 1996 budget deficit)." (*Reuters News*, 20 January 1995). The primary aim of his next government, if he was elected, was loud and clear: "It is necessary to do everything to remain in the leading band of European Union countries. Belgium must join EMU from the start."[15] (ibid., 9 February 1995). He added that he wanted the new government to make social security reform a priority and that the aim of such reform would be to help Belgium cut its budget deficit to a level acceptable for the EMU (*Reuters News*, 15 February, 7 April 1995).

In April, in the run-up to the election, Dehaene prepared a 111-page government program, *Sleutels voor Morgen/Clés pour demain* (Keys for Tomorrow), which was adopted by his party. The program featured the policy priorities of the new government, if it were elected, including "modernizing social security" and "bringing Belgium into the European top group." The Socialists, too, agreed that the program could constitute an acceptable starting point for coalition negotiations (*Reuters News*, 21 April 1995; Deschouwer and Platel 1996, 532).

Strikingly, almost all political parties agreed that Belgium must meet the Maastricht criteria. With respect to budgetary policy, there was a consensus on the need for additional budget measures; however, views differed on the timing of fiscal consolidation and the means of achieving it. Among the coalition partners, while the Christian Democrats agreed that spending cuts were needed, they were against raising the tax burden, which was already the highest in the EU. The Socialist parties advocated debt reduction, too, but they were against a rigid and rushed timetable. All parties agreed that additional austerity was needed to enter the EMU, but, except for the Flemish Liberals, no party dared attach a price tag to the additional budgetary effort.

There was also a consensus among the parties on the urgent need to reform the social security system. All broadly agreed that it was the system's high costs that were aggravating Belgium's debt problem. While the coalition parties ruled out dismantling the system altogether, views differed on how to reform it, and debates revolved around questions of regionalization, privatization, and alternative ways to finance it. While the parties offered different proposals for achieving reform, all emphasized that the system must be sustainable (*Reuters News*, 8 May, 10 May, 12 May, 14 May, 15 May 1995).

Interestingly, none of the political parties (save the Flemish Liberals) promised to overhaul the social security system, and, in fact, by 1994, it was almost in balance. Press reports, however, showed that the new government was expected to make "further [social security] cuts in order to reduce Belgium's budget deficit for European economic and monetary union" (*Reuters News*, 14 May 1995). The press depicted Dehaene as "desperately trying to trim Belgium's staggering debt to qualify for European monetary union this decade." To achieve his goal, reporting continued, he would have one "major target": "social security" (*Wall Street Journal Europe*, 22 May 1995). The common expectation was that social security would be the prime target for cuts in the 1996 budget, which, many expected, would be the new government's first major task (*Reuters News*, 29 May 1995).

The Dehaene II Government

The parliamentary election held on 21 May 1995 was a personal victory for Dehaene. The results made him the obvious candidate to return as prime minister, with the Christian Democrats and Socialists retaining control in the federal legislature. More importantly, the opposition Liberals, who had campaigned for a tougher budget policy and an overhaul of the social security system through regionalization, privatization, and large-scale cuts, made only very limited gains. Voters trusted the standing coalition's promise to keep welfare benefits intact and did not support the Thatcherite program of Guy Verhofstadt, leader of the Flemish Liberals (Marier 2008, 93). Perhaps the biggest surprise of the election was the solid support for Belgium's Socialist parties, even after the corruption scandals. The most likely explanation for their success, according to press reports, was other parties' election pledges to reform social security, which had frightened voters (*Reuters News*, 22 May 1995; *Financial Times*, 23 May 1995). Such concerns continued after the election, when Dehaene was negotiating with the other parties. "In spite of emotional election pledges by the socialists to safeguard Belgium's generous social security system," the *Financial Times* (15 June 1995) reported, many expected that savings were "to come mainly from pensions, health and social security spending."

After forming his coalition, Dehaene presented his government's declaration to Parliament on 28 June 1995. He noted six priorities: promoting employment and reducing unemployment by creating new jobs and ensuring a better distribution of existing jobs; reinforcing a more viable society by improving quality of life, consumer protection, and the fight against social exclusion; thoroughly modernizing social security by the end of 1995; taking the necessary measures to help Belgium join the EMU; enhancing Belgium's role on the international stage; and promoting democracy, justice, and state reform. The imperative of joining the EMU and the pursuit of the "European inspiration" were scattered throughout his declaration. Dehaene reiterated that Belgium "should be one of the first countries to participate in the EMU and that the government will take all the necessary measures to fulfil the conditions envisaged for 1997." To meet these goals, "The Government aims to bring down the government deficit to a maximum of 3 percent of GDP in 1996." He also announced that "a multi-annual program will be put in place with a view to stabilizing the difference between primary expenditures and revenues to the level envisaged for the end of 1996" (Dehaene 1995; translation mine).

On the issue of the long-overdue social security reform, Dehaene stated that "the objective of the government program is to modernize the social security system." Consolidating the public debt was the best guarantor of the future of the pension system. In modernizing the social security system, Dehaene stated, "the government would aim to preserve an egalitarian society whereby the pensioners, and in particular those with low income, would be able to benefit from the improvement in the standard of living" (Dehaene 1995; translation mine). He called on the social partners to help draft new legislation for developing a second-pillar pension scheme, while keeping the budgetary objectives and the financing of the social security on a sound basis.

The 1996 Budget: Raising Revenues, Postponing Social Security
Reform, Additional Austerity

The new government was prepared to make "whatever adjustments necessary to enter EMU" (Marier 2008, 94). On the day of his appointment as prime minister, Dehaene announced that his government would start working on the 1996 budget right away (*Reuters News*, 23 June 1995). Dehaene repeated on every possible occasion that he was determined to pursue even tougher austerity to reduce the 1996 deficit to 3 per cent (ibid., 25 July 1995). As the government was finalizing the budget, which was crucial for its hopes of joining the single currency, German Finance Minister Theo Waigel rejected any broad interpretation of the fiscal criterion by famously arguing that it must not exceed "*drei Komma null*" (three point zero) (ibid., 18 September 1996). He warned that Belgian[16] public finances would make it impossible for the country to join the EMU (ibid., 20 September 1995). In contrast with the reactions from Italian politicians (see chapter 5), Finance Minister Maystadt stated that "the message was rather clear" and Belgium "must make further efforts" to slash the budget deficit and public debt. Moreover, Maystadt also added that Belgium was "absolutely ready" to agree to tough, automatic sanctions against any prospective EMU member with an excessive deficit (*International Herald Tribune*, 30 September 1995).

In early October, in his budget speech to Parliament, Dehaene announced an austerity package in the 1996 budget equivalent to BEF 112 billion. The budget contained a mix of new, indirect taxes and a series of spending cuts in the social security sector. He promised, "The government will stick to the Maastricht Treaty, its criteria and its calendar. We are making a decisive move now in limiting the deficit to three percent." He added that the new austerity package was "absolutely necessary for [Belgium's] integration in the European Monetary Union" (*Reuters News*, 3 October 1995).

Unlike previous budget bills, this one included no increases in direct taxes. However, it introduced several indirect taxes, for a total of BEF 35.0 billion, including increases in the VAT, the withholding tax on fixed-income investments (such as bonds and savings accounts), and excise duties. At the same time, the government planned to raise BEF 14.5 billion from granting licences for a second mobile telephone. Other revenue raisers included new taxes on electricity production and a tougher stance on tax evasion, which would bring about BEF 3.5 billion into the state coffers. Another BEF 15 billion would come from cuts to various federal government departments. Moreover, around BEF 20.0 billion would come from savings in the social security system, including BEF 13.0 billion in the health insurance sector, BEF 4.0 billion from pensions, and BEF 4.0 billion from changes to unemployment insurance (*Reuters News*, 3 October 1995).

The government had already stepped up its campaign to privatize a range of state assets by announcing the sale of its controlling 50 per cent stake in the Société Nationale de Crédit à l'Industrie, an industrial credit bank. It also announced that it had approved the sale of its 41.4 per cent stake in the Institut National de Crédit Agricole, a rural credit bank. Dehaene, who had approved the sales, announced that the government expected to generate BEF 20.7 billion from privatization receipts in 1995 and 1996. The revenues, he argued, would help his government reduce Belgium's high budget deficit as it prepared for the EMU.

Dehaene was criticized in the media because the budget did not mention the social security reform he had promised. Analysts attacked the fuzziness of the changes in social security, the last-minute dropping of plans to raise fresh savings through a so-called generalized social-security contribution, and resorting to traditional revenue-raising techniques (*Reuters News*, 3 October 1995). Dehaene responded by arguing that the budget was a correction of the "unaccountable policies of the 1970s" (ibid., 4 October 1995). He denied that he was "dragging his feet on a reform of the social security system": "We have always said the modernization of the social security system will have to be tackled. ... I am sticking to that path" (ibid). He added that "it was just too early to do that in this budget" (ibid). He argued that "there's undoubtedly a lot of work left on the table, but we've got four more years to deal with that" before Belgium went to the polls in 1999 (*Reuters News*, 3 October, 4 October 1995; *Wall Street Journal Europe*, 4 October 1995).

It was at this juncture that social security reform reappeared as a "necessary element" to meet the fiscal convergence criteria (Marier 2008, 94; Anderson et al. 2007, 334). According to the government's declaration and the budget bill, social security reform was next in line. The issue became increasingly politically delicate, threatening to bring down the government. Belgium was rocked by strikes and demonstrations in response to the austerity measures, which many saw as never ending. Discontent was rooted in economic austerity and spending cuts, fear of job losses, and increased concerns about potential reductions in social security benefits. The government claimed repeatedly that Belgium had to undertake these measures to qualify for the EMU, and it was, in fact, absolutely clear to the public that austerity had its roots in the need to improve public finances to that end. The only factor that limited the political tension was the "widespread consensus that Belgium must be among the first wave of countries" to qualify for EMU (Economist Intelligence Unit, 1st Quarter 1996). Faced with intense pressure, referring to social security reforms, Budget Minister Van Rompuy conceded that "the government agreement says 'end of the year,' but I always thought this timing was too ambitious" (*Reuters News*, 8 November 1995).

Public-sector unions, which were outraged by the austerity measures, stepped up their pressure on the government in early January 1996, demanding that it reconsider its plans for sweeping social security reforms. The two main public-sector unions – the socialist General Confederation of Public Services (CGSP) and the Christian-Democratic Catholic Trade Union Confederation (CSC) – announced that they would call a twenty-four-hour strike unless their key demands were met (*Reuters News*, 8 January 1996). The government had announced plans to tackle the social security issue in the early part of 1996, but when January arrived, Dehaene refrained from specifying any time limit for the discussions: "We have to resolve this," "but I will not be pressured into a time" (Economist Intelligence Unit 1st Quarter 1996; *Reuters News*, 9 January 1996).

When the government was drafting the budget in October 1995, it aimed to reduce the budget deficit to 3.0 per cent of GDP based on projections of 2.2 per cent economic growth in 1996. After the economic outlook worsened, however, the official growth forecast was revised downwards, to 1.6 per cent. This meant that the resulting lower tax revenues and higher social security payments would automatically push up the budget deficit for 1996. The government was absolutely determined to meet its 3.0 per cent target. To bridge the gap between the projections and the actual deficit, in early May 1996, the government announced that it sought a supplementary austerity package of deficit-reducing measures amounting to BEF 25 billion on top of the adjustment of BEF 112 billion in the original budget. The package relied on BEF 4.4 billion of additional cuts in government departments' spending, BEF 5.8 billion of cuts in the social security system, BEF 5.0 billion from the recovery of unused reserves from the social security system, BEF 5.0 billion of additional receipts and savings from the National Bank of Belgium's arbitrage and other financial operations, and BEF 4.9 billion from other sources, including new measures for fighting social security fraud (Economist Intelligence Unit, 3rd Quarter 1996). Although the package tapped into "new sources of revenue," the additional austerity efforts did not rely on increases in taxes for the first time in years.[17]

Dehaene Obtains Special Powers for EMU Membership

The government was being tested on many fronts. Talks on employment measures among the government, employers, and unions came to a point of collapse, and the government had to postpone its plans to reform social security for a second time. On top of these chronic problems, attaining the deficit target for 1996 became impossible due to slower economic growth. Moreover, the new budget would certainly bring even more austerity. This was highly likely to provoke further tensions, although the government was clearly counting on the strong consensus in favour of qualifying for the EMU.

Coming under increasing pressure to meet the Maastricht deadline, Dehaene decided to ask Parliament for special powers. This was the first time since the early 1980s that a government had made a request for legislating by decree.[18] The government approved three draft "framework laws" (*lois-cadre*) (on government finances, social security, and employment) "with a view to reducing the budget deficit to three percent of GDP and to guarantee the financial balance of the social security system" (*Reuters News*, 13 May 1996). It began working on the decrees immediately because, with the EMU deadline fast approaching, there was no time to lose. When requesting special powers, Dehaene warned the deputies that the 1997 budget was "one of the most important in Belgium's history" as it would constitute the "basis for the EU decision on whether the country can be in the first group to join EMU" (ibid.; *Financial Times*, 10 May 1995).

At the end of May 1995, the government issued a statement, announcing that the Council of Ministers had approved the three draft laws, "which should make it possible to realize the conditions for Belgium's participation in EMU." The laws set out "that the government, for the implementation of the 1996 budget and for the drafting and implementation of the 1997 budget, can take the necessary measures to realize the membership of the EMU and notably respect the Maastricht Treaty's budget deficit norms." Invoking the urgency of the EMU deadline, the government stated that these laws were necessary because it wanted "to have the instruments to be able to act quickly … to reach the Maastricht Treaty budget deficit targets" and that "any risk [of not meeting them] must be excluded" (*Reuters News*, 28 May 1996).

By resorting to executive decrees in the form of framework laws, Dehaene obtained a *carte blanche* to carry out whatever austerity measure was needed to meet the criteria. These powers were exactly what he needed at a time when the EU was putting constant pressure on Belgium for its public imbalances. Meanwhile, the ECOFIN Council was warning Belgium to cut its budget deficit below 3 per cent of GDP in 1997 if it wanted to qualify for the EMU (*Reuters News*, 8 July 1996).

In justifying the framework laws, the government repeatedly stressed that to meet the criteria, Belgium would have to "modernize" its social security system. Finance Minister Maystadt emphasized that the special powers were obtained to implement "changes in the social security system which would allow Belgium to meet the Maastricht criteria for EMU" (*Reuters News*, 19 June 1996). In justifying social security reform, Dehaene stressed that the laws would smooth the way for the budget cuts necessary to improve the country's chances of joining the single currency. However, when news leaked out that Pensions Minister Colla was working on a new reform plan, the public reacted strongly. Even women's organizations affiliated with the coalition partner Wallonian Socialist Party insisted on the removal of all measures related to pension reform (*Le Soir*, 18 June 1996, quoted in Marier 2008, 95).

Despite this strong opposition, Parliament approved the three framework laws in July, giving the government special powers to legislate by decree in budgetary matters (the EMU Law), reform of the social security system (the Social Framework Law), and wage settlements. Now that the government had obtained decree power, it expected that drafting the 1997 budget would be an easy task; moreover, it could swiftly reform the social security system without having to seek parliamentary approval at every step (*Reuters News*, 10 June 1996). However, persistent differences among the coalition partners about how to reform social security, especially pensions, made it extremely difficult to draft the budget (Couttenier 1997, 527–8). The political mood turned increasingly bitter that summer, when the government was working on the 1997 budget. Due to austerity fatigue, the government's approval rating dropped to less than 20 per cent. Nevertheless, Dehaene continued to insist that there was "no alternative" to urgent measures, including social security reform, if Belgium wished to meet the Maastricht criteria.

Drafting a tight budget for 1996 resulted in protracted public unrest as well as strikes and demonstrations throughout the summer months. The riots of 1 May and the subsequent unrest in reaction to the pension-reform proposal revealed significant discontent and demonstrated the broad base of the opposition to reform. In July, the government decided that large social security cuts were urgently needed because the 1997 social security budget would otherwise have a sizeable deficit. The government faced even more bruising battles with the unions, when news broke that BEF 50 billion of spending cuts were to be made in the social security sector. The unions called for protests in several cities and brought angry workers out into the streets (*Reuters News*, 30 September 1996).

After the framework laws passed, both public service unions (CGSP and CSC) held large-scale protests across the country in response to fears that the government would roll back public service pensions and health care benefits with the new budget. Finance Minister Maystadt reassured them that they "should not fear for a social massacre" (*Reuters News*, 26 September 1996). However, the CGSP threatened the government with massive protests and strike action, as did other public service unions, and declared that union leaders would meet after the government presented its budget to decide on possible courses of action (ibid., 30 September 1996).

Faced with such determined opposition and continuous pressure, the government had to abandon its reform plans. It had an incentive to keep the Maastricht timetable on the agenda because the goal of joining the EMU had always enjoyed wide and sustained public support. Although budgetary austerity was widely unpopular, the EMU provided a unique *vincolo esterno* that rendered austerity palatable. The EMU also served as a convenient tool for diverting public attention away from a series of scandals rocking the government. The government's use of the EMU strategically paralleled how the government in Greece used it in 1996. As we will see, the Simitis government's focus on the Maastricht deadlines proved to be a successful strategy to divert attention away from the diplomatic crisis with Turkey. (See chapter 6.) The EMU saved the day for both of these ruling governments.

From the "Budget of the Century"[19] to "Typical compromis à
la Belge"[20] in Social Security Reform

Towards the end of July 1996, the coalition partners reached an agreement on the 1997 budget. The new budget "aimed at paving the way to Europe's economic and monetary union." The EMU Law had given the government executive powers until the end of August 1997 to take a wide range of measures necessary for Belgium to join the EMU (Couttenier 1997). The government presented its budget in October, promising that it would guarantee entry to the EMU in 1999. In his speech to Parliament, Dehaene promised that "thanks to this budget, [Belgium] will comply with the Maastricht Treaty criteria for monetary union." He added that "with this budget we are de facto members of EMU." Parliament safely approved the budget, which included a sizeable package of corrective measures amounting to BEF 80 billion (about 1 per cent of GDP).

The budget aimed to cut the total public-sector deficit to 2.9 per cent of GDP from an estimated 3.3 per cent in 1996. The government deliberately kept the deficit target below the 3 per cent benchmark because, given the usual slippages, it believed it needed a margin of safety in case interest rates rose or economic growth weakened. To achieve the 2.9 per cent, the government introduced an austerity package worth BEF 80 billion, half of which consisted of tax increases and half of spending cuts. It would realize BEF 17 billion by cutting subsidies for future pensions at the state-owned postal service and subsidies to state-owned companies as well as reducing the international relations and defence budgets. This represented a decline in primary spending of 1.7 per cent in real terms. Cuts to social security expenditures, worth BEF 23 billion, were mainly to health care (by limiting spending on medication, hospitalization, and wages); there were other, smaller cuts to unemployment and early retirement benefits.

On the revenue side, the BEF 40 billion of new revenues would come largely from an increase in taxes worth BEF 23 billion: levying new taxes on the physical delivery of securities and savings accounts, closing tax loopholes used by companies, and imposing higher excise duties on petrol, beer, and spirits. Another BEF 7 billion would come from new taxes on company cars and an increase in social security charges for the self-employed. Non-fiscal receipts would increase with a sizeable sale of public assets (mainly public buildings and land), which was expected to yield BEF 7 billion.

The budget also included an unprecedented debt reduction package, which aimed to slash BEF 370 billion from the country's mountain of debt and reduce the debt-to-GDP ratio to 127 per cent by 1997. The most important of the measures was the use of a foreign exchange surplus on the sales of official gold reserves. The proceeds would be used, with the consent of the EMI, to reduce foreign currency–denominated debt (OECD 1997, 44–6).

Meanwhile, the Social Framework Law of 26 July 1996 had given the government extraordinary powers to tackle the pension schemes for wage earners and self-employed workers. The government wanted to "modernize" social security by ensuring a sustainable financial balance in the social insurance system, modernizing its administration, increasing administrative control and reducing fraud, and improving living standards for those with minimum benefits. Another goal was to ensure equality of pension benefits between men and women, first proposed by Willockx. On the financing side, to reduce the government's reliance on payroll taxes, a burden borne mainly by labour, the law raised extra revenues for the social insurance system. These "alternative means of financing" included additional indirect taxes and federal subsidies (Anderson et al. 2007, 335).

According to the original plans, the government would introduce an austerity package, worth BEF 80 billion in savings, with the 1997 budget. It planned to rely on BEF 50 billion in savings from the social security budget. This meant that the government planned to raise more than half the savings through spending cuts in social security (*Reuters News*, 27 September 1996). The government aimed to realize these cuts through a set of new measures, the most visible of which was a gradual increase in women's retirement age to sixty-five years (from sixty) over a thirteen-year period. It had also decided on a 2 per cent tax on all early retirement pensions. Most of the measures appeared highly technical, making it very difficult to trace the actual changes. They included a reduction in family allowances for teenagers, lower unemployment benefits for older people, and some targeted measures in the health sector (ibid., 27 September 1996). The government unveiled the reform in late September. The resulting law reflected numerous concessions (Marier 2008, 96–7) and included the following significant changes (Festjens 1997):

- The legal retirement age for women would be gradually raised from sixty to sixty-five, with a transition period of thirteen years. At the same time, the duration of the career on which access to a full pension is based would be increased from forty to forty-five years. The age limit for women to obtain access to other forms of replacement income would be raised to the legal retirement age.

- Early retirement (from the age of sixty) would be subject to a career condition, gradually raised from twenty years in 1997 to thirty-five years in 2005 (in two-year increments).
- A "minimum claim per year of career" would be introduced. This minimum pension right would be linked to the minimum wage.
- The wage ceiling would be raised every two years, based on growth in real wages. The possibility of selectively awarding a welfare adjustment to certain categories of pensioner (apart from automatic indexation) would be provided.
- Pensions would be revalorized during the period 1955–74 by a coefficient of 3.6 per cent, which would be gradually eliminated by 2005.

The changes to the pension scheme for self-employed workers were similar to the reform of the wage earners' pension scheme with respect to the increase in the retirement age, the calculation fraction for women, and the introduction of a career condition for men and women in case of early retirement between sixty and sixty-five years of age. The main goal of raising the legal retirement age for women and introducing the career condition was to increase women's participation in the labour force.

Due to opposition from the unions, numerous measures that the government had initially announced did not make it into the reform. For example, Parliament did not pass the reconsideration of the non-contributory benefits for sickness and unemployment. The early retirement scheme was also not altered, except that women would have to wait longer to obtain it. For all items, the transition periods for phasing in the reforms were much longer than the government initially intended. Moreover, implementation of the measures was postponed to 1 July 1997. Significantly, the powerful *vincolo esterno* played a crucial role in allowing the reform to pass (Anderson et al. 2007, 335).

In terms of its impact, the reform did not introduce any dramatic change. A Federal Planning Bureau working paper estimated that affected individuals would see a less than 1 per cent reduction in the value of their pensions (Festjens 1997). The paper predicted that the long-term effect of these measures on spending would be zero, if not positive. Most of the negative effect of giving women more time to make pension contributions was, in fact, compensated for by the newly introduced "minimum pension right" for individual career years. The worst-affected group was non-married women pensioners, and the impact of the measures on them would amount to a 1 per cent reduction in their pensions, starting in 2010. The most significant savings would come from the gradual elimination of the revalorization granted between 1955 and 1974 (ibid.). Marier (2008, 97), who analysed the impact of the reform, claimed that it actually increased the burden on other social security spending in areas such as unemployment, disability, and early retirement, and that the impact on these programs would amount to more than BEF 20 billion by 2007.

In fact, when the budget was announced, it became clear that the total savings in the social security budget was limited to only BEF 23 billion – less than half the initial goal of cutting back BEF 50 billion. Analysts and opposition politicians criticized the budget, which, they concurred, delayed the long-awaited fundamental reform of the social security system once more. Belgian newspapers complained that the government had missed an important opportunity to introduce the reforms it had announced earlier, fiercely criticizing the government for not having used its powers of executive decree to push through more radical social security reforms. For example, *Le Soir* (2 October 1996, digest repr. in *Reuters News*, 3 October 1996) remarked, "This budget is terribly flat, without imagination, without brilliance, a repetition of previous budget exercises." Referring to the decrees, the newspaper questioned whether "it [was] really necessary to give special powers to the government and muzzle the parliament for this." It argued that aside from gradually increasing the retirement age for women to sixty-five from sixty over thirteen years, most other measures were so technical that even specialists were having trouble explaining them. It added that the measures consisted largely of blocking future increases in benefits rather than scaling back existing ones. It concluded, "The Maastricht project has been reached, but with a disputable budget ... [where] the promise of a fundamental reform of the social security has not been kept."

La Libre Belgique (2 October 1996, digest repr. in *Reuters News*, 3 October 1996) concurred: "The Maastricht target has been reached, but without glory. In this budget there are no traces of measures which will ensure the long-term financing of social security. And we are still trying to understand why Dehaene demanded special powers to draw up a budget like this." *De Morgen* (2 October 1996, digest repr. in ibid.) answered the questions the other papers had raised. It claimed that Dehaene's piecemeal approach was inspired by fear of street protest: "This budget is not revolutionary. ... This way, Dehaene avoids a French scenario whereby the whole country grinds to a halt because of strike actions." *De Standaard* (2 October 1996, digest repr. in ibid.) was sharply critical of the budget, which, it argued, "again includes tricks and 'one-shot' measures" without any genuine reform of the social security system. It added that "this budget hurts nobody, especially not those big groups which could organize social protest." The Economist Intelligence Unit (4th Quarter 1996), too, agreed with these newspapers by stating that "the government had missed a golden opportunity to make more drastic reforms to the social security system" because, wary of more discontent, "the government chose to play safe." Finally, the *Financial Times* (30 September 1996) commented that the budget was "politically 'very good' since the Maastricht criteria would be met and it contained hardly any controversial or politically sensitive measures."

The government had a loud and clear promise to legislate radical changes to the social security system; this was why it had obtained special powers. However, facing popular unrest and intense pressure from the unions, and once he realized that he could raise savings in areas other than social security, Dehaene changed his original plan. Thus, the government shied away from a radical reform of the social security system. Economists and analysts had already been warning that the budget would have to contain one-off measures should the government wish to avoid unpopular cuts to social security (*Reuters News*, 30 September 1996). In fact, Dehaene himself confessed later that the government had designed the social security budget in such a way as to minimize political protest. Observing that social security reforms required in the context of Euro-austerity had led to massive unrest in France, causing the Juppé government to resign, Dehaene admitted that he had had to opt for a more cautious approach to reform: "If I slowed down and postponed certain reforms planned for the end of last year, that's exactly because I was convinced that, in the climate created by the French situation, if I had gone too fast I would have found the same situation [in Belgium]." He stated that, instead, he preferred "the pragmatic approach, going step by step, which avoids breakdowns." He did "not believe in *La Reforme* of the system, with a capital L and a capital R. The social security system is so complicated, like a kind of spider's web touching all parts of society, so that you have to modify it in successive stages." Dehaene added that he was capable of realizing structural reforms in other areas – for example, the partial privatization of public enterprises such as Belgacom, the national airline Sabena, and other state-owned enterprises (*Financial Times*, 19 November 1996).

The government's piecemeal reform strategy paid off politically in the end. While Euro-austerity measures helping Belgium pass the Maastricht test provoked strikes and demonstrations, their extent was more limited than the mass unrest that had plagued France a year earlier. When the European Commission published projections for the budgetary positions beyond 1997, it predicted that all member states, except

Greece, would be able to meet the 3.0 per cent rule in 1998. And when it announced that the prediction for Belgium was 2.5 per cent, Dehaene felt even more reassured that the budgetary strategy had worked without having to retrench social security altogether.

After reforming private pensions, the government contemplated tackling public-sector pensions – the bigger-ticket item by far. Given the budgetary constraints that had been imposed on the road to the EMU, reforming public pensions would certainly mean huge savings in the budget. Immediately after it introduced the budget in early October, the government caught a rare policy window, where a consensus emerged among its coalition partners on reforming public pensions. It seemed that this could be politically feasible only if reform measures were phased in during a long transition period. At the end of January 1997, while discussions on reform options were continuing, the three major unions staged a strike in Brussels, paralyzing the capital. The unions demanded that the government respect their pension rights. This put the reform proposal on the back burner for another six months (Marier 2008, 99–100).

In June, reports began appearing in the press that the government was preparing a reform proposal similar to the one originally proposed by Willockx. Pension benefits would no longer be automatically indexed to wage increases – instead, increases would be held to a ceiling of 1 per cent per year – and there would be an increase in the *tantièmes* (the pension denominator). Minister of Pensions Colla denied press reports that reform preparations were underway, and Dehaene called a press conference to deny the rumours. Dehaene added that his government would negotiate the terms of the reform with the unions if and when they decided to take the initiative. The response from the unions was loud and clear: touching the indexation mechanism and increasing the *tantièmes* would be a declaration of war. They warned the government that they would take strike action against any initiative. To prove their unwavering opposition, the unions staged two weeks of strikes and demonstrations. It was clear that this round of reform attempt, too, would end in a cul-de-sac (Marier 2008, 100).

After several of his earlier initiatives were defeated, in January 1998, Colla once again called on the unions for another round of negotiations. Signalling that he would be ready to grant concessions, he announced that "even if we vote in a year, I am ready to make a reform that is socially acceptable" (*Le Soir*, 7 January 1998, quoted in Marier 2008, 100). When his proposal received no response, the public-sector-pension reform initiative came to an absolute halt. After rounds of frustrating attempts,

Colla redirected his attention to the issue of health care, which was also in his portfolio – and which eventually proved even more difficult.

Second Convergence Program, Fiscal Gimmickry, "Painless" Austerity, and the 1998 Budget

In December 1997, the government had presented Belgium's second convergence program, which would provide the framework for the next four years' budgets (1997–2000). Putting Belgium on track to enter the EMU, the program envisaged cutting the budget deficit to 2.9 per cent in 1997, 2.0 per cent in 1998, 1.6 per cent in 1999, and reaching 1.4 per cent by 2000. It also estimated that Belgium's mounting debt would be slashed by 10.0 percentage points, from 130.4 per cent in 1996 to 120.5 per cent by 2000. In presenting the convergence program, Finance Minister Maystadt claimed that "Belgium already fulfills most of the Maastricht convergence criteria; price stability, exchange rate stability, convergence of long-term interest rates ... therefore the thrust of this document is on budgetary convergence." He reaffirmed Belgium's "clear commitment" to following prudent budgetary policies for participating in the single currency and stated that the main way the government aimed to achieve debt and deficit reductions was by raising primary surpluses (*Financial Times*, 21 December 1996).

Following the lead of the European Commission and the Monetary Committee, the Council stated that the program's strategy was "ambitious," but "credible" and "adequate." It appreciated the policies Belgium had followed in the framework of the first convergence program (1992–6), which had resulted in considerable progress towards meeting the budgetary criteria. While it was reassured by the government's commitment, it urged Belgian authorities to take every opportunity to make maximum progress in reducing the debt ratio (*Reuters News*, 17 February 1997; *Agence Europe*, 18 February 1997).

In the meantime, a series of reports appeared in the press, stating that Belgium had "cooked the books." They said that the Belgian Treasury had secretly carried out a complex swap with an arm of the central bank to make it appear that its net public debt had fallen more than it actually had and that the purpose of the swap was "to reduce the net state debt in order to fulfill the EMU criteria" (*Wall Street Journal Europe*, 9 January 1997). This accounting trick amounted to anywhere from BEF 80 billion to BEF 150 billion (1.0 to 1.8 per cent of GDP) (*Financial Times*, 10 January, 29 January 1997; Economist Intelligence Unit, 1st Quarter 1997). Finance Minister Maystadt officially denied that this was a covert operation because the government had informed Parliament about the transfer.

Belgium's success in reducing its debt was, in every sense, vital for gaining entry to the EMU. The country was already meeting the other criteria on inflation, interest rates, currency alignment, and budget deficit. The government hoped that if it could demonstrate that its debt met the Maastricht definition of being "sufficiently diminishing and approaching the reference value at a satisfactory pace," Belgium would qualify for the EMU. It just so happened that Eurostat announced that there was no rule preventing governments from using gold to pay down public debt, a strategy that the Belgian Treasury had used extensively in 1996 (Savage 2005, 122). After this endorsement, the Council assessed the convergence program favourably. The Belgian economic bureaucracy saw this as a positive sign: the government had finally managed to convince its European partners that its fiscal consolidation strategy was credible.

In early January 1997, the government announced that the 1996 deficit had fallen to 3.4 per cent of GDP – 0.4 percentage points higher than projected. The government attributed this slippage to disappointing economic growth and a rising deficit in the social security budget. Budget Minister Van Rompuy quickly declared that this was a small margin. The government announced that it would impose a further BEF 10 billion of fiscal tightening during 1997 in addition to the BEF 80 billion in supplementary measures undertaken in 1996 (Fiers and Deweerdt 1998, 382–3). Van Rompuy was quick to add that the government had carefully chosen "painless" measures that would not directly affect the public – mainly raising revenues and reining in spending. As expected, these further austerity measures did not provoke much opposition (Economist Intelligence Unit, 2nd Quarter 1997).

When the ECOFIN Council was conducting the EDP in May 1997, it recommended that the Belgian government pay close attention to social spending and tax revenues in order to meet the EMU requirement of 3.0 per cent. In particular, the Council warned Belgium to focus its consolidation efforts on limiting the expansion of social security expenditures. It also stated that "the Belgian government must, as soon as possible, address its current excessive deficit so that Belgium may be ready to participate in the third phase of monetary union according to the timetable fixed in the Treaty." The Council's recommendation followed a European Commission report on measures that should be adopted by the EMU candidates running deficits higher than the reference limit (*Market News International*, 12 May 1997). The government, somewhat rattled by the Council's statement, decided in July to sell off a further 24.7 per cent of its shares in a banking and insurance group, ASLK-CGER. Finance Minister Maystadt stated that the government was planning to use the money raised from the sale and bourse listing to pay down its public debt. Budget Minister Van Rompuy announced that "we will 100 percent certainly participate in the European monetary union" (*Reuters News*, 25 July 1997).

The government was expecting the preparations for the 1998 budget to be much easier than those in earlier years. The fact that the country was already heading for a budget deficit target that was comfortably below the Maastricht target left a large amount of fiscal room in which to manoeuvre. The government thought that only a few additional measures would be required to offset higher-than-expected spending. Speaking to Parliament, Dehaene stated that, with the 1998 budget, Belgium was "sure to take part in EMU." To maintain a high level of primary surplus that year, the new measures amounted to BEF 17.0 billion (or 0.2 per cent of GDP) in both expenditure cuts and additional receipts: an extension of levies imposed in 1997 on pharmaceutical companies and electricity producers, and one-off initiatives, such as the sale of a licence for a third mobile phone operator (OECD 1999, 45–6).

Van Rompuy announced that, in addition to these new measures, the 3 per cent surcharge on personal and corporate income taxes (the "crisis tax" that had been levied to meet the Maastricht criteria in 1993) was to remain in force (Economist Intelligence Unit, 4th Quarter 1997). The government intended to contain social security spending, which was set to increase by BEF 46.9 billion in 1997. This tremendous increase stemmed almost entirely from expanding health care benefits. In fact, when the budget was being drafted, the Finance Ministry insisted on imposing limits on the health care budget, and eventually, the government announced that the increase in health care spending would be capped at 1.5 per cent. The National Fund for Health and Disability Insurance objected to this measure and pressured the government to reconsider the cap. After negotiations, the health care budget was permitted to increase by about 3.4 per cent (ibid.). The budget was approved in the Chamber of Representatives in December 1997.

With the fiscal measures introduced with the 1998 budget, the authorities expected Belgium to be one year ahead on its deficit reduction path, and nearly two years ahead in its debt reduction path, compared with the targets set out in its convergence program. Austerity packages worth about BEF 100 billion in each of the five previous budgets had given the state a primary surplus of 5.3 per cent of GDP. Only the BEF

660 billion needed to pay the interest on Belgium's BEF 9.882 trillion debt pushed fiscal balances into the red. There was consensus in Belgium (and in Europe as well) that the 1998 budget would safely deliver entry to the EMU.

Belgium Enters the EMU Safely, with Little Drama

In February 1998, Finance Minister Maystadt announced that the budget deficit for 1997 had dropped to 2.1 per cent and the debt ratio had fallen to 122.2 per cent (*Reuters News*, 16 February 1998). A few days later, he and Van Rompuy announced together that the 1998 deficit would fall to 1.8 per cent of GDP (ibid., 20 February 1998), while Dehaene added that the debt ratio would decline to around 118.5 per cent. Although the government was within a safe margin, Dehaene warned that Belgium should continue its budgetary discipline so as to reduce its debt ratio, which was still almost double the Maastricht norm (ibid., 20 February 1998). In March, when the government was conducting the annual quality control of the budget, it announced that Belgium would be able to further reduce the deficit, to 1.7 per cent of GDP, due to higher levels of economic growth and lower interest rates.

Selling gold reserves also helped. In March, the National Bank announced that it would be selling BEF 110 billion of gold from its reserves. In May, Maystadt emphasized that these sales had been undertaken to reduce Belgium's national debt ahead of the EMU. He added that other measures would be forthcoming, including more privatization (*Reuters News*, 1 May 1998). The proceeds of the previous four gold sales, which had generated a profit of BEF 222 billion, had already been used to help Belgium reduce its public debt to meet the Maastricht criteria (Economist Intelligence Unit, 2nd Quarter 1998; Fiers and Deweerdt 1999, 270).

Ahead of the EMI and the ECB publishing their convergence reports on the assessment of the EMU candidates, the German Bundesbank and Dutch de Nederlandsche Bank criticized Belgium and Italy, seeing them as "a burden and a risk." These central banks called on both governments to make additional commitments to reduce their debt ahead of the final selection process in May (*Reuters News*, 27 March, 20 April 1998). In a news conference, however, Commissioner responsible for Economic, Monetary and Financial Affairs de Silguy defended high-debt Belgium (along with Italy), stating that asking the Belgians to achieve more than they had done already would be "unreasonable" (ibid., 25 March 1998).

When the European Commission and the EMI published their convergence reports, the Commission stated that the budget deficit in Belgium had declined substantially and continuously, reaching a level below the Maastricht reference value; the primary surplus remained at a high level; and the debt ratio expected to decline further in the future. Thus, it recommended to the Council "the abrogation of the decision on the existence of an excessive deficit for Belgium" (European Commission 1998, 97). The EMI's report, however, expressed concern because it predicted that Belgium would not be able to meet the debt-to-GDP ratio of 60 per cent before 2031. It warned that "there is an evident ongoing concern as to whether the ratio of government debt to GDP will be sufficiently diminishing and approaching the reference value at a satisfactory pace ... and whether sustainability of the fiscal position has been achieved" (EMI 1998, 14). Despite the warnings of the EMI and the protestations of the Germans and the Dutch, the European Council decided on 2 May 1998 that Belgium was qualified to enter the EMU with the ten other EMU candidates.

Euro-Austerity and the Political Economy of Reform in Belgium

This chapter showed that Belgium made great strides in bringing its public finances under control in the early 1990s, despite widely held expectations to the contrary. The budget deficit declined from about 7 per cent of GDP in the early part of the Maastricht decade to around budgetary balance by the end. The two Dehaene governments had a clear agenda for how to meet the Maastricht convergence criteria: a firm determination to reform the Belgian welfare state. In fact, at the beginning of the 1990s, the social security budget had a surplus, which the governments used to finance the central government budget. But the welfare state was time and again accused as the main culprit behind Belgium's notorious fiscal imbalances. Once the Maastricht convergence criteria were announced, however, the fate of the Belgian social security system appeared to be sealed: everyone expected the welfare state to be the prime target under Euro-austerity.

Such expectation was vindicated throughout the convergence process: in domestic public debates, the welfare state had been systematically charged by politicians and policymakers as the main cause for the severe budgetary problems that would thwart Belgium's entry to the EMU. In addition to acting as the most powerful structural constraint on the budgets, the EMU provided Belgian politicians with the much-needed discursive instrument – the *vincolo esterno* – for justifying any kind of radical reform. As a powerful political instrument, the EMU had the potential to support their case for retrenching the Belgian welfare state, and it would certainly shield them from powerful opposition on their path to radical reform. Thus, many had expected that Belgian governments could easily push through an overhaul of the country's social security system.

In the end, both Dehaene governments *did* push through comprehensive reform of the social security system. After rounds of reform attempts, however, the Belgian welfare state could only be characterized as maintaining the status quo. Every reform initiative aimed at retrenchment had faced massive strikes, demonstrations, and protests by opposition groups, at times bringing public life to a standstill. Opposition came from a broad range of societal groups, mobilized mainly by organized labour: interest groups (e.g., women's organizations), coalition partners (mainly the Socialists), and working and middle classes taking to the streets. At times, even Cabinet members opposed the initiatives.

The Belgian case shows that even the most intense Euro-austerity and the all-powerful EMU card were insufficient to retrench the Belgian social security system. Radical initiatives were categorically abandoned even before they were brought before Parliament. The "long overdue" pension reforms originally proposed by Minister of Pensions Willockx and subsequently by Minister Colla under both Dehaene governments are prime examples. The plan to standardize the retirement age for men and women in the public sector was proposed by successive ministers to no avail. If it had passed, the reform would have brought immediate savings during the Maastricht time frame because public pensions constituted the largest item in the social security budget.

But during the first attempt by Willockx in 1993, women's associations and unions put up a powerful protest. Cabinet members themselves joined them to oppose the initiative even before the Cabinet debated it. When that attempt failed, Colla attempted to implement the same reform in 1994. This time, massive opposition by the unions blocked the legislation after it had reached the Senate, a move that eventually led to the reform being shelved again. The Dehaene II government put the issue on the agenda again as part of the government's cost-containment strategy. Colla made two attempts at reform in 1997, but the unions took them as a declaration of war, and Brussels was paralyzed by strikes and demonstrations. As a result of such opposition, therefore, the government had no choice but to withdraw the reform plan.

In other cases, Belgian politicians did not even attempt to introduce wholesale reform because they were intimidated by their punitive electoral consequences. In both elections during the Maastricht decade (1991 and 1995), social security reform became *the* hot potato. Whichever political party proposed radical plans before an election, it was simply cast out from the ruling coalitions. Electoral support for all these parties plummeted, so none of them could join newly forming governing coalitions. Although all parties believed that the social security system needed urgent reform to enable Belgium to join the euro on time, radical reform was the thorn in the side of Belgian politics all through the Maastricht decade.

In the few cases where reforms were passed, it was only after the Dehaene governments had dramatically scaled back their reform ambitions. The 1993–4 reform, introduced with the Global Plan, and the 1996 social security reform, passed through extraordinary powers, are cases in point. In the former, the government had called for a pact with its social partners to introduce reform based on the Verplaetse Report. The report stated that, for Belgium to attain EMU membership, social security spending had to be curtailed. It proposed that, in the fiscal consolidation process, two-thirds of the entire burden of the fiscal effort should be borne by the social security budget until Belgium entered the EMU. This would mean massive cutbacks in virtually all welfare programs. The unions were frustrated by what they saw as a massive attack on social security and walked out of negotiations. Dehaene insisted on his plan and tried to sell it as a *sine qua non* for meeting the Maastricht targets. Successive strikes paralyzed Belgian public life for the first time since the 1930s, forcing the government to invite the unions back to the negotiating table. The reform was passed, but only after the unions had obtained very significant concessions.

The case of the 1996 social security reform under the Dehaene II government is at least as striking as the first. The government was equipped with special executive powers, giving it a mandate to carry out social security reform (as part of the government's declaration) and extraordinary legislative power (the Social Framework Law) to reform Belgium's social security system. The original plan was to raise BEF 50 billion through cuts in social security programs, but, facing popular unrest and intense pressure from the unions, many of the proposed measures were scrapped. Once the government realized that there were alternative ways to create savings, it shied away from taking radical measures. When asked why the government had not stuck to its stricter original plan, Dehaene confessed that he had deliberately designed the reform to minimize political unrest. Thus, once again, radical reform plans were scaled back due to union opposition or the threat of social and political unrest – even when the government was equipped with extraordinary powers to carry out any reform plan whatsoever.

The Belgian case study shows that, after rounds of reform attempts on the road to the EMU, neither fundamental restructuring nor wholesale retrenchment of the welfare state proved possible. In some cases, governments had not been able to bring reform initiatives to Parliament; in others, they simply did not dare to proceed for fear that opposition would threaten the life of their government; in still others, reforms were passed only after the government had watered down its original plans. Paradoxically, instead of saving money in the short term, governments felt obliged to push the bitter impact of the reforms down the road to make them palatable. Instead of relying on cutbacks that would produce immediate savings, they resorted to alternative means of financing, including taxation measures, increases in social security contributions and privatization receipts, and fiscal gimmickry to help them meet the requirements of the Maastricht Treaty.

The Belgian case study demonstrates that, in spite of the large stock of public debt, governments managed to rein in their budgetary balances. Both Dehaene governments were determined to implement austerity, and, in the end, they successfully corrected large fiscal imbalances. Throughout the Maastricht decade, the treaty's timetable hung over their heads like the sword of Damocles. By the end of it, the general government deficit had declined from a level that was more than double the Maastricht norm in the early 1990s to a level comfortably below the 3 per cent benchmark.

When successive attempts to reform the Belgian social security system failed to produce the planned savings, governments had to resort to other fiscal strategies to comply with the criteria. Instead of cutting social spending, which was their declared goal, they generally relied on obtaining ever-higher levels of revenue from privatization and taxation, as shown in table 10.

The Belgian fiscal consolidation strategy centred largely on increasing revenues, especially in the first half of the 1990s, and public revenues rose from 46.1 per cent of GDP in 1991 to a record 49.4 per cent by 2001. As episodes of fiscal consolidation show, both Dehaene governments

Table 10. Belgium: General Government Accounts, Social Expenditures, and Privatization Revenues (% of GDP)

	1991	1992	1993	1994	1995	1996	1997	1998	1999	2000	2001
Total government expenditures	53.9	54.1	55.3	52.9	52.4	52.7	51.2	50.6	50.1	49.0	49.2
Social expenditures	25.2	24.2	25.2	24.7	25.2	25.7	24.7	24.7	24.6	23.5	24.0
Non-social expenditures	28.7	29.9	30.0	28.2	27.2	26.9	26.5	25.8	25.5	25.5	25.2
Total government revenues	46.1	45.6	47.4	47.4	47.9	48.7	49.1	49.6	49.5	49.0	49.4
Privatization receipts	–	–	0.4	0.2	1.0	0.5	0.7	0.8	–	–	–
Government deficit	–7.4	–8.2	–7.5	–6.2	–4.4	–3.9	–2.1	–0.9	–0.6	–0.1	0.2
Public debt	126.9	128.5	134.1	132.1	130.5	128.0	123.2	118.2	114.4	108.8	107.6

Source: OECD (2002, 2016a, 2016b, 2017a, 2017c); European Commission (2017); privatization figures: author's calculations.
Note: A dash (–) denotes zero or a negligible amount.

introduced large increases through non-indexation of tax brackets, a reduction in tax benefits, increases in direct and indirect taxes, and fighting tax evasion. In particular, the government imposed a crisis tax in 1993. As a result of these measures, the tax burden in Belgium remained the highest in the EU. Among non-tax measures, Belgium recorded some hefty proceeds from privatization, mainly from 1993 until 1998, when the European Council announced that Belgium qualified for EMU membership.

Although Belgium's fiscal consolidation strategy mainly relied on raising revenues, the Dehaene governments repeatedly imposed spending restraints to qualify for the EMU. They justified all attempts to reform the social security system by referring to the EMU and stating that all savings achieved would contribute to the fiscal consolidation strategy. However, because they scaled back their social security reforms, they could not raise appreciable savings from social spending. As table 10 shows, the governments did manage to reduce total public outlays, from 53.9 per cent of GDP in 1991 to 49.2 per cent in 2001. Although these outlays decreased by a sizeable amount, social expenditures remained rather stable, with only minor cutbacks.

The table also shows that non-social spending declined notably, from 28.7 per cent of GDP in 1991 to 25.2 per cent in 2001. These figures confirm the finding in this chapter that when facing opposition to welfare reform, governments resorted to reducing non-social expenditures and that, despite their political discourse and scholarly expectations, it was these reductions, along with revenue increases, that brought in the largest savings. In addition, governments took one-off measures such as increasing privatization receipts. There were also reports that they were engaged in various forms of fiscal gimmickry including gold sales, but these actions were subsequently cleared by Eurostat.

This chapter aimed to test the Euro-austerity hypothesis using a case study of the political economy of reform in Belgium. As discussed in chapter 1, the EMU was conceived of as the most direct and pressing constraint on Europe's social protection systems. And the most direct and significant mechanism through which economic and monetary integration was expected to pressure welfare states was the stringent fiscal rules governing the Maastricht transition period. Thus, the Euro-austerity hypothesis implies that the extent to which welfare states change depends on their level of need to reduce deficits and public debt. With the largest debt-to-GDP ratio in the EU and very high deficit-to-GDP ratio at the beginning of the convergence process, Belgium was destined to undergo a process of dramatic fiscal retrenchment if it was to qualify for the EMU. Such a process would bring intense pressure on budgets, which would effectively downsize the Belgian welfare state by forcing policymakers to retrench social expenditures. Moreover, many expected that Maastricht would provide Belgian governments with a trump card, empowering them in their reform attempts and insulating them from powerful opposition pressure.

Whether welcoming or resisting such severe pressure, Belgian governments made every effort to retrench their welfare state. The evidence presented in this case study demonstrates that part of the conventional expectations – the structural pressure stemming from the EMU and the discursive opportunities it would provide – were largely confirmed. On the road to EMU membership, Euro-austerity did, in fact, force Belgian governments to make strong declarations about their retrenchment plans, and in all electoral pledges and eventually in the *déclarations gouvernementales*, the imperative of welfare reform constituted the centrepiece of government programs.

However, conventional expectations of the actual reform outcomes (i.e., entry to the EMU leading to massive welfare state retrenchment) are not borne out by the evidence of Belgian welfare state trajectories in the 1990s.

5 Euro-Austerity and the Political Economy of Reform in Greece

Seen from the vantage point of the early 1990s, with deficit and debt levels so far off from the Maastricht Treaty requirements, Greece was, along with Belgium and Italy, certainly a basket case. By 1990, its inflation rate exceeded 20 per cent, and interest rate differentials with the other EU member states was exceedingly wide. With deficit ratios quadruple those of the Maastricht benchmark and public debt levels fast approaching the size of its national income, Greece's public imbalances were disastrously large. The goal of entering the EMU looked virtually impossible. As one of the three highly indebted EMU candidates, Greece faced dramatic fiscal austerity. However, by the end of the Maastricht decade, Greece became the twelfth member of the eurozone, two years after the initial eleven member states had adopted the single currency.

The case study presents each government's reform attempts and their outcomes during the Maastricht decade. I show that while Euro-austerity led to significant reforms in fiscal policy and politics in Greece, reform efforts did not go far enough to bring radical change to the Greek welfare state. First, I trace how Greece qualified for EMU membership despite having exceptional fiscal imbalances. I review the budgetary strategies adopted by each government and present the institutional changes that resulted in a larger capacity to rein in the budget. By analysing episodes of fiscal consolidation, I discuss the role of the EMU, as both an impending constraint on and a *vincolo esterno* for policymakers desperately wishing to join the euro. Second, I review each attempt at welfare state reform in this pension-heavy state and emphasize the large gap between the original plan and the reform outcome. By the end of the Maastricht decade, Greece had secured its eurozone membership. Its welfare state had largely escaped radical retrenchment; in fact, it had even seen some expansion! The case study concludes that this was possible mainly due to successful opposition by the unions and other societal actors, which blocked the politicians' reform attempts.

The chapter begins by describing how EU authorities and observers alike viewed the Greek candidacy during the early 1990s in relation to the treaty requirements. It reviews the election of the New Democracy (ND) party under Constantine Mitsotakis, following a period of corruption scandals and economic crisis, and the Mitsotakis government's attempts to introduce fiscal austerity for the first time in years through Greece's first convergence program and two successive episodes of social security reform. Although these reforms were to bring about significant changes, the governments that adopted them found themselves thrown out of office. Incoming governments often chose to quietly disregard them when the time came to implement the measures.

The chapter then follows how the Panhellenic Socialist Movement (PASOK) governments led by Andreas Papandreou and Costas Simitis continued with Euro-austerity, albeit somewhat half-heartedly, until the general election of 1996. It traces the efforts by the second Simitis government to meet the Maastricht requirements and its two attempts at social security reform. While the first attempt was subsequently shelved, the second in fact expanded the Greek welfare state. It follows the third, short-lived Simitis government, which proposed pension reform, paradoxically, after having secured entry to the EMU, and traces the Maastricht effect on the process of fiscal consolidation in Greece. The chapter concludes by providing an analytical overview of the political economy of welfare state reform in Greece and discusses the implications of these developments for the empirical validity of the Euro-austerity hypothesis.

Greece "On the Fringe"

Although, for Belgium and Italy, joining the euro would be a miracle, it was only a question of when. In the case of Greece, however, it was a question of *if*. By the early 1990s, only a few thought that Greece had any hope of qualifying for the EMU. At home, seasoned observers of Greek politics called Greece "on the fringe" because "it was not, nor did it expect in the foreseeable future to be, a member" of the eurozone (Featherstone, Kazamias, and Papadimitriou 2000, 396). Abroad, when treaty negotiations were launched, the country was seen as either Europe's "black sheep" (*Financial Times*, 8 December 1990) or a "lost cause" (Featherstone 2005a, 224).

Even before treaty negotiations began in March 1990, European Commission President Jacques Delors, in a very harshly worded letter, warned the Greek government to take urgent action. No other member state received such a cold, formal, written warning from the highest level. Given the grave problems characterizing Greece's fiscal balances, Delors strongly warned the government that the country was lagging behind the rest of the EU, to the point where its "course toward the single market, monetary union and European unification [was] in danger of being permanently undermined" (*Financial Times*, 27 March 1990). He urged the government to take "drastic measures" to permanently reduce the soaring deficit and debt (*Agence Europe*, 28 March 1990).

When the treaty negotiations began that December, Greece's reputation was at an "unprecedentedly low ebb" (Featherstone 2003, 924) and its credibility as a future EMU member "at rock bottom" (Featherstone, Kazamias, and Papadimitriou 2000, 396). Judging by the convergence criteria during the early 1990s, Greece was clearly identified time and again as one of the three laggards, along with Italy and Belgium (Dyson 2000, 114–17). In fact, of the three, it was the member state whose chances for EMU participation were clearly the lowest. As the state "most divergent" from the convergence criteria (Featherstone 2005a, 224), economic forecasts for Greece's participation in the single currency during the early 1990s remained "dire" (Featherstone 2003, 928). The fiscal criteria were, in fact, specifically designed to exclude Italy, but, surprisingly, not Greece, from entering the third stage of the EMU. This was because there was a widely held, open secret that, as "the sick man of Europe" (*Economist*, 9 May 1992), Greece was either "out of the first round" (McNamara 2003, 343) or "not yet in the running" (Dinan 2004, 301, 248).

In July 1991, the European Commission sent a communication to the Council (European Commission 1991), giving Greece the lowest marks of all member states: two black marks for inflation (negative situation), one black for the budget deficit (negative situation), two grey for the official debt (partially unsatisfactory situation), and two black for external accounts (negative situation) (*Agence Europe*, 4 July 1991). Greece was at the bottom of all the blacklists, not only in the EU but also across the entire OECD. Its budget deficit was at 20 per cent and inflation at 20 per cent, causing the OECD's *Economic Survey* for the country (ibid., 11) to identify it as "practically the worst in the OECD area." Its fiscal balances were deteriorating at a time when Greece was a net beneficiary of the EU budget.

When the time for EMU convergence assessment came in March 1998, Greece still remained far from approaching any of the convergence criteria. Accordingly, the Commission concluded that Greece fulfilled "none of the necessary conditions for the adoption of the single currency" (Decision No 98/318/EC). This meant that, of all the candidates that aspired to join the single currency, only Greece failed to meet the convergence criteria. Although Prime Minister Simitis quickly declared that Greece would meet the criteria by 1999 (*Agence France-Presse*, 23 April 1997), the chances of even a delayed entry looked bleak, if it were possible at all.

Greece Enters the 1990s: The Mitsotakis Government

Greece entered the 1990s in political turmoil. Andreas Papandreou's PASOK government, which had dominated Greek politics since 1981, ended in corruption scandals and economic failure. The election of June 1989 led to a hung Parliament with an ephemeral coalition government, and the November election brought about no change. The economy grew so fragile that political parties were forced to form a grand coalition. This broad-based government, led by the former governor of the Bank of Greece, Xenophon Zolotas, had an explicit mandate to secure economic recovery. His attempts to cut costs in 1989 proved unsuccessful because the party leaders in the grand coalition could not agree. Greece was facing a fiscal crisis, and Delors's letter arrived at a time just when Greece was desperately in need of an external emergency aid package.

In the election of April 1990, the main centre-right party, ND, headed by Constantine Mitsotakis, managed to form a government, but with a paper-thin majority. The message of Delors's letter had been received loud and clear: putting the economy back on track became the single most important priority of the new government. In his inaugural address to Parliament, Mitsotakis announced wide-ranging reforms to improve Greece's ailing government finances by drastically reducing the size of the public sector. The *apokratikopoisi* (reduction of the state) program involved cutting large subsidies and instituting other measures, including tax reform, price liberalization, and privatization of state-owned enterprises (OECD 1992).

In May, the government presented the delayed 1990 budget, which contained medium-term fiscal targets that aimed to achieve a primary surplus. At the same time, it prepared a legislative package enabling the privatization of state enterprises. The unions were furious about the austerity program; the General Confederation of Greek Workers (GSEE) condemned the government's austerity program and organized a series of strikes in the late spring. In the summer, the government managed to introduce a single omnibus bill bundling the 1990 budget with other measures.

The "First Phase": Souflias's Social Security Reform
(Law 1902/1990)

Soon after taking office in April 1990, Mitsotakis instructed Minister of National Economy George Souflias to draft a bill that would address the pension problem. Souflias prepared a comprehensive overhaul of the public pension system, and the government introduced the bill in September. The radical plan provoked harsh reactions from organized labour, and the strikes that followed were among the largest and most disruptive in living memory. During the three weeks that the bill was being debated in Parliament, the GSEE and other unions organized continuous strike action, causing severe disruptions and nationwide chaos. The massive demonstrations brought Athens to a standstill (Triantafillou 2007, 127).

The government insisted on passing the reform and announced that it would proceed with its plan to implement it (*Reuters News*, 28 September 1990). But when reaction to the bill ultimately threatened to bring economic life to a halt, the prime minister believed he had to announce significant concessions. Mitsotakis declared that his government would re-examine the measures and postpone any decision regarding structural changes (Venieris 1996, 266). In an effort to appease the unions, the government watered down the draft and withdrew the strictest measures. It decided not to tinker with the privileges of "protected categories," especially public-sector employees.

In the end, the bill could not address the long-term problems of the pension system, nor could it tackle its fundamental structural deficiencies. Even the most heavily indebted pension funds managed to escape the changes brought about by the reform. Thus, the bill targeted only the beneficiaries of the Institute for Social Insurance (IKA), the largest social security fund, which covered the lowest-income workers (Matsaganis 2002, 114; Papadimitriou 2001, 4–5). Once these modifications were announced, the GSEE dropped its opposition. The resulting watered-down Souflias law (1902/1990) was passed in October – by just one vote (Triantafillou 2007, 128). The bill introduced the following reform measures (ibid., 119; Papadopoulos 1997, 200):

- An increase in the retirement age (to sixty-five for men and sixty for women) and in the minimum retirement age for public servants.
- Increases in minimum contribution periods, the reference period, and contribution ceilings.
- Stricter eligibility criteria for invalidity pensions.

- Changes in pension indexation rules based on a wage increase for public servants.
- Disincentives for early retirement.

The government had initially aimed to undertake a comprehensive review of the social security system and put the pension deficit on a permanent downward trend. But due to the fierce opposition to the initial radical reform plan and the subsequent amendments to the legislation, the reform could not achieve any of these objectives. This round became the "first phase" of the pension problem, and the government announced that a comprehensive solution would be discussed again in another round of negotiations with its social partners in 1991 (OECD 1991, 61). Souflias himself admitted that the reform had to be incomplete and that a more comprehensive, radical reform of the pension system was needed (Featherstone, Kazamias, and Papadimitriou 2001, 469). Although the law passed, the process proved politically costly. Souflias, its chief architect, asked the prime minister for a leave of absence and never returned (Papadimitriou 2001, 5). As one commentator observed, history will record the Souflias law not just as "the first law which introduced changes in the pension system after years of 'pending' reform, but it will also be remembered for the social upheaval it produced" (Triantafillou 2005, 10).

The ECOFIN Council Warning, the Medium-Term Adjustment Program, and Minor Pension Reform (Law 1976/1991)

The 1991 budget, presented to Parliament at the end of November 1990, anticipated a revenue-based consolidation. Its ambitious targets included increasing revenues by 44 per cent by instituting tax measures, outlined in a separate tax bill, to achieve a primary budget surplus as early as 1991. Expenditures would increase by 25.5 per cent, even with additional restraints on spending.

In the meantime, Greece was negotiating a new loan facility with Brussels. In December 1990, the ECOFIN Council refused Greece's demand for the first time, concluding that its austerity policies were not adequately detailed (*Agence Europe*, 29 January 1991). The government then co-drafted the Medium-Term Adjustment Program, 1991–1993 with the Monetary Committee, which fulfilled the condition of the loan (26 February 1991) and was designed to prepare Greece for "full participation" in the EMU (OECD 1992, 11). The Council reluctantly agreed to grant Greece ECU (European currency units) 2.2 billion in January 1991. The loan was payable in three tranches, the first of which was disbursed immediately. However, the Council stated that the disbursement of the second and third tranches was strictly conditional on Greece fully adhering to the medium-term fiscal targets (*Agence Europe*, 26 February 1991). The new Minister of National Economy, Christodoulos Christodoulou, reassured the Council that the loan would help Greece "follow the other eleven Member States on the road to EMU" (14 March 1991). Thus, although the Adjustment Program was not formally submitted as a convergence program, Commission Vice-President Henning Christophersen announced that Greece had entered "surveillance" (9 July 1991).

When attempts to reform many of the social security items failed, the government announced that it would seek a comprehensive solution with its social partners. Having learned the lessons of a go-it-alone strategy, it carefully avoided confronting the unions. In October 1991, Mitsotakis set up a special committee to study the social security system under the chairmanship of Professor Rossetos Fakiolas. The committee incorporated representatives from the social partners, including the two largest labour unions: GSEE, representing private-sector employees, and the Confederation of Public Employees' Unions (ADEDI), representing public-sector workers. The report delivered by the Fakiolas Committee would subsequently provide the basis for tripartite negotiations (Featherstone, Kazamias, and Papadimitriou 2000).

Once the committee was established, however, the unions walked out. They claimed that the government would use the report to hide its agenda of overhauling the pension system. (Information had been leaked that the government had secretly requested technical help from the IMF.) The government did plan to use this report to justify its own radical reform priorities. In November, Mitsotakis announced that the government had decided to introduce some minor modifications and implementation measures instead of overhauling the system. The government drafted a bill without consulting the unions and introduced it in Parliament. Law 1976/1991 contained the following limited measures (Triantafillou 2007, 118):

- Restrictions on eligibility conditions for pensions provided to members of the National Resistance.
- Implementation measures for categories that were "trapped between" previous legislation and the recent Law 1902/1990.

It became clear that the 1991 budget had missed its revenue targets and included expenditure overruns (*Financial Times*, 5 November 1991). Nevertheless, revenues rose faster than expenditures. New measures were introduced to tighten up tax collection and accelerate the privatization of public companies. In an effort to contain spending, the government cut investment grants and subsidies to the private sector. Advocating his austerity program, Mitsotakis vowed that the adjustment effort had not been abandoned. He also repeatedly warned that time was running out if Greece wanted to be a part of the EMU (*Reuters News*, 7 September, 26 September 1991). As daunting as the warning sounded then, the government believed that the Maastricht constraints could open a policy window for pushing through fiscal austerity. Since domestic support for the EU had received a further boost at a time when public dissatisfaction with the ND government was plummeting, the government conveniently appealed to the *vincolo esterno* (Featherstone, Kazamias, and Papadimitriou 2000; Featherstone 2003). In his budget speech, Mitsotakis warned that the 1992 budget was essential for Greece to keep pace with its EU partners (*Reuters News*, 21 December 1991).

Immediately after passing the 1992 budget, Christodoulou announced that the government would submit to the EU a revised economic adjustment plan in April 1992 in an effort to make preparations for the EMU, and he called on all political parties to commit themselves to the Maastricht plan (*Reuters News*, 22 December 1991). At this critical stage, Mitsotakis replaced Christodoulou with Stefanos Manos as his minister of national economy. Manos was a former minister of industry with strong neo-liberal credentials. He immediately announced that the government was speeding up the reform process with plans to implement widespread privatizations, a five-year pay freeze in the public sector, and a radical reform of the pension system (*Financial Times*, 10 March 1992).

The European Commission's report of March 1992, assessing the first year of the ND's Adjustment Program, slammed the government's dismal economic track record: it had failed to reduce public deficits, delayed privatization, made inadequate efforts to root out tax evasion, and endlessly postponed reforming social security. The report concluded that the only way Greece could meet its Maastricht commitments was through "further continuous and sustained adjustment measures" focused on curtailing spending and increasing taxes (*Reuters News*, 16 April 1992). The harsh tone of the report signalled that the second tranche of the Commission's loan would not be released until Greece had submitted its first convergence program.

Mitsotakis's popularity had been severely undermined by the austerity measures. Despite its pre-election pledge to make sweeping reforms to bring the Greek economy into line with those of its European partners, the government had missed all its targets, and the prospect of joining the single currency seemed even lower than a year earlier. Moreover, the Cabinet was divided, largely about the prime minister's stringent economic policies. In about a year, Mitsotakis had lost more than half a dozen top ministers, who had harshly criticized the austerity program. The European Commission's refusal to release the second tranche of its loan was a serious embarrassment for the government.

The process of drafting the first Greek convergence program began with technical assistance from the Commission, aided by a committee of economic planners assembled by the government. The first draft aimed to achieve a savings of GDR 200 billion a year over the next five years. These measures aimed, first and foremost, to reduce the budget deficit, which, in turn, would help reduce the debt (*Financial Times*, 3 June 1992).[1] In the meantime, the tax system underwent some changes. Parliament passed a mini-tax bill in February and, in June, a new tax bill introducing sweeping changes (lowering nominal tax rates, eliminating exemptions, and simplifying how taxes were calculated to reduce bureaucratic delays in collection). At the end of July, Parliament ratified the Maastricht Treaty with an overwhelming majority of 286 out of 300 deputies (*Reuters News*, 31 July 1992).

*The "Second Phase": Sioufas's Social Security Reform
(Law 2084/1992)*

The Fakiolas Committee, which had been struck in October 1991 to study the social security system, submitted its report in May 1992. It contained inconclusive results and no estimate of the potential impact of any reform. When the unions reacted, the government distanced itself from the report, rejecting its recommendations. Although this initiative failed, the government insisted on continuing with the reform process. Minister of National Economy Manos initiated talks with the unions in June 1992 (Triantafillou 2007, 130–1). When the Fakiolas Committee began its work, the government had secretly requested a report from the IMF on its proposed social security reform. That report had warned Greece that it was the country furthest away from the Maastricht fiscal criteria, and it emphasized the urgent need for radical reform of the Greek social security system to approach the treaty's benchmarks. Manos himself leaked the report, which was supposed to remain confidential because he wanted to use it during his negotiations with the unions – independent evidence of the acute nature of Greece's economic problems (*Financial Times*, 28 July 1992).

The already fragile dialogue between the unions and the government grew increasingly untenable over the summer. The unions walked out of negotiations in August, and the following month saw rounds of walkouts and strikes. Blaming the reform effort on Euro-austerity, the secretary general of the GSEE complained that the government was "blindly follow[ing] the orders of the European Community for harsher austerity measures" (*Reuters News*, 3 September 1992). Hundreds of thousands of Greek workers joined a twenty-four-hour general strike in early September, causing power cuts; disrupting transport, telecommunications, postal services, and state hospitals; and closing down state banks and government offices. Rounds of nationwide general strikes followed. Greece was in chaos, with growing labour unrest and riot police clashing with demonstrators. By mid-September, employees of state banks, telecommunications, postal services, and the public power corporation had been on strike for more than three weeks, but it was not yet over.

Even so, the government tabled a new social security bill before Parliament, proposing to raise the retirement age and contributions to health and pension schemes, while lowering benefits. This unilateral move galvanized workers into widespread defiance of the government's economic program (*Reuters News*, 8 September 1992). In response, the government dropped its plan to standardize the retirement age at sixty-five for all, leaving the pensionable age for women at sixty (*Agence France-Presse*, 17 September 1992). However, the GSEE and ADEDI called for another general strike to maintain their pressure on the government (*Associated Press*, 18 September 1992). The government was under fire from all opposition parties as well: some senior ND members threatened to withdraw their support, which would overturn the party's paper-thin majority. Even the new governor of the Bank of Greece, the former minister of national economy Christodoulou, remained highly sceptical of the government's unilateral approach.

The government managed to push through its pension-reform bill (2084/1992), although it was much more modest than the government's original radical plan. The proposed measures had included raising the pension age, limiting the total pension paid from state sources to no more than final earnings, ending subsidized contributions, increasing transferability, making benefits dependent on contributions, pooling the differential of contributions to auxiliary funds to level them, and eventually abolishing special levies. However, only a handful of these planned changes passed in Parliament, and virtually all of them passed in modified form.

The watered-down version of the bill certainly did not jibe with Manos's neo-liberal profile (Featherstone, Kazamias, and Papadimitriou 2000), nor did the method of passing it suit his well-known "bull-in-a-china-shop" reputation. In the difficult days of forcing the reform through Parliament, he, as minister of national economy, had had to transfer much of his responsibility to the minister for health, welfare, and social security, Dimitris Sioufas, who was considered to have a more consensual style. It seemed that had Manos insisted on his radical, adversarial approach, it would have been impossible to overcome even internal opposition from prominent members of the ND, let alone endless attacks from the unions and opposition parties (ibid.).

Like the Souflias law of 1902/1990, this second phase of social security reform did not attain its goal, and Law 2084/1992 left the structural characteristics of the Greek pension system untouched. The reforms passed in the period 1990–2 introduced contributions for individuals entering the public service or increased them for those already working there. Other measures included levying a progressive tax on high-income pensioners, gradually lowering replacement rates, extending minimum contribution periods, and gradually raising the minimum pensionable age for public-sector workers. But perhaps the most important change was switching the basis of indexation for private employee pensions from minimum wage increases to increases in public servants' pensions.

Bowing to political pressure, the government phased in these new measures gradually, from 1993 to 2007 (OECD 1993, 46). Additionally, those already affiliated with an insurance regime as of 31 December 1992 would continue to be subject to the existing provisions, while those entering the pension system for the first time after 1 January 1993 would be subject to the stricter conditions of the new regime. The major provisions applying to only the post-1992 labour market entrants included the following (OECD 1997, 86–7; IMF 2002):

- The retirement age was set at sixty-five for both men and women and fifty-five for women with underage children.
- The replacement ratio was determined to be 80 per cent for combined primary and supplementary pensions, with the pension assessment base to be extended to five years.
- Employer and employee contribution rates were not changed, but the government provided an additional contribution of 10 percentage points (or one-third of the total).
- Spouse and child dependency allowances were trimmed.
- Survivor pensions became means-tested unless the survivor was disabled.
- If recipients continued to work, their pensions were either reduced by one-third or eliminated (for recipients receiving a minimum pension).

Although some of these parametric changes could prevent a future explosive situation, the reform was no more than a stopgap measure

(OECD 1997, 81). Even for new labour market participants to whom the law would apply, pensions continued to be very generous, compared with contributions, in actuarial terms. In the meantime, while the government announced that it would take the measures necessary to put an end to subsidized contributions to social security institutions, government subsidies remained broadly unchanged (OECD 1993, 53). Moreover, the structural aspects of the system remained as fragmented as before because the pensions provided by different funds were still different. Instead of attempting to unify the social security institutions, which would have provoked strong opposition, the government preferred to harmonize the insurance systems by gradually standardizing the level of benefits, entitlement conditions, and contributions (Stergiou 2000, 89).

With respect to the time frame of the expected benefits, the law could ensure the financial stability of the system only for the next two decades. The retirement-age differentials between the IKA, on the one hand, and "special funds" (public servants, workers in nationalized industries, banking employees), on the other, were to be gradually eliminated, taking full effect for the cohort retiring in 2007. However, the law could claw back virtually none of the privileges enjoyed by powerful groups of public servants due to strong opposition; employees of the electricity company DEI and state-owned banks were given special exemptions. Likewise, workers in other professions – engineers, doctors, lawyers, and the military – retained their full benefits. Moreover, after the 1993 budget passed in November, the government announced that the strict limits on pensions and wages would be selectively relaxed for categories that had experienced a marked fall in real incomes (OECD 1993, 57).

The government also introduced expansionary measures in other programs. Following a pro-natalist policy, the government expanded new family benefits for families with three or more children. It extended the duration of unemployment benefits from nine to twelve months to soften the impact of actual or planned privatizations. It attempted to shift the financing of hospitals from the Treasury back to the social insurance institutions and abolished the decade-long freeze in the per diem rate paid by sickness funds for hospital care (Guillen and Matsaganis 2000, 125).

New Tax Measures, the 1993 Budget, and the First Greek Convergence Program

By mid-1992, the government was concerned that there would be large deviations from the medium-term Adjustment Program targets if it took no further fiscal measures. Despite the earlier passage of the mini–tax bill, which had introduced significant legislative taxes, large budgetary shortfalls took place in the first half of that year. Accordingly, the government introduced another fiscal package in August to raise indirect taxes; this amounted to significant savings – 1.25 per cent of GDP in 1992 and 3.75 per cent of GDP in 1993. When discussing the bill in Parliament, Manos remarked that it was the only way to bring Greece up to the strict convergence criteria and, by passing the bill, the government would be able to adhere to its program (*Reuters News*, 14 October 1992). Meanwhile, privatization proceeds turned out to be sizeable in 1992 for the first time, exceeding 1 per cent of GDP. As a result of these changes, the government accounts showed a primary surplus for the first time since 1973. The budget deficit would have been twice as high, however, had the GDR 496.5 billion of debt interest payments not been rescheduled and privatization proceeds not budgeted.

The 1993 budget was unveiled in November. It was clear that it, too, was geared towards further austerity, aiming to increase the primary budget surplus to 4.25 per cent (OECD 1993, 55). The deficit reduction plan was based on a growth in total revenues of 30 per cent in 1993, while limiting growth in total expenditures to 18 per cent. This consolidation was largely based on GDR 330 billion in privatization revenues and GDR 300 billion in extra revenue raised by direct taxation. Part of this increase in taxes was to be obtained through a new law that cracked down on tax evasion (*Financial Times*, 9 December 1992).

In the meantime, ND became increasingly divided over the government's austerity measures and unfolding external events. In particular, party backbenchers who feared that adhering to a harsh reform program would cost them their seats in Parliament in the next election began to put pressure on Mitsotakis. A large group of MPs sought a change in leadership to enable the party to follow a more expansionary strategy. However, a series of Cabinet shuffles did not help the prime minister quell backbench dissent. When the budget came before Parliament, a large group of ND deputies did not attend the session (*Financial Times*, 9 December 1992). Mitsotakis then moved to suppress the revolt by making the budget vote a confidence vote (*Reuters News*, 16 December 1992). Despite their frustration with the austerity budget, and given ND's majority of just one seat, none of the deputies dared to be the cause of an early election. They closed ranks and backed the government in passing the budget (ibid., 22 December 1992).

After the 1993 budget was approved, the government presented Greece's first convergence program (1993–8) to Parliament as a draft law. The program envisaged that Greece would meet the Maastricht criteria (except for the debt criterion) by 1998 and that its mountainous debt would begin to decline in 1994. In presenting the program, Manos proclaimed that the goal was to "drastically cut state expenses" so that "convergence with Europe can be achieved" (*Reuters News*, 4 December 1992). At the ECOFIN Council meeting, Manos emphasized that he was also expecting a "dramatic rise" in government revenues, not only by raising taxes but also by "legalizing the underground economy" (ibid., 15 March 1993). The minister's statement foreshadowed Greece's consolidation efforts throughout the 1990s, which would rely heavily on expanding revenues.

Convergence Program Derailed, Additional Revenues Raised,
and Election Approaching

The policy performance of the ND government did not live up to the new budget's expectations. In early 1993, there were fears of significant slippages in the deficit. The projected primary surplus of 5.1 per cent of GDP for that year was turning out to be much lower because the economy was growing more slowly than expected and Greeks were reluctant to declare their full incomes. Moreover, expenditures were exceeding projected levels. Fiscal slippage, which was becoming more apparent as time went on, invalidated the underlying macroeconomic assumptions and thus derailed the convergence program.

Manos had promised that no new taxes would be levied in 1993 after the heavy tax packages introduced in 1992. However, in the summer, Parliament approved a new package to compensate for the unexpected shortfalls in revenue. Also, the government sought to raise additional revenues by imposing road taxes, selling casino licences, levying special taxes on fuel oil, increasing excise taxes on alcohol and tobacco, raising the withholding tax on investment receipts from bank deposits, and levying special taxes on cars and motorcycles (*Financial Times*, 9 June 1993; OECD 1993, 53). In June, the government also introduced a modest package of expanded social security benefits. Among other measures, the pensions of agricultural workers were increased by 25 per cent in 1993 and 40 per cent beginning in 1994. Pensions to mothers with large families were extended to cover all mothers rather than only those who had had their children after 1979. The family benefits of all public servants were doubled, and the monthly salaries of various public-service groups were increased (*Kathimerini*, 5 June 1993; Economist Intelligence Unit, 3rd Quarter 1993, 16–17).

These expansionary policies, brought in on top of the unpopular tax measures, foreshadowed a general election. In fact, a few months later, the ND government lost its parliamentary majority when two influential deputies defected to a new, smaller, right-wing party named Political Spring. Although the Mitsotakis government did not succeed in achieving its economic targets, its desperate efforts at austerity had put Greece firmly on the path to the EMU. Even though these policies aligned with ND's ideological program, they were repeatedly presented as the "ticket for Maastricht," especially in the face of not only strong opposition from the other parties in Parliament and the unions but also the ever-growing, intra-party dissent over the government's austerity policies. It was these very policies that would eventually bring about Mitsotakis's electoral defeat.

Papandreou's PASOK Returns to Power

The election in October 1993 returned Andreas Papandreou and a more pragmatic PASOK to power. In the run-up to the election, Papandreou had refrained from making overly generous, populist promises and had frequently repeated his commitment to the EMU (*Financial Times*, 6 October 1993). The government immediately announced its intention to carry on the fiscal consolidation process. However, Papandreou promised an "easier path to EMU" (Featherstone 2005a, 228): the Greek state would take on the role of "guarantor of social security," with an explicit commitment to "pension stability," while keeping up with fiscal austerity. In his first policy speech in Parliament under the Maastricht strictures, social democrat Papandreou promised restraint in macroeconomic policy (*Reuters News*, 23 October 1993).

The first priority of George Gennimatas, the new minister of the economy, who had also been appointed minister of finance, was to draft the 1994 budget, and he presented it in November. The budget was premised on revenues of GDR 7.2 trillion and spending of GDR 9.8 trillion. The deficit ratio would exceed the Maastricht benchmark by four times. Gennimatas also pledged to wage a battle against tax evasion, which would be central to his government's policy. He was quick to announce that the biggest spending increases were being allocated to the welfare state (*Reuters News*, 30 November 1993; Economist Intelligence Unit, 1st Quarter 1994, 14). Strikingly, however, prime minister Papandreou suggested that there was a clear trade-off between the overarching EMU goal and expanding the Greek welfare state. In his speech in Parliament in December, ahead of the vote on the budget bill, he emphasized that the urgency to improve the economy and remain on course for the EMU had to be prioritized over the need to reverse ND's cutbacks in social programs (*Reuters News*, 21 December 1993).

Faced with a major fiscal slippage, in mid-April 1994, the government presented a tax reform bill in Parliament that levied new taxes on the wealthy and openly declared war on a powerful group of tax evaders (OECD 1995, 23, 84). The bill raised the top marginal personal income tax rate and taxed income using various financial instruments (ibid., 20). Tax brackets were not adjusted for inflation, allowing for "bracket creep," which automatically led to higher tax revenues (OECD 1996, 25–6). Taxes on tobacco and duties on automobile licence plates were increased, and a withholding tax was introduced on purchases by the public sector from the private sector (OECD 1995, 84). Although these reforms increased the tax burden, they sparked less opposition than the previous episodes of pension reform. Despite a round of strikes, the government successfully pushed the bill through Parliament (*Reuters News*, 27 April 1994).

Updated Convergence Program (1994–9), Further Austerity
Emphasizing Revenues, and Some Expansionary Measures

Now that the 1994 budget and additional measures were approved, it was time to revise the convergence program. The updated version (1994–9) was presented to the ECOFIN Council in mid-June. Its central pillar was reforming Greece's public finances. Announcing the plan, the minister of national economy, Yannos Papantoniou, maintained that "the government's fiscal policy … aim[ed] to adapt the Greek economy to the fiscal terms of the Maastricht Treaty in the next four years" (*Reuters News*, 21 June 1994). In its first phase, the program envisaged that policies of fiscal restraint would be coupled with high levels of public investment (which would be supported by the regional development transfers from the EU). These would put the economy on a higher growth path until 1996.

The second phase anticipated that the fiscal consolidation program would be completed, the debt reduced significantly (von Hagen, Hughes Hallett, and Strauch 2001, 99), and the deficit reduced to below the Maastricht guideline of 3 per cent, but only by 1999. In March, the Ministry of National Economy had announced that the Greek national accounts had been revised to bring them into line with the European System of Accounts. This revision had substantially reduced government debt in 1993. The government admitted that the Maastricht criteria would not be met on time, and, therefore, Greece could hope to join the EMU only in a second wave of countries.

There was no legal requirement to debate the convergence program in Parliament. To garner support for his government's EMU goal, however, Papandreou called a parliamentary debate in late July. In the meantime, the ECOFIN Council endorsed the program but reminded the Greek government of its treaty obligations (*Reuters News*, 19 September 1994). Moreover, the Council had other carrots: Greece had also successfully concluded negotiations for the Community Support Framework (CSF), bringing in GDR 8.38 billion in development projects over the next five years. In addition to these funds, the European Commission had earmarked some of the Cohesion Fund (CF) for Greece on the proviso that it would disburse it only when Greece complied with the targets announced in its convergence program (Economist Intelligence Unit, 3rd Quarter 1994, 22–3).

Preparations for the 1995 budget began, and Papandreou announced that it was being drafted "in a spirit of austerity." He added that it was "entirely consistent with the convergence plan and [was] especially tough on public spending." He defended his economic policy by stressing the urgency of meeting the Maastricht criteria, and he emphasized that the government was carefully following its convergence program (*Reuters News*, 10 September 1994). In October, when the ECOFIN Council was conducting its EDP exercise, the finance ministers again warned Greece to limit its budget deficit to 10.7 per cent. The European Commission joined the Council in warning Greece that the 1995 deficit would exceed the target announced in its convergence program. In response, in November, the government presented a new, tighter budget. In presenting the budget, Finance Minister Alexandros Papadopoulos stated that "the 1995 budget is of historic importance. The country cannot afford another disappointment over its convergence plan" (ibid., 14 December 1994).

The budget was designed to restrict spending and increase the primary surplus to 3.4 per cent of GDP without imposing new taxes; however, it was premised on increasing tax receipts using a more efficient collection system. After the budget was brought down, hundreds of thousands of workers joined a twenty-four-hour, nationwide general strike to protest against the ongoing austerity. The strike, the first of its kind since the Socialists had returned to power, shut down state banks, schools, and factories, and disrupted hospitals, transport, telecommunications, and the postal service (*Reuters News*, 14 December 1994).

In response, the government made some concessions to pensioners and public servants: pensioners contributing to the IKA would receive a 3 per cent raise. Pension funds that paid less than the IKA minimum could raise their payments in line with their finances. People with special needs were eligible for raises of up to 20 per cent (*Reuters News*, 30 November 1994). The budget also contained increases in family benefits, teachers' benefits, and overtime pay for the police, and it allocated resources for reinstating the pensions of those who had fought with the National Resistance during the Second World War (OECD 1996, 27).

In the process of drafting this budget, the government was justifying unpopular austerity with repeated references to the EMU. In fact, all economic policy decisions seemed to have been formulated, justified, and implemented in the shadow of convergence. Appealing to pressure from the EU for fiscal consolidation, for example, Papandreou emphasized that the 1995 budget was balancing economic stabilization "ordered by the European Union" with growth and social welfare (*Reuters News*, 23 November 1994). Parliament easily passed the budget towards the end of December. There was no public opposition because it was clear to the public that the budget was designed to meet the EMU criteria (ibid., 21 December 1994).

When the national accounts for 1994 were made public in 1995, they showed that the general government primary balance had recorded a surplus of 2.1 per cent of GDP. This figure, however, included sizeable transfers from the EU, averaging approximately 5.3 per cent of GDP per year since 1990.[2] Still, there was an air of optimism – inflation had fallen to single digits for the first time since the 1973 oil shock, and interest rates had begun to decline. Budget figures for the first half of 1995 showed revenues running ahead of target due to the government's successful efforts at enforcing taxes, and spending was increasing at a slightly higher rate than expected. Nonetheless, Minister of National Economy Papantoniou and Minister of Finance Papadopoulos announced that austerity would have to continue through 1996. The government also announced new taxes on tobacco, casinos, and mutual funds. Moreover, it formed a committee to discuss abolishing tax relief on special interest groups. The Finance Ministry also announced new, "objective" measures for valuing property, effective July 1995, with the aim of increasing public revenues.

From the 1995 Budget to the 1996 Budget and Plans
to Restructure the Greek Welfare State

In September, the government drafted yet another austerity budget for 1996. It, too, was designed to reach the Maastricht objectives in accordance with the convergence program targets. In his annual state-of-the-economy address in September, Papandreou reassured the public that fiscal austerity would not be achieved by cutting back the welfare state: "We are not stabilizing the economy in order to destabilize social cohesion." He added that his campaign to boost tax revenues would be intensified, but, at the same time, there would be improvements in pensions in real terms (Economist Intelligence Unit, 4th Quarter 1995, 12).

The budget bill presented to Parliament at the end of November targeted a deficit of 7.0 per cent of GDP, compared with the 7.6 per cent announced in the first convergence program, and predicted a primary surplus of 3.2 per cent of GDP. Revenue-raising measures included increased vehicle registration fees, higher taxes on petroleum products and alcohol, significant upward revaluation of property, and tightening of the criteria for calculating the income of self-employed individuals and farmers. In the meantime, the government intensified its efforts against tax evasion and took some further measures that would come into effect in 1996 (Economist Intelligence Unit, 4th Quarter 1995, 15–16). In defending the budget, Minister of National Economy Papantoniou repeatedly stressed that Greece could join the third stage of the EMU in 1999 only by pursuing an austere economic policy (*Reuters News*, 19 December 1995). In the meantime, the chief architect of Papandreou's austerity plan, Costas Simitis, was also seeking support for the 1996 budget, urging strict adherence to the convergence program (ibid., 21 December 1995). Although Papandreou could not attend the budget debate for health reasons, Parliament passed the budget easily on the last sitting day before the Christmas recess.

When the budget was being drafted, the government had announced preliminary plans to restructure the public health care and social welfare system. The Greek "system" consisted of some 385 separate funds – the main pension funds, auxiliary pension funds, health funds, welfare funds, and mutual assistance funds – and five ministries (Health, Labour, National Defence, Finance, and Merchant Marine) were responsible for overseeing their activities. The government intended to merge some of the smaller funds so that they could be managed more efficiently and effectively (Economist Intelligence Unit, 4th Quarter 1995, 17). Fearful of inciting further opposition to social security reform in an already tense environment, however, and although it had been discussing the reform for a long time, Cabinet halted debate on the initiative, declaring that it would be brought up again in 1998. The Ministry of Health then announced that it would hire new doctors and staff, at a cost of GDR 120 billion. So as not to overburden the budget, the government decided that this initiative would be financed off budget, either by revenues from state lotteries or by a special tax on tobacco products (Economist Intelligence Unit, 3rd Quarter 1995, 15). At the same time, the government announced that farmers' pensions were to be increased by GDR 4,000 per month as of September 1995 (OECD 1996, 30).

The First Simitis Government

An ailing Papandreou stepped down in January 1996, and Costas Simitis, a university professor, socialist politician, and the architect of Papandreou's austerity program for the EMU, was elected prime minister. When putting together his Cabinet, to ensure the continued economic restraint required for the EMU, Simitis kept the key policymakers, Minister of National Economy Papantoniou and Minister of Finance Papadopoulos, in place. Referring to the urgent need for fiscal austerity, Simitis announced that his government's economic policies were already aligned with the convergence program. He pledged to keep Greece on track with the rest of the EU and repeated his commitment to the EMU on several occasions: "Our immovable goal is European Union convergence and European Monetary Union" (*Reuters News*, 29 January 1996). However, referring to a "new social state," he added that "the country's problems need swift and coordinated action but with a sensitivity to social conditions." He also signalled his intention to reinforce the "social" character of the Greek state.[3] Aware of the sensitivities caused by Euro-austerity, he continued that the government had to reconcile measures to alleviate social inequalities with the need to cut the budget deficit and continue with fiscal adjustment on the road to the EMU (*Financial Times*, 19 January 1996).

In May, Cabinet approved an official document, setting out measures for cutting expenditures, that would have a significant impact on future budgets. According to this document, all ministerial funding proposals, including those for social security, were to be accompanied by structural changes that would rein in spending. Cabinet was not permitted to approve any law, and ministers could not issue any decision, that would require unforeseen spending. State subsidies to several hundred autonomous public entities were cut, and these public entities were no longer permitted to borrow in their own right. There were other measures for controlling runaway spending: the government hoped to save GDR 250 billion per year by reducing the pharmaceutical costs paid through social insurance agencies, cutting the operating expenses of state agencies, closing down redundant public-sector agencies, and eliminating state subsidies. Papantoniou had the final word on all spending decisions of all ministries, including those related to social spending.

Despite its original plan to maintain fiscal restraint, the PASOK government managed to expand some welfare state programs, as it had promised in its election campaign. In June, it proposed to increase pension payments to the lowest-paid IKA pensioners. It was under growing pressure to restore the link between basic pensions and the national minimum wage, which had been broken by the outgoing ND government. However, the government resisted this pressure and also announced that pensions were to be automatically indexed to inflation as of the beginning of 1996 (*Reuters News*, 6 June 1996).

At the same time, Papantoniou repeatedly declared that there was no plan to levy new taxes in 1996 (*Reuters News*, 23 July 1996). However, the government drafted legislation to curtail extraordinary tax exemptions for groups of state employees and professionals, which would increase total taxable income by GDR 30 billion. The government also proposed to make tax evasion a crime. Fines would be increased for not remitting the VAT on time, and retail outlets issuing false invoices or receipts would have their business licence revoked. A special financial police force was to be established.

Following Papandreou's death in June, PASOK convened its party congress. Two groups were competing for party leadership: the first, led by Simitis, saw Greece's future firmly aligned with the EU and subscribed to Euro-austerity, while the second opposed Euro-austerity and preferred a self-reliant Greece with its own style of government and large amount of public ownership. The pro-EMU camp won the leadership race, and Simitis was elected the new president of the party. Three weeks later, he called for an early summer legislative recess, signalling an early election.

Before drafting another tough and unpopular budget, Simitis wanted to ensure that if his party won re-election, it would give him a free hand to push through the further austerity needed to enter the EMU. Emphasizing that he was calling the early election to speed up Greece's progress in meeting the Maastricht criteria, he stated that "only a government with a public mandate can deal effectively with the challenges." Greece "must take all necessary measures and decisions so that it does not become marginalized" (*Reuters News*, 23 August 1996). In his election campaign, Simitis made it clear that he would continue with fiscal austerity, unlike his ND opponent, who was campaigning on populist policies. The tables were turned. The promise of joining the EMU had dramatically shifted the traditional party approaches: it was now PASOK that was calling for austerity, while ND had embarked on Papandreou-style, populist promises (ibid., 9 September 1996). The EMU was the single most important issue on Simitis's agenda. Throughout his election campaign, he and his team repeatedly stressed the need for tighter austerity if Greece wanted to join the EMU.

The Second Simitis Government: The "Modernizers"

After PASOK won the election in September 1996, the new Simitis government was widely hailed as a "Cabinet of Reformers" (*Reuters News*, 23 September 1996) and *"eksynchronistes"* (modernizers) (*Financial*

Times, 25 November 1997). A common expectation, reflected in press reporting, was that Greece was ready to undergo unprecedented economic and social reform to achieve its EMU targets, and Simitis's first task was to prepare an austerity budget for 1997 to achieve this goal. When he announced his Cabinet, he gave Minister of National Economy Papantoniou the Finance Ministry portfolio as well. Thereafter, Papantoniou was nicknamed Greece's economic "czar" (*New Europe*, 6–12 October 1996).

The 1997 Budget and Opposition to Euro-Austerity

In October 1996, the European Commission predicted that all member states except Greece would meet the deficit rule in 1998. This latest report on convergence made clear that Greece had made the "least progress" towards meeting the Maastricht criteria. Simitis admitted that the inability to reduce the massive imbalances had been a key factor precluding Greece from joining the EMU from the start (*Dow Jones International News*, 19 November 1996). He announced that the crucial 1997 budget would be designed to meet the convergence program targets with an ambitious package of revenue and expenditure measures.

With respect to revenues, the budget aimed to make the tax system more equitable and efficient by broadening the tax base to include under-taxed sources such as real property and government securities. The government would eliminate some 824 tax exemptions for the high-income classes, the self-employed, and special interest groups without reducing other exemptions of a social or developmental nature (Kypris 1997, 204–6). The budget also anticipated increases in personal income taxes through bracket creep and higher corporate taxes for the financial sector. It continued the previous government's efforts at fighting tax evasion and expected increases in non-tax revenues as a result of larger dividend transfers from public entities and public banks. In terms of expenditures, the budget aimed to improve efficiency in the areas of personnel, interest payments, and the expenditures of public entities receiving government transfers (OECD 1997, 46–7). It forecast a deficit of 6.2 per cent of GDP and a primary surplus of 4.5 per cent, both of which were in line with Greece's convergence program targets.

In defending the new budget, Simitis vowed to take all measures necessary to enable Greece to enter the EMU by 2000 or 2001. "If we fail to participate in the EMU by that date, we will lose everything we conquered in the past 15 years with our membership in the EU." This, he emphasized, would condemn Greece to "second class citizen" status (*Wall Street Journal of Europe*, 20 November 1996; *Reuters News*,

25 November 1996). Papantoniou added that Greece was preparing the "toughest budget in 15 years" to make sure that the country would be ready to enter the EMU by the end of the decade (*Reuters News*, 25 November, 29 November 1996).

When the budget was announced at the end of November 1996, workers crippled transport, schools, hospitals, and public services with a one-day strike. They protested against the abolition of tax exemptions and the introduction of new taxes. The loudest slogan chanted at the demonstration by public servants and bank employees, held in Athens on the day the budget was presented to Parliament, was "No to Maastricht and its criteria" (*L'Echo*, 29 November 1996, quoted in Pakaslahti 1997, 47). The government was facing successive waves of unrest from teachers, pensioners, students, and dockworkers. These were followed by demonstrations and farmers blockading highways and railroads with tractors and chanting slogans against the EU. Simitis tried to appease these groups by stressing that sacrifices must be made by everyone to meet the convergence targets or else it would be a "disaster" for Greece (*Reuters News*, 28 November, 5 December 1996).

Approval of the 1997 Budget through Expanded Social Security Benefits and the Vincolo Esterno

PASOK deputies, too, joined the unions in opposing austerity. This ever-growing opposition forced the government to take some "corrective" measures so that its approach – a commitment to social cohesion as well as its overriding aim to achieve the EMU – could see some early results (Matsaganis 2004, 9). Accordingly, the government adopted a selective policy approach with an emphasis on means testing. It made some minor changes in tax exemption abolitions, benefits to large families, and the timing of other provisions coming into effect (*Imerisia*, digest repr., *Reuters News*, 29 November 1996). In particular, in the area of family benefits for mothers with many children, Simitis announced that cancelling their tax-free pensions would be compensated for by increasing the allowance for each child (OECD 1997, 48; *Financial Times*, 4 December 1996). At the same time, while rejecting farmers' demands in other areas, the budget increased their pensions by GDR 44 billion. Subsidies to the Farmers' Pension Fund were increased with state co-financing (*Reuters News*, 5 December 1996). A means-tested, "social solidarity" pension supplement, the Epidoma Koinonikis Asfalias (EKAS), was introduced to a large proportion of low-income pensioners (Venieris 2003, 137). This new benefit worked as a quid pro quo, helping the government step back from an earlier pledge to restore the link between minimum pensions and the minimum wage (Matsaganis 2002, 115).

During the budget negotiations, Simitis emphasized repeatedly that the tax-heavy budget was absolutely necessary on the way to the euro. Time and again, he referred to the *vincolo esterno* – "There is no alternative to this budget" – because failing to meet the convergence criteria "would lead to a national disaster" (*Reuters News*, 21 December 1996, 22 December 1996). In his speech before the vote, he pointed to the fact that Greece ranked "rock bottom" on the list of EMU candidates and said that "participation in Economic and Monetary Union is a matter of national survival, development and security" (*Athens News Agency*, 23 December 1996).

Having skilfully played the Maastricht card, the government finally managed to pass the budget in October 1996. All strikes, demonstrations, and roadblocks came to an end when the unions and the public accepted the compensatory measures. In January 1997, the government pushed through Parliament most of the new tax legislation required to implement the 1997 budget. Then, despite another wave of disruptive strikes by farmers, public servants, teachers, and sailors, it passed a bill clawing back some groups' special privileges.

The government planned to reinvigorate economic growth by increasing public investment expenditures. Until 1997, in the face of rising social expenditures and high defence spending, one key strategy for containing the budget deficit had been to limit or reduce public investment despite the incentive that the EU would match the amounts allocated through the CSF and CF. Beginning in 1997, the government did its best to commit all available funds to investment and thus benefit fully from the CSF and CF before the programs expired.[4] Despite Greece's ever-rising spending, increasing portions of the deficit were being financed through capital transfers from the EU. Moreover, reduced interest payments on the public debt and the use of equity acquisitions in lieu of capital transfers to public enterprises (moving public investment off the balance sheet, thereby eliminating its adverse impact on the deficit) contributed to smaller deficits (OECD 1998, 48–50).

The Spraos Committee's Report on Pensions: From "Overblown Promises" to Shelved Reforms

Immediately after having won the vote of confidence in Parliament for his 1997 budget, Simitis convened an ad hoc committee of academics and technocrats. Named the Committee for the Examination of Economic Policy in the Long Term, it was chaired by Professor Yannis

Spraos. The purpose of the committee was to produce a set of reports on the state of Greece's competitiveness, pension reform, health care, and public administration with a view to its participation in the EMU (Papadimitriou 2001, 7).

One of the reports, *Pensions and the Greek Economy: A Contribution to the Public Debate*, was submitted in September 1997. It reiterated the findings and recommendations of a "40-year long history of reports which, in amazing unison, [had] identified the same problems and proposed the same solutions" (Greece. Spraos Committee, 33). It pointed to widespread tax evasion and a fragmented pension system composed of a multiplicity of funds with varying provisions, leading to wide disparities in benefits. It warned that adverse demographic developments and "maturing" privileges would render the pension system unsustainable as early as 2010. It identified the "overblown promises" made by various governments as the root cause of the problems in the social security system[5] and claimed that the debt criterion had effectively eliminated the option of higher budgetary spending as a means of supporting the pension system. Moreover, it argued that the savings achieved through a future reform would contribute to reducing the deficit. Each deadline suggested in the report was based on the timetable for Greece's participation in the EMU by 2001.[6]

The report refrained from proposing any specific recommendations; in fact, the recommendations were "left open to be decided through the process of social dialogue" (Greece. Spraos Committee, 6). Moreover, there was room for "political choice" with respect to the "strategies" adopted. It insisted that reform options would reflect the politics of choice, whereby "political priorities matter." The report argued that "although the problem is serious, solutions and alternatives *do exist*, as long as there is the courage and determination to search for them." (8). It provided a striking example of the different options available: as long as the government was committed to an overarching cost-containment strategy for achieving the EMU targets, "It makes no difference if [one drachma saved] is at the Ministry of the Interior, Public Administration and Decentralization or at TSMEDE [Engineers' Pension Fund]. A single drachma entering TEBE [Greek Fund for Craftsmen and Small Traders] or collected as VAT has the same impact on the fulfillment of the EMU requirements" (31). With respect to the reform strategy, the report rejected a reform style carried out in "instalments" but cautioned that "any hurry will be harmful." To ensure a smooth reform process, the report advised the government "to establish a tranquil climate" (33).

The press framed the report as proposing "radical" and "harsh" changes. In fact, out of the seven reports that the committee produced, only the report on pensions provoked fierce opposition from organized labour, the left, and other segments of society (*Athens News Agency*, 14 October 1997). The GSEE, for example, argued that it had created a "climate of panic," amounting to a violent overthrow of all the "conquests of working people" (17 October 1997).[7] The response from other unions, civil society groups, and left-wing political parties was virtually the same. The Athens Labour Centre, several unions of retired workers, the Union of Postal Workers, the Communist Party of Greece, and the Democratic Social Movement (DIKKI) unequivocally rejected the report (*Avriani*, 14 October 1997; *Avgi*, 14 October 1997; *Eleftheri Ora*, 14 October 1997; *Athinaiki*, 14 October 1997; *I Niki*, 14 October 1997, quoted in Featherstone, Kazamias, and Papadimitriou 2001, 473–4).

Facing growing opposition from all sides, the government distanced itself from the report, although it considered it "a contribution to the processes of the social dialogue" (*Eleftheri Ora*, 14 October 1997; *Athinaiki*, 14 October 1997; *O Logos*, 14 October 1997; *Eleftherotypia*, 14 October 1997, quoted in Featherstone, Kazamias, and Papadimitriou 2001, 474, 474n16). Reaction was so intense that Labour and Social Security Minister Papaioannou had to declare, "There is no question of an increase in age limits for pensions, there is no question of an increase in contributions and there is no question of a decrease in pensions" (*Athens News Agency*, 17 October 1997). Finally, when Simitis's spokespersons officially distanced the government from the report, it became clear that the attempt to clarify Greece's financial position had been officially withdrawn (Featherstone 2005b, 743). Hitting a cul-de-sac, the government announced that social security reform would take place only after the next election in 2000 (OECD 1998, 55).

With the proposals of the Spraos Report effectively shelved in the face of such severe opposition to pension reform, the government turned to focusing on achieving its shorter-term fiscal targets. Although he was not able to achieve welfare reform, Simitis had to find an alternative fiscal strategy for pushing Greece into the EMU in 2001 or 2002. Thus, when playing the Maastricht card did not work for pension reform, the government turned to other austerity measures that could "fly under the radar."

From the Convergence Program Update to the "Convergence Budget"

When the European Commission released its forecasts on the state of convergence in the EMU candidates in April 1997, Greece remained the only "ugly duckling" (*Reuters News*, 22 April, 23 April 1997). The measures that the Commission now demanded from Greece called for "superhuman efforts" (*Kathimerini*, digest repr., *Reuters News*, 24 April 1997).[8] In July, the government submitted a revised convergence program (1994–9). The document retained the initial convergence targets, with the exception of the deficit target for 1999, which was revised upward, to 2.0 per cent. Although the direction of general economic policy remained unchanged, the program stated that the new government had decided to accelerate its efforts at fiscal consolidation so that Greece would be able to achieve the Maastricht criteria in 1998 or 1999.

In line with the convergence program, the 1998 draft budget aimed to reduce the deficit from 4.0 per cent of GDP in 1997 to 2.4 per cent in 1998 through a primary surplus of 4.7 per cent of GDP. The deficit target was below the Maastricht benchmark. This strategy relied on expanding the tax base even further, making the tax system more equitable by taxing assets at a higher rate and taking stronger action to contain current outlays. For the first time in years, the budget placed a greater emphasis on controlling public outlays. Total revenues were planned to rise by 11.7 per cent, while total spending was to rise by only 5.9 per cent. A sizeable, thirteen-item package of new revenue measures was also announced.

The prime minister's resolve to join the EMU was manifest in his speeches. In his annual economic policy speech, for example, Simitis warned that "the improvement in the economy … does not allow for relaxation or for a halt in our efforts. We must go even further in a short period of time" (*Reuters News*, 8 September 1997). Responding to the breaking news that Greece's bid to host the 2004 Olympic Games had been successful, he capitalized on the joyful moment by emphasizing that "the [monetary] award can help the Greek economy, which continues to have its first aim as entry to EMU" (ibid., 7 September 1997).

The government presented the 1998 budget two weeks ahead of schedule. Papantoniou announced that "this [was] a budget of convergence" (*Reuters News*, 12 November 1997). In fact, public perception that the budget was "tailor-made" to meet the EMU criteria was reflected across all news sources (*Imerisia*, 13 November 1997; *Kerdos*, 13 November 1997; *Naftemboriki*, 13 November 1997; *Kathimerini*, 13 November 1997).[9] Simitis used every media platform to stress that the "convergence budget" should be seen as a strong signal of his government's unwavering commitment to the EMU (*Reuters News*, 18 November 1997). He warned that "if we fail to join EMU within this two-year period, we will suffer destabilization, backtracking and the undermining of years of collective efforts." His economic czar, Papantoniou, added that they were "running the last 100 meters" to the EMU finish line (ibid., 25 November 1997).

In the meantime, economic life in Greece came to a halt again, this time in late November, when ADEDI launched a twenty-four-hour strike against the "never-ending austerity measures" (*EIRR* 1998, 288: 8). When Parliament began debating the 1998 budget, the GSEE and ADEDI led a nationwide strike protesting the government's belt-tightening policies, bringing the country to a standstill again. Public services and transport were paralyzed along with banks, tax offices, and schools, and all services shut down (ibid.; *Reuters News*, 18 November 1997).

Armed with the *vincolo esterno*, Simitis was determined not to give in. In Parliament, he responded to the critics of his austere "EMU-conscious budget" by arguing that his government could not "afford to stand in the middle of the road and debate whether to go on or not." He appealed to the deputies: "I ask you to vote for this budget, which expresses Greece's determination to win an equal place in Europe" (*Reuters News*, 21 December 1997). In the end, Parliament approved the tight 1998 budget. Thus, although playing the EMU card had not been enough to help the government carry out social security reform in the past, this time it proved effective in justifying unpopular austerity.

ERM Membership, the Structural Reform Package, and the
Revised Convergence Program: On Course to the EMU

By early 1998, the financial turmoil in Southeast Asia had spilled over to Greece, and the drachma came under attack amid speculation that it would soon be devalued. In fact, following a sharp devaluation, in March 1998, the government applied to join the ERM. The move was another clear signal that the government intended to join the EMU at the start of 2001. To garner support from other ERM participants whose central banks would have to support the drachma to maintain its value close to its ERM central rate, the government immediately promised a package of reforms (*Reuters News*, 13 March 1998), which were intended to ensure that Greece would meet the qualifying criteria for joining the single currency on 1 January 2001 (*Reuters News*, 16 March 1998; *EIRR* 1998, 292: 7; 296: 7).

A package of budgetary measures was introduced. They included cutting back primary current expenditures by reducing transfers to public enterprises and utilities and increasing social security revenues by increasing contributions (OECD 1998, 54; *Reuters News*, 16 March 1998). At the same time, Papantoniou announced a structural reform package based on an eighteen-month timetable leading up to EMU entry. The government would sell its 100 per cent stake in state-owned banks and 49 per cent stake in public utilities, a move made possible by passing an amendment to the privatization law. It would also sell three banks and ten small public enterprises as well as a third tranche of equity in the partly privatized state telecoms operator, Hellenic Telecommunications Organisation (OTE). These measures would bring in revenues of almost 2.0 per cent of GDP. The reform package would also implement restructuring programs in public enterprises that were incurring losses, introduce more flexibility into the labour market, and implement small-scale social security reform in 1998 (OECD 1998, 55; *Reuters News*, 16 March 1998; *EIRR* 1998, 299: 7).

With respect to social security reform – the most politically contested of all these measures – Papantoniou tried to convince the unions that he had to make spending cuts in health and welfare and that these saving were absolutely imperative for Greece to meet its 1998 deficit target for EMU entry (*Reuters News*, 16 March 1998). The government announced that the reform would be undertaken in two stages: in the first stage, minor organizational changes would be introduced during 1998 based on an agreement with its social partners. The second stage, which would attempt a major overhaul of the pension system, would be implemented after the next election took place in 2000.

The drachma was devalued and entered the ERM in March 1997, and the Greek government announced a number of budgetary measures and structural reforms. However, when it presented its updated convergence program to the European Commission that July, it was asked to revise it once again. The new set of convergence targets had been drafted with the aim that Greece would meet all the criteria by 2000 except for the debt benchmark. The government decided to insert into this revision the measures announced in March, and work began immediately (*Reuters News*, 23 March 1998).

The revised program was designed to bolster Greece's credibility in the eyes of its European partners, and presenting the structural measures as a commitment to the ECOFIN Council would help the government justify its austerity policies to the Greek public. Simitis was cautious when he announced that he would take no new measures beyond those set out in the program, whose contents "ha[d] been already set and measures ... announced." Invoking a *vincolo esterno* discourse again, the prime minister added that the government was adamant about sticking to its convergence plan and that it incorporated a structural reform package to make Greece an "equal EU partner" despite public opposition. He warned that Greeks "must be in combat mode to implement all that [the government] has decided" as "the country's strength and development are at stake." He also stressed that Greece had no option but to move forward towards the EMU so that it could achieve a steadily developing economy and better quality of life for its citizens (*Reuters News*, 7 May 1998).

The revised program was submitted to the Commission in June 1998. The government proposed to cut expenditures amounting to GDR 320 billion by reducing subsidies and public investment. In terms of structural measures, it committed to making drastic changes in the pension system and making the labour market more flexible. It also proposed a timetable for the privatizations already announced. At the ECOFIN Council meeting, the finance ministers pressed for additional urgent action, and they warned the government that it should realize the spending reductions forecast in the program as soon as possible (*Dow Jones Online News*, 12 October 1998).

From Non-implementation of Earlier Pension Reforms to the "Mini–Social Security Reform Package"

In the face of growing protest against fiscal austerity, the government decided *not* to implement the cost-containment measures introduced by the Fakiolas report and Sioufas reforms of 1990–2, which were to have come into effect in January 1998. Some measures were postponed indefinitely – for example, limiting supplementary pensions to a maximum of 20 per cent of the pension base, raising the minimum age for workers receiving a pension early due to performing work in arduous and unhygienic environments, and raising the number of years of service required for eligibility for a full pension in public enterprises and state-owned banks. Another measure not implemented was the planned reform of means-testing the very costly lifetime pensions for mothers with more than two children, which the earlier plan would have restricted to women over the age of sixty-five. At the same time, the government announced that the eligibility for the EKAS supplement of low-income pensioners, introduced in 1997 for pensioners over sixty-five, would be extended to cover pensioners over the age of sixty in general as well as other pensioners in certain categories (such as survivors with underage children) with no fixed age limit. Moreover, it significantly raised the base amount used to calculate invalidity pensions for individuals entering the labour force after 1993. In effect, by not implementing these planned reforms and by announcing additional benefits, Simitis's Socialist government effectively reversed some harsh measures introduced by the conservative government during the 1990–2 period.

In March 1998, the government announced a new set of social security reforms as part of the structural adjustment measures that it had inserted into the convergence program it submitted to the European Commission in July 1997. During the first stage of the reform, the large number of pension funds would be reduced to simplify the system and make it more transparent, and the funds that were in deficit would be merged with others that were financially sound. This efficiency would take place in four phases: (1) seven deficit-ridden supplementary funds would be merged with the large supplementary fund for private-sector employees; (2) twelve supplementary funds for public servants and 48 funds for rural lawyers would be brought under a single fund; (3) a new fund would replace the three large primary funds for the self-employed; and (4) a unified fund would be created for employees of state-controlled banks. These measures, however, would not create savings in pension spending because they would not reduce individual pension payouts; on the contrary, they would allow an expansion of pension benefits (OECD 1998, 78).

In addition to this organizational restructuring, the reform included cost-containment measures to generate financial savings. First, the reform would reduce contribution evasion, in part, by hiring labour inspectors. Second, beginning in 2001, pensioners under fifty-five years of age who were working would no longer receive a pension. Others above the age of fifty-five would receive only 30 per cent of that portion of their pension that exceeded GDR 200,000 per month. This measure, however, would effectively protect more than 80 per cent of private-sector pensioners from any cut. Third, as a result of a ruling by the Constitutional Court on equality between the sexes, survivors' pensions would have to be provided to male survivors, who had previously been ineligible.

In October 1998, Simitis asked the GSEE and ADEDI to help the government meet its EMU targets. In particular, he was seeking support for his government's structural reforms in the areas of social security, the labour market, and taxation (*Imerisia*, digest repr., *Reuters News*, 6 October 1998). Despite the fact that Simitis had reversed the Mitsotakis government's reforms, his own round of social security reforms had undermined his popularity. His government emerged that month weakened from local elections; they were considered a referendum on government austerity policies, and the results were widely interpreted as popular disenchantment with the government's austerity measures (*Dow Jones International News*, 29 October 1998). Bowing to massive political pressure, the weakened government decided to postpone any radical overhaul of the state pension system until Greece had achieved its goal of joining the single currency. Instead, it pushed through Parliament a "mini-reform" package of pension measures in late November that contained the following measures (Economist Intelligence Unit, 1st Quarter 1999):

– Supplementary social security funds would be merged, whereby 68 of 160 funds would disappear.
– A single fund for the self-employed would be created.
– The funds of public employees would be amalgamated.
– Entitlements for persons with pensions exceeding GDR 200,000 a month would be reduced.
– Benefits for those under the age of fifty-five who were entitled to a pension but who continued to receive work-related income would be eliminated, but only after a transition period of several years.

Although the mini-reform bill remained modest in scope and content, strikes erupted immediately after it was introduced in Parliament, and they continued during the entire fourth quarter of 1998.[10] Simitis warned the unions that he would not budge. He emphasized the eventual rewards that the EMU would bring and asked the unions and the public to accept the changes that were needed to qualify Greece for Europe's single currency: "We are here to accomplish something. If we can't do that we should all go home" (*Reuters News*, 3 December 1998).

Despite Simitis's efforts, the strikes spread to all parts of the public sector, including the banks, utilities, and public transport, as well as private businesses. When it became clear that they were not coming to an end, Simitis resorted to a rare emergency decree to halt the strikes in some sectors (*Reuters News*, 4 December 1998). Still strike action continued, culminating in a one-day general strike on 15 December called by the GSEE and ADEDI and other supporting unions. The strike paralyzed Greece, halting public transport and disrupting state banks, hospitals, and other public services (ibid., 14 December 1998).

The mini-reform package was designed to improve the organization of the pension system, raise revenues, and lay the groundwork for the second phase of reforms. In January 1999, the government passed a bill that consolidated, unified, or abolished some sixty funds to improve their financial viability. It also finally amalgamated the three funds for self-employed workers; however, the proposal to create a unified fund for public bank employees was postponed due to widespread opposition (Petmesidou 2000, 319). In fact, even after the three funds had been amalgamated, each one retained its own administrative and financial autonomy. This was another example of the difficulty of implementing reforms in the social security area (Tinios 2003, 33; Sotiropoulos 2004, 276).

Because of the difficulty of passing even the mini-reforms of the social security system, the government decided that it had reached its reform capacity. Simitis decided that the political cost of trying to bring in more reforms would be too great at a time when he was maintaining the tight fiscal and wage policy required to qualify for the EMU (*Financial Times*, 8 December 1998). Unwilling to provoke successive rounds of confrontation with the unions, the government announced that it would postpone the second phase of more radical reforms until after Greece had entered the EMU (Guillen and Matsaganis 2000, 126). It was clear that although Simitis had put Greece's fiscal house in order with an iron fist, he was not "tough" on social security reform. In the face of growing unrest, he was widely seen to have "caved in to the trade unions" when they "jibbed at his plans to reform pensions" (*Financial Times*, 23 January 1999).

Towards the "Budget for EMU Entry"[11]

In his annual address on the state of the economy in September 1998, Simitis announced that Greece was about to meet four out of the five criteria necessary to join the single European currency (*Reuters News*, 5 September 1998). After the unfavourable results of the local elections, Simitis called for a confidence vote to consolidate parliamentary support ahead of presenting the next "EMU-targeted" budget later in November. Although he faced severe criticism from the opposition parties over his austerity measures, during the parliamentary debate leading up to the vote, the government eventually won Parliament's confidence (ibid., 4 November 1998).

When Papantoniou brought the 1999 budget before Parliament, he called it "Greece's EMU entry budget" (*Reuters News*, 11 November 1998). Greece was expecting an assessment in March 2000 based on its debt and deficit figures for 1999. The budget called for a deficit of 1.9 per cent of GDP at the end of 1999, reduced from an estimated 2.2 per cent at the end of 1998. Ordinary revenues were expected to rise by 6.1 per cent, while revenues from direct taxes would rise by just 6.6 per cent and indirect taxes by only 5.3 per cent. The budget aimed to contain expenditures, which it forecast to grow by 4.5 per cent. The largest single expenditure item for the previous five years – interest payments on the public debt – would begin to decline substantially. The state had sold its controlling shares of four publicly controlled banks and a sizeable share of its largest bank holding as well as large tranches of stock in Hellenic Petroleum and the OTE; these sales amounted to additional receipts of GDR 1.02 trillion. The government would also increase, by about 15 per cent, the pensions of persons receiving benefits below the average of approximately GDR 105,000 a month. This "social solidarity upgrade" of GDR 67.5 billion was the only significant real expenditure increase in the budget (Economist Intelligence Unit, 1st Quarter 1999). In an environment of growing popular resentment against Euro-austerity, this upgrade proved helpful in securing the approval of the budget bill in Parliament.

The government was facing opposition from the unions and the public, and political pressure in Parliament was increasing. The main opposition party, ND, charged that the government had done very little to restructure the economy and had squeezed in fiscal austerity on the eve of entering the EMU. It also accused the government of having relied extensively on accounting tricks to try to meet the EMU budget targets (*Dow Jones International News*, 21 December 1998). While Parliament was debating the budget, press reports appeared of instances of serious creative accounting.[12] Apparently, the comment by the *Financial Times* shortly after the approval of the 1999 budget was no exaggeration: "Greek statisticians have learned from their Spanish and Italian colleagues how to fudge accounts to the satisfaction of people in Brussels" (*Financial Times*, 23 January 1999).

A Weakened Simitis Appeals to the EMU

By 1999, the government was further weakened by the endless rounds of fiscal austerity. The party congress was convening in March, and the general election was coming up in 2000. PASOK was divided into two factions advocating alternative election strategies: the "modernizers" and the "populists." The modernizers believed that PASOK could carry on with Euro-austerity until 2000; then, after Greece's entry to the EMU was secured, it could be relaxed. In an alliance with left-leaning parties DIKKI and Synaspismos, PASOK's populist faction demanded a halt to austerity (*Financial Times*, 18 March 1999; Economist Intelligence Unit, 1st Quarter 1999, 9–11). The government, represented by the modernizers, decided to continue its austerity measures, thereby staking its credibility on Greece's EMU bid, the outcome of which would be decided before the election in spring 2000.

In the meantime, a series of incidents unsettled the government. Throughout, however, Simitis aptly used EMU entry to save his government. First, in February, three senior Cabinet ministers resigned after what many saw as the government mishandling the "Ocalan affair."[13]

This triggered the most vociferous criticism against Simitis since he had assumed office (*Financial Times*, 18 March 1999). Amid calls for his resignation, he announced that he would continue to serve until the end of his term in order to secure EMU entry. His economic czar, Papantoniou, added that "we are only a breath away from the EMU" and that "the country will not tolerate any more back-stepping or deviations" (*Dow Jones International News*, 24 February 1999).

Second, at the party congress in March, delegates rebelled against the PASOK leadership. Simitis quickly warned members that party unity was crucial at a time when Greece was fighting to secure euro entry (*Dow Jones International News*, 18 March 1999). Third, in June, Simitis faced opposition again when PASOK lost seats to other political parties in the European Parliament election. He refused to bow to pressure to resign on the grounds that the government still held the mandate to carry Greece into the EMU by 1 January 2001. The *vincolo esterno* proved instrumental yet again: EMU entry was being used as a foil, shielding the government from rounds of criticism. It was also being used as blackmail: the government later threatened to resign if it were further challenged.

The Expansionary "Simitis Package" on Social Security

By late 1999, when the 2000 budget was being prepared, it seemed almost certain that Greece would meet all the Maastricht criteria except for the one concerning the inflation rate. The budget deficit for 1999 was below 3.0 per cent, and although aggregate debt was still far above 60 per cent, it was showing a declining trend. Long-term interest rates remained around 2.0 percentage points of the benchmark German rates, and the drachma had remained stable within the ERM since March 1998. Moreover, during the first half of 1999, public revenues had risen by 12.4 per cent, more than double the rate of 5.8 per cent targeted in the 1999 budget. Surveying the 1998–9 period, the OECD (2001, 38) reported that the "budgetary outcomes were close to target or even better since 1997, mainly due to positive surprises on the revenue side." Endless austerity was finally paying off.

The government took advantage of this favourable position to introduce a social security package, the "Simitis package," along with the 2000 budget, which was estimated to cost GDR 320 billion (1.2 per cent of GDP). On the revenue side, the package included indirect tax cuts worth about GDR 150 billion, the first round of which would apply to 1999 earnings and profits. On the expenditure side, the unemployed and pensioners were to receive a sum of GDR 150 billion as a result of the following measures (*Kathimerini English Edition*, 3 September 1999; OECD 2001, 40):

– An across-the-board increase of GDR 10,000 in old-age pensions was to begin on 1 January 2000 for an estimated 800,000 pensioners.
– Pensions were to be fixed at GDR 43,000 monthly from the current GDR 33,000; this would be a great help to all farming families around the country.
– A uniform increase of GDR 3,000 per month in the "social solidarity allowance" was introduced. This meant that the special subsidy for low-income pensioners (EKAS), which was being paid out to around 360,000 people, would rise from its monthly benefit of GDR 18,000 to GDR 21,000.
– The 350,000 recipients of public-sector pensions would receive up to GDR 250,000 per month, a 4 per cent increase.
– The unemployment allowance would be increased by 10 per cent, giving recipients an estimated GDR 112,000 more every year. Unemployed workers who were registered with the Manpower Employment Organization would be eligible for free medical care and medicines, irrespective of their age.

These increases in social security benefits were incorporated into the 2000 budget. The package was widely seen as a move to improve the government's popularity ahead of the election in 2000.

The 2000 Budget and the Convergence Program Update

The prospects for Greece entering the EMU had brought optimism to the country. In his annual state-of-the-economy address in September 1999, Simitis announced that Greece would meet all the necessary criteria by 2000 (*Reuters News*, 5 September 1999). Papantoniou presented the 2000 budget in Parliament in early November, nearly four weeks ahead of schedule. The aim of the budget was to ensure that Greece was removed from the EU's EDP blacklist of candidates with derogation. Papantoniou stressed, "The 2000 budget is a budget of EMU" (*Dow Jones International News*, 3 November 1999).

In October, the press began reporting that the budget targets were being made to look within reach of the EMU using "tricks" and "creative accounting" (*Kathimerini English Edition*, 11 October 1999).[14] Nevertheless, the Commission decided that the government's efforts to comply with the Maastricht parameters had been successful, and, in early November, it recommended that Greece be removed from the EDP list

(*Dow Jones International News*, 11 November 1999). In mid-November, the ECOFIN Council reversed its 1994 decision that an excessive deficit existed in Greece (29 November 1999).

The government aimed to give the budget a "social character" by incorporating the Simitis package, a mix of tax-relief measures and higher social welfare payments (Economist Intelligence Unit, 1st Quarter 2000, 19). The budget would record a primary surplus of 4.9 per cent of GDP in 2000, limiting the government deficit to 1.2 per cent of GDP. The debt ratio was projected to further decline to 103.9 per cent of GDP in 2000 by speeding up the privatization program (*Dow Jones International News*, 3 November 1999). Budget expenditures would amount to GDR 8.7 trillion, and all spending items had been restricted, with the exception of defence and social welfare spending.

The Simitis package, therefore, was among the big-ticket spending items in the budget (*Kathimerini English Edition*, 20 September 1999). Its expansionary effect was cushioned by an increase in the tax rate on stock exchange transactions, amounting to a revenue increase of around 0.5 per cent of GDP. The government also announced that it would increase property taxes by 14.2 per cent and collect taxes in arrears to bring in GDR 285 billion. Additional revenues were forecast to come from computerizing the tax offices, speeding up the activities of the Financial Crimes Investigation Bureau, and doubling down on efforts to enforce the VAT (Economist Intelligence Unit, 1st Quarter 2000, 19–20).

During the parliamentary debate on the budget, the EMU was the focal point of Simitis's speech: "This is the EMU entry budget, ... the outcome of years of efforts ... to make Greece a true member of Europe." The budget passed 160–133 in the 300-member Parliament, in which PASOK held 153 seats (*Dow Jones International News*, 21 December 1999). That day, the government also submitted its *1999 Update of the Hellenic Convergence Program (1999–2002)* to the European Commission (Greece 1999). The program's goal was "the completion of the process of nominal convergence by satisfaction of all five Maastricht criteria at the beginning of 2000" (ibid., 23). It emphasized that the government had been pursuing a tight fiscal policy to achieve its policy objectives. Strikingly, the document stated that the fiscal consolidation process would continue without having to sacrifice the welfare state: "The government is following a prudent fiscal policy while at the same time is trying to meet social needs in those areas which fall within state responsibility" (ibid., 4).

The ECOFIN Council approved the updated Greek convergence program at the end of January 2000. Although it congratulated the Greek government on the measures it had taken to date, it warned of the need for continued austerity. At the end of the meeting, triumphant Papantoniou said that this approval constituted the penultimate step for Greece on its path to membership in the eurozone (*Dow Jones International News*, 31 January 2000). In March, Simitis announced that the government had submitted a formal bid for membership of the EMU. In a letter to the president of the ECB, Papantoniou formally requested that Greece's application for the abrogation of its status as a member state with derogation be evaluated. In a euphoric mood, Simitis proclaimed, "It is a historic moment for Greece. ... A 25-year effort to bring Greece in line with the rest of Europe is complete" (9 March 2000). In March, immediately after having formally submitted its EMU application, Simitis called an early election, arguing that the country needed a government with a clear mandate to negotiate its entry to the eurozone.

The Third Simitis Government: EMU Entry Secured and Giannitsis Pension Reform Withdrawn

The general election took place in early April 2000. PASOK prevailed over ND by a very slim margin, winning 43.8 per cent of the vote against the latter's 42.7 per cent. In May, European Commissioner for Economic and Monetary Affairs Pedro Solbes endorsed Greece's bid to participate in the final stage of the EMU. He announced that having failed the euro-entry test in 1998, Greece had since achieved "a high degree of sustainable convergence." Drawing attention to the distance that Greece had travelled since then, he reminded his audience that the country had met none of the economic convergence criteria for the EMU just two years before. Since then, however, it had made "striking progress" in bringing its inflation rate, long-term interest rates, budgetary balances, and exchange rate stability into line with the requirements of the single currency (*Financial Times*, 4 May 2000).

Meanwhile, the reports from both the Commission and the ECB had endorsed Greece's application to become the twelfth member of the eurozone, and following these recommendations, the European Parliament (*Dow Jones International News*, 18 May 2000) and the ECOFIN Council endorsed Greece's bid (5 June 2000). At the European Council meeting in Santa Maria da Feira, Portugal, EU leaders agreed to welcome Greece as a eurozone member as of 1 January 2001 (*Dow Jones International News*, 19 June 2000).

The narrow margin of PASOK's victory in the April election had revealed discontent with Euro-austerity, although, overall, it seemed that the Socialist government had struck a fine balance between austerity and achieving re-election. Interestingly, during the election campaign, neither PASOK nor ND had addressed the controversial issue of social security reform, which was due to be tackled by the next Parliament. The reform, which had been postponed in 1998, would require higher levels of contributions and an increase in the pensionable retirement age. PASOK promised that whatever changes were made, they would be carried out through tripartite consensus among social partners (Economist Intelligence Unit, 2nd Quarter 2001, 15).

Upon assuming office, Simitis quickly pledged to press ahead with far-reaching reforms and privatizations despite his tarnished image (*Dow Jones International News*, 10 April 2000). He acknowledged that his austerity policies in the run-up to EMU membership had alienated the unions and many socialist supporters. He declared that his new government would "put social welfare at the top of the agenda." In fact, he had already pledged a substantial increase in pensions, sourced from the sizeable revenue surplus projected for 2000. Earlier, following a bruising collision with the unions, he had decided to postpone overhauling the pension system until after Greece joined the eurozone. He believed, the press reported, that a more generous social policy would offset the bitter impact of austerity reforms (*Financial Times*, 11 April 2000).

But all this was not enough. Even EMU entry could not shield the government from public pressure. The unions were becoming impatient. The president of the GSEE warned that "the government's main priority ha[d] been the monetary aspects of economic convergence while the social dimension ha[d] been neglected." He quickly added that the GSEE supported the government in its bid to join the EMU, but that the government should adopt policies "promoting the social dimension and ensuring that social welfare [is] protected" (*EIRR* 2000, 315: 22).

Meanwhile, Simitis appointed his economic adviser, Tassos Giannitsis, as minister of labour and social security, with a brief to reform the nation's public pension system (*Financial Times*, 13 April 2000). Giannitsis immediately announced that the reform would be carried out through consensus. The government hired the British Actuary Service as a consultant to prepare an actuarial study on Greek pensions in the long term. The reform process would start with seven months of preparation and continue with two months of public consultations in the spring of 2001. The study would present "hard evidence" of the problems in the pension system and thereby serve as a "technocratic shield," protecting the government during the public consultations (Featherstone and Papadimitriou 2008, 96).

Although the government did not publish the study, leaks in the press revealed that the new wave of reform would bring longer contribution periods, later pension entitlement, and reduced entitlements over-all. The government knew the potential costs of introducing pension reform and announced that it would not trim the benefits of any pensions that had matured. Younger cohorts (those who had joined the labour force between the early 1980s and 1993) would receive lower benefits than older cohorts. However, their number would exceed one million over the 2010s, and they therefore constituted the bulk of the country's future pensioners. PASOK's electoral fortunes depended on them (Featherstone and Papadimitriou 2008, 97). The GSEE and ADEDI criticized the government for these proposals and mounted a unified front against the reform plan. Just as they had done in the early 1990s, the unions claimed that the government's efforts were being made in secret. They asked the Institute of Labour, the GSEE and ADEDI's joint research foundation, to deliver an independent report on pensions. It turned out that the findings and recommendations of its report were similar to those of the British Actuarial Service. The distrust among the unions towards the government assured that conflict was inevitable (Matsaganis 2006, 166).

The government considered the report's recommendations. Giannit-sis announced that the reform proposal would consist of only parametric changes – aimed at correcting some of the distortions in the pension system, minimizing differences in eligibility criteria, increasing inter-generational equity, and ensuring fiscal sustainability. The specific measures were as follows (Triantafillou 2007, 120):

– An increase in the retirement age (to sixty-five) for all retirement funds.
– An increase in the number of insurable years for seniority pensions from thirty-five to forty.
– Abolition of the retirement age (fifty) for mothers with young children.
– Extension of the reference period to the best ten out of fifteen years.

Although the reform proposals were not as comprehensive as the government had planned, public reaction was fierce. After having borne harsh austerity for an entire decade, and after the country had secured EMU entry, the Greek electorate found new rounds of austerity intolerable. The measures were framed as "the end of welfare as we know it" (Matsaganis 2006, 167). The GSEE called a general strike, and all the parties in Parliament (including the conservative ND) quickly dismissed the plan as unnecessarily harsh (Featherstone and Papadimitriou 2008, 99).

Reaction to the report was not confined to political opposition and the labour movement either; even Cabinet ministers and PASOK's own Central Committee members expressed frustration with the reform. The government was under siege from all sides. In March 2001, the government made a U-turn. Giannitsis announced a freeze on the reform process, and the government said that it would engage in public consultations "without preconditions." The "pension fiasco" of 2001 meant that the reform was "dead and buried" (ibid., 103).

In hindsight, analysing the Maastricht decade of limited and failed reforms reveals that reform was possible only during the early 1990s, when Euro-austerity was at its *weakest*. At that time, the Maastricht deadlines were far away, and Greece was not even in the running. It seems that the more acute Euro-austerity became, the more elusive the long-awaited systematic pension reform proved to be. In the political economy of reform, the euro drive "was a good hand, but it was played badly." Reforming pensions constituted "the hottest of all potatoes," even on an austerity agenda crowded with such contentious items as privatization of public utilities and state-owned banks, the traditional strongholds of PASOK support. Strikingly, "When it became evident that entry to EMU could be achieved even without it ... pension reform was quietly postponed" (Matsaganis 2006, 165–6).

Euro-Austerity and the Political Economy of Welfare State Reform in Greece

This case study has shown that Greece made remarkable progress towards controlling public finances beginning in the early 1990s. Successive convergence programs helped governments correct mounting fiscal imbalances. The literature on macroeconomic policy and governance in Greece corroborates this finding by emphasizing the unambiguous Maastricht effect on Greek fiscal behaviour (Andreou and Koutsiaras 2004, 93; Christodoulakis 2013; Ioakimidis 2001, 81; Liargovas 2000, 217). Joining the EMU meant enduring austerity, and all governments that came to power during the Maastricht decade – conservatives under Mitsotakis and socialists under Papandreou and Simitis – had a clear austerity agenda in the name of eurozone entry. To attain this overarching goal, every government was initially firmly determined to reform the welfare state. The rationale was clear: in domestic public debates and, more important, in policy circles, the Greek welfare state was commonly indicted by politicians and policymakers as *the* culprit for all financial problems that could forestall EMU entry. Thus, the EMU was the most powerful structural constraint on every government's budget. At the same time, it gave Greek politicians a desperately needed discursive shield, which, they assumed, could justify any radical reform whatsoever. Accordingly, all governments that came to power during the 1990s declared that they would address the thorny issue of pensions.

Despite having weathered waves of reform attempts, however, the Greek social security system averted large-scale retrenchment. In fact, it even saw reforms resulting in *expansion*! As this chapter showed, at each attempt at reform aimed at retrenchment, and regardless of the size of the proposed cutbacks, the Mitsotakis and Simitis governments faced massive strikes, demonstrations, and protests by opposition groups that brought public life to a standstill. Such opposition encompassed a large constellation of societal groups, including organized labour, traditionally protected groups (above all, public-sector employees), professional groups (including doctors, lawyers, military personnel), and people from all walks of life. All these groups were mobilized under the unions and other civil society organizations. In almost all cases, they were supported not only by the opposition parties but also by senior members of the ruling party. Such opposition rendered any radical retrenchment strategy beyond the reach of any government.

None of the reform plans aimed at making radical cutbacks passed Parliament successfully. No attempt at fundamental restructuring proved successful either. For example, neither the Papandreou nor the Simitis government had the audacity to even *attempt* retrenchment – they were simply intimidated by potential opposition. When Papandreou floated the idea of restructuring the fragmented social security system, Cabinet refused to discuss it for fear that it would provoke further opposition in an already tense environment defined by austerity fatigue. The reform was put on the back burner, like so many ideas before. Likewise, even after Simitis requested the Spraos Committee to propose pension-reform options, the government was overwhelmed by fierce reaction from the unions, public service organizations, left-wing political parties, and other groups, and it was forced to distance itself from the findings of the report and postpone the reform altogether. Later, Giannitsis planned to introduce a radical reform in 2000–1 – the second stage of an earlier mini-reform. The potential political costs, however, compelled the government, yet again, to withdraw the proposal.

In the few cases where reforms passed, they did so only after governments substantially scaled back their ambitions. These cases were the 1990–2 reforms under Mitsotakis and the mini-reform of 1998 under Simitis. In the case of Mitsotakis, the prime minister had included a "comprehensive revision" of the Greek social security system in his election platform. He intended to overhaul the pension system swiftly, with an ambitious reform agenda. When he faced severe reactions from the unions and other groups, he made significant concessions. A watered-down version of the reform passed only after the government postponed the measures bringing in structural changes and withdrew others that would tinker with the privileges of protected groups. Mitsotakis then made a second, even bolder move, with the initial participation of the unions. But when the unions walked out of negotiations, the ensuing nationwide strikes and popular unrest threw the country into chaos. The opposition parties and even senior members of his own party joined in opposing the reforms.

In the case of Simitis, his government was hard pressed to find savings on the road to the EMU. After the process began, the prime minister bowed to pressure and dropped many of the more important measures; at the end of two rounds of reform, only a handful from the original much longer list had been passed. With powerful groups unable to claw back any privileges, and with long transition periods, these measures left the structural characteristics of the Greek welfare state virtually intact. Because these reforms were not bringing in the savings that Greece desperately needed to join the EMU, the government decided to increase savings through tax reform and privatizations.

Likewise, when Simitis planned to introduce a radical overhaul of the Greek pension system in 1998, he had to postpone it, initiating instead a mini-reform aimed at reorganizing the social security funds and resulting in modest cutbacks. But opposition was once again fierce: the unions staged strikes and demonstrations virtually every day, reactions of such dramatic proportion that they forced the government to rule through emergency powers to halt the strikes. By the end of the reform process, Simitis had to withdraw some of the proposed measures, and the funds retained their own administrative and financial autonomy.

Ironically, despite the inexorable fiscal pressure stemming from the EMU, the Greek welfare state experienced some *expansionary* measures, all aimed at appeasing growing public opposition to the fiscal austerity. Successive governments resorted to measures that expanded some welfare benefits as a means of buying off submission to budgetary austerity. To compensate for his austerity policies, Mitsotakis introduced new benefits to families and other groups. Papandreou made concessions to some pensioners, including farmers and IKA.

After having increased the benefits of IKA pensioners during his first term, Simitis sought approval for his 1996 austerity package by granting additional social security benefits, which would expand benefits for families and give them a pension supplement (EKAS). These benefits included delaying bringing these provisions into effect and not implementing some of the measures introduced by the Mitsotakis government. Again in 1997, when growing resistance to fiscal austerity threatened to undermine public support for the EMU, the government decided not to implement the 1990–2 reforms, which were to take effect in 1998. It also expanded the eligibility for EKAS and other benefits as a deliberate move to appease growing opposition against budgetary austerity.

Once EMU entry was guaranteed in 1998, the government introduced the Simitis package, which expanded benefits again. In times of general budgetary austerity, many governments had to *augment* welfare benefits to appease public and political opposition. Otherwise, governments believed, such opposition would easily derail their fiscal austerity strategies. Consequently, the OECD (2001, 38) observed that the reforms had not even "dented" Greece's social spending; in fact, thanks to expansionary strategies (such as the Simitis reforms), social expenditures grew, even throughout the otherwise austere Maastricht decade.

This case study also showed that, after many reform attempts, political strategies aimed at bringing about across-the-board welfare state retrenchment were futile. In some cases, governments could not even bring some of their reform initiatives to Parliament; in others, they had to scrap their plans altogether for fear that they would provoke fierce opposition. In still other cases, when reforms were passed, it was only in seriously scaled-back form. In particular, although these reforms were initially intended to bring in the short-terms savings desperately needed for EMU entry, their budgetary impact remained far below the threshold originally planned. While strategies for postponing the bitter impact, or non-implementation, of previously legislated reforms paid off by rendering Euro-austerity more palatable, the reforms that did go through achieved no significant savings to meet immediate budgetary goals.

The present case study also demonstrated that Greek governments made remarkable progress in controlling their fiscal balances beginning in the early 1990s, despite the creative accounting strategies they resorted to. All governments that came to power during the Maastricht decade were committed to Euro-austerity, and, eventually, Greece corrected its large fiscal imbalances with the help of successive convergence programs. When repeated attempts at welfare reform failed to produce the projected savings, politicians resorted to alternative fiscal strategies to comply with the Maastricht criteria. Instead of cutting social spending, they switched to their Plan B: greater fiscal and non-fiscal revenues,

Table 11. Greece: General Government Accounts, Social Expenditures, and Privatization Revenues (% of GDP)

	1991	1992	1993	1994	1995	1996	1997	1998	1999	2000	2001
Total government expenditures	46.7	49.4	52.0	49.9	46.1	45.2	43.8	45.2	46.2	46.3	45.9
Social expenditures	15.2	15.4	16.2	16.3	16.6	17.0	16.9	17.5	18.0	18.4	19.7
Non-social expenditures	31.5	34.0	35.8	33.6	29.5	28.2	26.9	27.8	28.2	27.9	26.3
Total government revenues	35.6	37.2	38.6	40.7	36.3	36.9	37.6	38.9	40.4	42.4	40.5
Privatization receipts	–	–	0.1	0.1	0.1	0.6	1.3	3.4	3.6	1.0	1.0
Government deficit	−11.1	−12.2	−13.4	−9.2	−9.7	−8.2	−6.1	−6.3	−5.8	−4.1	−5.5
Public debt	74.0	79.1	99.2	97.2	99.0	101.3	99.5	97.4	98.9	104.9	107.1

Source: OECD (2002, 2016a, 2016b, 2017a, 2017c); European Commission (2017); privatization figures: author's calculations.
Note: A dash (–) denotes zero or a negligible amount.

lower non-social expenditures, and, as confirmed later by EU authorities, a variety of creative accounting practices, as shown in table 11.

Just as in the Belgian case study, the table shows that the most striking aspect of the Greek fiscal consolidation process was its strong emphasis on rising public revenues. In the Maastricht decade, total revenues increased from 35.6 per cent of GDP in 1991 to 40.5 per cent in 2001. As this chapter described, *every* government introduced a combination of large-scale tax reforms and other measures to improve tax compliance, broaden the tax base (by abolishing tax privileges and taxing previously untaxed incomes), and modernize tax administration. Among non-tax measures, the privatization program that began in 1994 as part of the first convergence program (1994–9) became a policy priority after 1996 as the EMU deadline approached (OECD 2002, 73). The Simitis government accelerated the process by implementing the structural measures introduced with the second convergence program (1998–2001).

Table 11 also shows that, in 1999, which was the critical window for Greece's assessment for EMU entry, privatization receipts skyrocketed, reaching record high levels – some 3.6 per cent of GDP! This jump in revenue placed Greece among the highest in the EU for this marker (OECD 2002, 73). Privatization was seen as the most convenient way to raise revenue without having to rely on politically treacherous social security cutbacks or unpopular tax increases. It is significant that when EMU entry was guaranteed, the privatization process decelerated, bringing in declining receipts. Additionally, at the beginning of the convergence period, Greece was the poorest EMU candidate, a position governments exploited to secure massive transfers from the EU. By the end of the Maastricht decade, Greece had received the highest amount in transfers of any EMU candidate. In fact, researchers argued that the expansionary trend in social expenditures during the otherwise austere decade was partly thanks to the massive resources flowing into the country from the EU (Petmesidou and Mossialos 2006, 8).

In terms of expenditures, although Greece's fiscal consolidation strategy actually relied on rising revenues, successive governments followed the EU's guidance by insisting that they had to curtail spending to satisfy EMU convergence. All social security reforms were justified by the imperative of exercising restraint to contribute to desperately needed fiscal savings. The political economy of reform, however, forced governments to scale back their initial ambitions, and any eventual savings that accrued in the social security account failed to contribute to the consolidation effort.

As table 11 shows, governments managed to rein in public outlays. It is very interesting to note that, despite cutbacks in public expenditures, social expenditures increased by about 30 percentage points, from 15.2 per cent of GDP in 1991 to 19.7 per cent by 2001. Whenever the option of raising revenues through welfare reform was foreclosed by public opposition, governments resorted to retrenchment measures focused on non-social expenditures, which were politically less troublesome. They raised budgetary savings mainly by reducing spending on general public services (through wage freezes and tighter personnel policies) and defence spending (which had been highest in the EU). Moreover, governments found ways to move substantial parts of defence spending off budget so they would not appear in government accounts defined by the Maastricht Treaty. As a result, non-social expenditures declined markedly, from 31.5 per cent of GDP in 1991 to 26.3 per cent in 2001.

This confirms our finding that, under the double bind of Euro-austerity and strong opposition to welfare reform, Greek governments retrenched only non-social expenditures. This demonstrates, once again, that, despite the political discourse of successive governments to the contrary, it was reductions in *non-social* outlays that brought in savings on the road to the EMU. Finally, sharply declining interest rates in

Greece during the Maastricht decade eased the pressure on government borrowing and contributed to the consolidation effort.

Once Greek governments had reached the political limits of regular fiscal measures, they resorted to creative accounting. After Greece entered the EMU, the European Commission and Eurostat discovered that there had been serious budgetary irregularities during the 1990s. With the Maastricht deadline fast approaching, Greek governments under-recorded defence expenditures, over-recorded surpluses in the social security account, and incorrectly reported transfers from the EU and privatization receipts. As a result of the large discrepancies between the originally reported and the actual deficit and debt levels, the Commission revised these levels upward, but only long after Greece had entered the EMU (OECD 2005). According to the revised figures, Greece had *never* satisfied the fiscal benchmarks defined by the Maastricht Treaty.

In conclusion, this chapter showed that as it faced severe fiscal imbalances at the beginning of the 1990s, Greece was a prime candidate for undergoing draconian fiscal retrenchment on the road to the EMU. Many expected that this pressure would force governments to cut welfare state programs in general and the immense pensions program in particular. They could do so easily given the *vincolo esterno* – the Maastricht convergence imperative. The evidence presented here demonstrates that the austerity drive compelled successive governments to *initiate* major social security reform, but they repeatedly failed to accomplish it. Opposition from large constellations of societal groups – organized labour, traditionally protected groups, professional groups, and various sectors of society mobilized by the unions and civil society organizations – precluded any serious reform whatsoever. These coalitions were sometimes supported not only by the opposition parties in Parliament but also by senior members of the ruling party. In most cases, resistance led to the complete shelving of reform plans; in others, it resulted in only limited, parametric changes in some welfare state programs.

Facing the austerity imperative but wary of the potential political consequences of retrenchment, Greek governments devised alternative ways of curtailing spending (such as cutting back on non-social spending) and raising revenues (raising tax revenues, increasing privatization receipts and EU transfers). All these strategies diverted pressure away from the welfare state budget. In fact, growing opposition to fiscal austerity, undertaken in the name of the EMU, forced governments to resort to expansionary measures aimed at compensating for losses elsewhere and to buy off public submission to budgetary austerity.

6 Euro-Austerity and the Political Economy of Reform in Italy

By the early 1990s, the consensus among scholars, experts, and policymakers was that Italy had virtually *no chance* of qualifying for the EMU: its budget deficit and public debt levels deviated too wildly from the stringent rules imposed by the Maastricht Treaty. It was another EMU candidate at the treaty-negotiation table whose candidacy Germany did not even take seriously until the very last minute. Epitomizing the case of the "extreme misfit," Italy's chances of completing the fiscal adjustment and meeting the convergence criteria were considered to be virtually nil.

At the end of the convergence process, however, Italy had succeeded in achieving fiscal consolidation, reducing its budget deficit and public debt, and squeezing through the narrow gates of Maastricht to become an EMU member on 1 January 1999. It made it to the first round of the EMU, although the government had been repeatedly named and shamed by its EU partners for failing to comply with the Maastricht criteria. In this chapter, I show that the euro drive led to a paradigm shift in fiscal policy and politics in Italy. But it did not lead to a radical overhaul of the Italian welfare state. I argue that while some changes in the Italian welfare state occurred, these were far from the across-the-board retrenchment that the Euro-austerity hypothesis would predict.

I develop my argument in two steps. First, I show how Italy qualified for EMU membership in spite of its mounting deficit and public debt, present the austerity policies adopted by Italian governments during the Maastricht decade, and trace the institutional changes in fiscal policy and politics that allowed Italian governments to gain increased control over the budget. By analysing episodes of fiscal consolidation during the 1990s, I describe how Euro-austerity was a structural constraint on Italian budgets. I also show how policymakers used the EMU as a discursive opportunity to catch the "Euro train."

Second, I examine the efforts by each Italian government in the 1990s to reform welfare state programs in general and pensions in particular. I outline the goals of Italian policymakers and show that reform outcomes were significantly less ambitious than the original plans. By tracing each government's attempt at welfare reform, I show how these attempts faced powerful opposition from a constellation of societal groups. In most cases, these groups were led by the unions, which effectively managed to limit retrenchment efforts. The Italian case shows that, as in Belgium and Greece, Italian governments were very successful at introducing remarkable changes in fiscal policy, but they were largely unsuccessful in restructuring their welfare state. They failed to bring about reform despite both the structural constraints imposed and the discursive opportunities provided by Euro-austerity.

The case study on Italy is structured as follows. It begins by describing how EU authorities and experts viewed its candidacy for the EMU during the early 1990s and how far it was from complying with the Maastricht criteria. Next, it outlines the background to Italy's budgetary problems and the political crisis that led to the fall of not only the Andreotti government but also the First Republic. It then follows the formation of Amato's technocratic government after the emergence of Italy's Second Republic, tracing the reversal of Italy's fiscal path after the government obtained emergency powers and made a first attempt at reforming the welfare state.

The case study reviews the continuation of fiscal austerity under the caretaker government of Ciampi and the reversals of some of the measures brought about by Amato's welfare reforms. Next, it traces the Berlusconi government's coming to power and its frontal attack on pensions. It shows how this led to a series of strikes, which resulted in not only the withdrawal of the reform but also the collapse of the government. It then follows the reforms introduced by the technocratic Dini government and discusses the consensual style it used to further the welfare reform process.

It goes on to review the reform episodes under the Prodi government and shows how the Ministry of Treasury was strengthened throughout the Maastricht decade to steer fiscal policy from the centre. It reviews the Italian budgetary strategies (including the Euro-tax) that made it possible to meet the Maastricht targets on time. It also traces how the Prodi government tried to introduce pension reform as a last-ditch effort before the EMU deadline, the resistance it met, and how it could be passed only in significantly amended form. In conclusion, the chapter gives an analytical overview of the political economy of welfare state reform in Italy and its implications for the empirical validity of the Euro-austerity hypothesis.

Italy as the Misfit

Seen from the point of view of the early 1990s, Italy's prospects for joining the euro would be described in different ways. Many thought it would be a miracle; others viewed it as impossible. Its macroeconomic fundamentals were notoriously different than those of the other members of the European Community. As late as 1996, *none* of the Maastricht criteria had been met! Just a short while after the treaty was signed, in September 1992, the Italian lira was ousted from the ERM. Interest rates remained much higher than those in Germany, and this had extremely adverse effects on Italian public finances. Such a differential indicated that the financial markets viewed Italy, by any measure, as an unsuitable candidate for the EMU.

Although indicators of price stability, interest rates, and exchange rates diverged wildly from the Maastricht criteria, both the Italian government and European institutions deemed them largely unproblematic (see, e.g., EMI 1996). Convergence was the least successful in the area of public finances (OECD 1992, 50); the fiscal criteria alone sufficed to seal Italy's fate as an outsider. After all, the Italian fiscal imbalances had been a primary source of concern from the first day of treaty negotiations on the EMU. Although Greece was in the worst position, the main focus of attention in the official documents was on the Italian fiscal imbalances (European Commission 1993, 72). The fiscal situation in Italy was so precarious that experts concurred that the *raison d'être* of the fiscal criteria themselves was to effectively exclude Italy from entering the third stage of the EMU (Moravcsik 1998, 443; Dinan 1999, 174–5; Heisenberg 1999, 164; Sbragia 2001, 80; Dyson 1994, 149; Dyson and Featherstone 1999, 9). Between 1991 and 1992, Italy (along with Greece and Belgium) was seen as a member state facing "acute problems" (Buiter, Corsetti, and Rubini 1993, 64), to say the least, and the required adjustment would be "massive" (as in Belgium and Greece) (71–2).

In a communication to the Council in July 1991, in which the European Commission reviewed member states' progress towards convergence, Italy received the second-worst marks after Greece: two grey marks for inflation (partially unsatisfactory situation), one black for the budget deficit (negative situation), two black for the official debt (negative situation), and one grey for external accounts (partially unsatisfactory situation) (*Agence Europe*, 4 July 1991). In its survey of the Italian economy in 1992, the OECD (1992, 12) commented on the hopeless prospects of

Italian participation in the euro: "Meeting the Maastricht convergence rules implies for Italy a speed of fiscal consolidation which has no precedent among major countries."

Experts, too, concurred that the feasibility of Italian adjustment was simply "slim when judged by the markets, nil in the eyes of our European partners, as well as of economists and opinion makers" (Chiorazzo and Spaventa 1999, 2–3). There was consensus that Italy, facing more than triple the Maastricht deficit reference value, would almost certainly not be able to join the EMU, even at a later date. Sbragia (2001, 85) summarized the expert consensus this way: "Italy came to symbolize an extreme misfit – a member state whose public finances were so incompatible with the European standard that its chances of adapting in time to join the first wave of EMU entrants were thought to be nil."

When the time came to assess convergence in 1998, however, Italy squeezed through the narrow gates of Maastricht in the first wave, "defying widespread adverse expectations, technical disbelief and political hostility" (Chiorazzo and Spaventa 1999, 150). It managed to do so through what the Commission's *Convergence Report* (European Commission 1998, 130) praised as "a far-reaching budgetary consolidation." The stance of the primary budget balances revealed how dramatic the change was: "From a 1990 primary deficit-to-GDP ratio that was the second highest in Europe, Italy in 1997 achieved a primary surplus that was the highest in Europe" (Kostoris Padoa-Schioppa 2001, 118).

Italy Enters the 1990s: The Andreotti Government

Italian fiscal performance stood out as "anomalous," even among the other member states with major fiscal imbalances (European Commission 1993, 72). There had been attempts to introduce fiscal discipline starting in the late 1970s, but these were modest. Budget deficits remained consistently above 10 per cent of GDP throughout the 1980s, and only as late as 1988 did the government take a more effective step and introduce a new institutional instrument, the Economic and Financial Planning Document (*Documento di Programazzione Economico-Finanziara*, or DPEF). The DPEF was designed to set public finance targets and limits within a multi-year framework.

Although the DPEF was meant to serve as an institutional constraint on policymakers, its implementation until the second half of the 1990s was rather weak.[1] It was in itself insufficient to bring order to Italian public finances (Felsen 2000, 161–2).[2] Budget deficit spirals resulted in ever-rising public debt. Debt ratios rang alarm bells, especially in the second half of the 1980s, when they were growing at a higher rate than those of the other member states (with the exception of Greece); by the end of the 1980s, they had reached 100 per cent of GDP. In 1991, the Commission warned that "the Italian government borrows each year almost as much as all the other member state governments put together" (*Reuters News*, 7 November 1991). In 1992, public debt exceeded the country's entire GDP for the first time since 1924 (except for its wartime level of 1943); it accounted for 40 per cent of the total standing debt of all EU members states combined and the total combined debt of Germany, France, and the United Kingdom (OECD 1992, 38).

Chronic deficit slippage had been another constant feature of the Italian fiscal scene since the 1980s: between 1981 and 1991, with the exception of 1986, sizeable deficit overruns appeared each year. Although, during the late 1980s, the ruling elite saw fiscal austerity as a *"scelta obbligata,"* a choice "with no degree of freedom" (Radaelli 2002, 216; see also Walsh 1998, 96; Felsen 2000, 162), any serious effort at consolidation proved futile. The literature on Italian fiscal problems pointed unequivocally to *partitocrazia* – political parties intruding into every aspect of social, political, and economic life. *"Partitocrazia* and sound public finance were largely incompatible," concluded one keen observer of Italian politics, and "those advocating the latter were no match for the power of the former" (Sbragia 2001, 89). It was only after the Maastricht Treaty was signed that Italian governments pushed for a rigorous fiscal consolidation strategy.

In an attempt to put the Italian fiscal house in order, the ruling government of Giulio Andreotti rushed to submit Italy's first convergence program in October 1991, while the treaty was still being negotiated.[3] This was the *first* national convergence program to be submitted by any member state to the ECOFIN Council within the framework of multilateral surveillance. In fact, Andreotti's finance minister, Guido Carli, had personally promised the ECOFIN Council in July 1991 that the government would submit a convergence plan to show Italy's commitment to the EMU (*Reuters News*, 7 November 1991). This was the first time that the Italian government had signalled its "good faith" towards its EU partners by pushing for fiscal austerity (Dyson and Featherstone 1996, 289).

The convergence program predicted an improvement in the government's fiscal balance by 4.5 percentage points in three years, from 10.0 per cent of GDP in 1991 to 5.5 per cent in 1994 (European Commission 1993, 61). To achieve this goal, it aimed for a strong, expenditure-based fiscal consolidation strategy that would reduce current expenditures from 28.8 per cent of GDP in 1991 to 28.3 per cent in 1994, along with increases in revenue. The program would be backed up by an institutional reform measure that would increase the powers of the executive vis-à-vis the legislature in budgetary matters.

In November 1991, the ECOFIN Council announced "its appreciation for the actions started in 1991 and for presenting this program." Its conclusions continued: "With regards to the need to establish sound public finance conditions, the Council particularly appreciates the explicit commitment to respect the deficit targets." Although it found the deficit targets "ambitious," "they [were] the minimum necessary." It called for the convergence program to be "more detailed on these issues in order to allow the Council to assess fully the adequacy of the measures proposed to achieve the targets." "In particular," it warned, the convergence program "will have to indicate the timescale and the extent of the proposed pension reform." The Council also called for institutional changes in the Italian fiscal system for budgetary discipline (Council of the European Communities 1991). Before the Maastricht Treaty was signed, therefore, the Council was already practising fiscal surveillance. Moreover, as this decision shows, it had begun to intervene in matters concerning Italy's welfare state reform.

Although the Italian government announced that it would rely on public pay restraint, pension reform, and privatization, it did not provide any concrete timetable for these reforms. Moreover, Parliament had watered down some items in the fiscal adjustment package, and the deficit had been hugely overshot (OECD 1992, 38–40).[4] It was clear in early 1992 that unless additional fiscal measures were taken, another massive deficit slippage would occur.

The budgetary outcome for the first half of 1992 confirmed these pessimistic expectations, and in May 1992, the ECOFIN Council increased its pressure on the government to take additional measures of fiscal restraint. Although it again welcomed the "explicit commitment of the Italian authorities to respect the annual budget deficit targets," it warned that Italy's budgetary situation was a "cause for serious concern" requiring "a substantial additional adjustment package." If "exceptional measures going beyond the normal framework of fiscal policy" were not taken, the Council concluded, "Italy would in all likelihood fail to meet the Maastricht criteria" (Council of the European Communities 1992, 7–8).[5]

The Amato Government and the *Annus Mirabilis*

Italians went to the polls in April 1992. The two political parties that had ruled post-war Italy, the Christian Democrats and Socialists, suffered setbacks in the election, although they still held a parliamentary majority. These losses were in large part due to the outbreak of the *Tangentopoli* (Bribesville) scandal. The following *mani pulite* (Clean Hands) investigation unveiled an entrenched system of political corruption. As scores of politicians were convicted, the prestige of the ruling parties was shattered. These were signs that the old political party system associated with the First Republic was disintegrating.[6]

The year 1992 represented a watershed moment in Italian political history. The electoral system was re-formed into a predominantly first-past-the-post system, and the elite that had ruled Italy since the First Republic was established in 1946 was largely swept away. A new era began, with new governments led by technocrats, mostly academics, who were not members of political parties, businesspeople, or senior public servants. All these developments led the OECD's (1993, 9) survey of the Italian economy to open by stating that "the speed and depth of political change which Italy has undergone since mid-1992 have defied all predictions." In May 1992, the president appointed Socialist Giuliano Amato prime minister. Amato had "unimpeachable economic qualifications" as a former Treasury minister involved in the workings of the EMS (Hellman 1993, 152).

Amato formed a new government in June 1992 in the midst of an economic recession and political turmoil. The European context, underpinned by uncertainties following the Danish referendum rejecting the Maastricht Treaty, was no more positive. Amato appointed non-political "technicians" to key economic posts, choices that reflected the major change in the nature of Italian politics as a result of the *mani pulite*. As the investigations deepened and the old system of *partitocrazia* collapsed, Amato could easily carve out a political space for executive power. These changes gave him a much greater political capacity than that enjoyed by Italian prime ministers during the First Republic (Hallerberg 2004, 189; Sbragia 2001, 90, 92; Hellman 1993, 155).

The Risanamento

Facing the crisis of Italian public finances and pressure from the ECO-FIN Council, the biggest challenge Amato faced was the insurmountable budget deficit, and much of his new government's energies were spent trying to introduce fiscal austerity (Pasquino and McCarthy 1993, 160). In fact, the main pillar of his government's program was redressing Italy's fiscal imbalances to prepare the nation for the EMU. He declared, "The government's economic policy will be centred on an immediate action to break inflationary pressures and reduce the budget deficit, with the objective of converging with the parameters of the Maastricht Treaty" (*Wall Street Journal Europe*, 25 June 1992). "The government must present as soon as possible a package of measures to meet the European objective which must accompany the ratifying of the Maastricht Treaty" (*Reuters News*, 24 June 1992).

Just one week after assuming power, in early July, the government announced an additional "corrective manoeuvre" amounting to 2.0 per cent of GDP. The aim of this mini-budget was to keep the 1992 deficit closer to the targets announced in the convergence program. Even if this mini-budget achieved its targets, this effort would still be dwarfed by the fiscal retrenchment required by the treaty, and the deficit would continue to hover at almost four times the Maastricht benchmark. The budget bill for 1993 still had to introduce draconian measures to put the Italian public finances on a sound footing. With pressure from the EU, the government made the vote on the crisis austerity plan a vote of confidence to show the urgency of the measures. The leaders of all political parties supported the bill (*Reuters News*, 14 July 1992).

In the meantime, along with the looming fiscal crisis, confidence in the lira was waning, pushing up the risk premium on the domestic interest rate and rendering fiscal consolidation more difficult. After a rash of financial speculation, the government had to devalue the lira in September for fear of sustaining substantial losses in its official reserves. As a result, the Italian lira was suspended from the ERM (OECD 1992, 13), a move that raised doubts as to whether Italy could *ever* reduce its budget deficit enough to meet the Maastricht criteria. Just a few hours later, Amato requested that Parliament grant him emergency powers so that he could impose a new package of fiscal restraint. The Democratic Party of the Left (PDS), the Lega Nord (Northern League), and other opposition groups accused him of pulling off an "economic coup d'état."

However, the harsh austerity program and devaluation of the lira increased Amato's personal standing (Pasquino and McCarthy 1993, 162). In defending his austerity package, he emphasized repeatedly that he needed emergency powers even more urgently after the EU had endorsed the free float of the lira (*Wall Street Journal Europe*, 18 September 1992). Warning Parliament not to tamper with the fiscal restraint package, he stressed that "the government's life depend[ed] on this budget" (*Reuters News*, 17 September 1992).

The government used many threats and warnings to suppress opposition to its austerity program and, in the end, managed to obtain parliamentary approval for it (Felsen 1998, 163). Parliament also passed a law conferring special powers on the government, which introduced a "break with the past practice of using one-off measures as a main vehicle for deficit reduction" (OECD 1993, 44). As a result, the influence of Parliament over the budgetary process was diminished; any future proposals for spending increases would have to be balanced by revenue gains. By strengthening the executive vis-à-vis Parliament in this way, the law became "the main instrument to promote fiscal convergence" (ibid).

The 1993 budget aimed to trim ITL 93 trillion – an unprecedented, massive cutback amounting to 6.1 per cent of GDP (OECD 1993, 45).[7] The OECD greeted this budget as "a landmark" in Italy's budgetary history (44). The convergence program submitted in 1991 was revised and resubmitted to the Commission.[8] At the same time, the government asked the Commission for a loan to support its budgetary reform; this was agreed to as long as Italy's performance was satisfactory, measured against the targets in the program.

The budget was perhaps the most rigorous in Italy's post-war history, and it began the process of *risanamento* (restoring the health of public finances). This strategy remained the main pillar of the fiscal policies followed by successive governments. In this sense, Amato's fiscal reforms are generally considered to be the first fundamental step in correcting the gross fiscal imbalances that had plagued Italy's post-war public finances. This strategy marked the beginning of a broad transformation not only in fiscal policy and performance but also in fiscal structure and politics, amounting to a "Copernican revolution" (Salvati 1997; Ferrera and Gualmini 2004, 66–7; see also Felsen 2000, 158; Antichi and Pizzuti 2000, 81; Fargion 2003, 313; Della Sala 1997, 24).[9]

After the Maastricht Treaty was signed in February 1992, Italy's fiscal crisis, compounded by the ensuing currency crisis, exerted powerful external pressure on Italy. Under the surveillance of not only the financial markets but also the EU, the fiscal criteria effectively dictated the government's fiscal policy choices. Until the treaty was signed, efforts to prune the deficit had been a signal to the financial markets only that the soaring debt would be tackled with; from 1992 on, however, doing so was a treaty obligation (Croci and Picci 2002, 227). As long as EMU was on course, the government believed, investors would feel confident that Italy would take action to correct its financial imbalances. At the same time, the treaty provided a discursive opportunity for the government because Amato was "able to instrumentalize" any warning from the EU: he could swiftly capitalize on the consensus about the acute need for fiscal restraint and be able to impose far-reaching fiscal measures (Felsen 2000, 162, 170).

The Amato Pact and Pension Reform

Reforming ailing pensions was a topic of discussion during the 1970s and 1980s. Many of these discussions, however, proved inconclusive and never evolved into successful reform initiatives. Although some initiatives reached Parliament, none were ever carried out. At the same time, social spending was on an upward trajectory and was, for many observers, largely responsible for the steep rise in public expenditures (Ferrera and Jessoula 2007, 396). Although revenues began to increase in the early 1980s, deficit spending was always the short-term solution to Italy's fiscal problems. Against the backdrop of the breakdown of the political system and the looming fiscal crisis, the last straw for the shaky Italian political economy was the ERM crisis of the summer of 1992. Stemming in large part from the unfolding fiscal crisis, the currency crisis severely shook the newly installed government, pushing it to take unprecedented measures. In this sense, the Amato reforms were not so much the outcome of the endless debates on the question of welfare as the result of the monetary and fiscal crises, which required urgent measures (Antichi and Pizzuti 2000, 89).

The government, through an emergency decree, introduced a set of austerity measures in an attempt to put Italy's fiscal house in order. Amato believed that the only way out of the crisis was through restrictive fiscal policies, and this required making cuts in the welfare budget (Ferrera and Jessoula 2007, 431). An immediate and large-scale cost-containment strategy was desperately needed to allow Italy to regain credibility in international financial markets and honour its treaty obligations. To curtail spending, Cabinet approved several bills, along with budgetary measures, to undertake reforms in the national pension system, national health system, public service, and local government finance. Struggling through the economic and political crises, Amato requested special powers (*legge delega*) from Parliament to carry out these reforms. In October, the Chamber of Deputies approved the legislative decrees (Law No. 421) that empowered the government to implement reform in these four policy areas with the passage of the 1993 budget bill (OECD 1994, 33). Under these circumstances, the approval of Parliament was not necessary, and this gave the government a large degree of autonomy from the political parties in the reform process.

In its original draft form, the government's reform plan was perceived to be "the biggest attack on health and social security spending since Italy's welfare state was set up" (*Financial Times*, 19 September 1992). The measures to reform pensions that were introduced in the budget bill provoked protests from the trade unions, which organized strikes and demonstrations through September and October. Hundreds of thousands of people took to the streets, resulting in a wave of industrial unrest not seen since the oil crisis of the 1970s. In early October, the unions threatened the government with a general strike.

Amato also came under strong pressure from his own coalition allies, on both the left and the right, to water down the cutbacks. To fend off the pressure, he repeatedly vowed to resign if his package was tinkered with, and he and his ministers justified the austerity measures by continually referring to the EMU. They insisted that whether Italians remained in the first, second, third, or fourth division of the EU would depend on passing the 1993 budget containing the proposed reforms. Facing hundreds of amendments from furious opposition deputies, Amato decided to make the approval of spending and welfare cuts a confidence issue.

Against this backdrop of protests, the government continued its informal, tripartite negotiations with the trade unions and the General Confederation of Italian Industry (Confindustria) (Regini and Colombo 2011). It was in this collaborative atmosphere that negotiations over the strategy to balance the budget deficit and secure the long-term sustainability of the Italian welfare state continued. Because of its technocratic nature, the government was politically weak, and Amato believed he had to seek legitimacy outside Parliament.[10] In his own account of these years, he admitted that it was very difficult to build consensus through conventional party channels and Parliament. In his own account of this reform, Amato shared his reasons for approaching the unions: "In a number of cases, this allowed me to follow a totally new procedure in pushing through my policy measures: I discussed them with the unions; on the basis of their total or partial consent I drafted a text which I then presented to Parliament, and – building on the consensus I had reached out of Parliament – I asked for a vote of confidence" (Fargion 2003, 314). In October, the unions won a set of concessions, and Amato revised his reform plan. In the so-called Amato Pact, the unions accepted the revised version of the reform, and, after Law No. 421 was adopted, the strikes and demonstrations subsided.

The resulting revisions included the following: First, the government agreed to raise the ceiling on pensions proposed for 1993, and payments would rise by 3.5 per cent. The government then had to introduce additional revenue measures to cover the extra expenditure. Second, the government lowered the proposed ceiling for annual household income from ITL 40 million to ITL 35 million for singles, but raised it to ITL 65 million for large families because the measure would have denied free health care to twenty million Italians. Third, the government dropped its proposed freeze on indexing pensions for 1993; the resulting semi-indexing (just over 1 percentage point below the rate of inflation) would cost an extra ITL 3.6 trillion. Fourth, workers with a minimum of fifteen years of contributions as of 1992 were not covered under the new rules except for the new rule on linking contributions to the consumer price index (CPI). Fifth, Amato withdrew his original proposal of increasing the minimum contribution requirement of seniority pensions for private employees from thirty-five to thirty-six years.

The government insisted, however, that the overall target of holding the deficit to ITL 93 trillion remained unchanged. The extra revenue would be raised through an increase in national insurance contributions and making the national electricity authority cover its own debt-service costs. Moreover, new taxes were introduced, including the largely unpopular "minimum tax" (*Financial Times*, 16 October 1992; Ferrera and Gualmini 2004, 110). Thus, the government found alternatives to cutting back pensions, allowing it to achieve its budgetary targets without inflaming social tensions.

In its final form, the pension reform included the following changes to the old system (OECD 2000, 100; Franco 2002, 219):

– Gradually increase the statutory retirement age from sixty years to sixty-five for men and from fifty-five years to sixty for women in private employment over ten years, to 2002. The official retirement age remained sixty-five for men and women in the public sector.
– Gradually extend the reference period for calculating pensionable earnings from five to ten years over ten years, to 2002. The reference period was extended to an individual's entire work history rather than the last few years of employment; this would especially help younger workers with fewer than fifteen years of contributions in 1992. Past earnings were to be revalued at a rate equal to the rise in the cost of living plus 1 percentage point per year.
– Raise the minimum number of years of contributions giving entitlement to an old age pension from fifteen to twenty over ten years, to 2002.
– Change the reference for indexing pension benefits from the minimum wage to the CPI, and the government was allowed to introduce discretionary adjustments through the budget.
– Gradually raise the minimum number of years of contributions required for public-sector employees to be entitled to a seniority pension to thirty-five.

All the reform measures that the social partners agreed to could have easily escaped notice; the unions and the general public did not quite realize their implications. In almost all cases, the changes did not touch the most visible elements of the current pension scheme, such as the multiplier (the 2 per cent accrual rate) for calculating pension benefits and the number of years to be completed to be eligible for entitlements (thirty-five years of contributions). Moreover, to stave off political opposition, cutbacks were designed to come into force gradually, after a certain period of time, so they would not be felt immediately (Antichi and Pizzuti 2000, 82; Pizzuti 1998, 46, 47). In addition to these political strategies, the sense of emergency created by the suspension of the lira from the ERM took pressure off the reform process.

These reform measures constituted the first significant step in containing pension costs in the long run. Their projected fiscal effects were limited, however, for several reasons. First, due to the introduction of long transition periods, many of the changes were phased in gradually (Ferrera and Jessoula 2007, 433); the effect was to limit the short-term impact of the reforms on budgets so that they had virtually no impact during the Maastricht time frame. The desperate need for measures with immediate and large-scale impact was in stark contrast with the long-phased-in character of the measures that brought savings only decades later. Second, the reform measures could not change the most salient features of the old system because its most serious inequities remained virtually untouched (Pizzuti 1998, 46). Third, although these reforms were designed to be phased in over the long term, they could not ensure the long-term sustainability of the system. Fourth, as the next section shows, the next (Ciampi) government did not implement some of the harshest measures in 1993–4, when the time came to implement them. Finally, the Constitutional Court ruled in June 1994 that the state should reimburse certain pensioners for their losses (see below).

Still, the reforms were significant. The government made these bold budgetary policy choices in an environment of great autonomy from the other political parties (Felsen 2000, 163). Amato capitalized on the acute sense of fiscal crisis and Italians' humiliation at the ERM crisis. He also sought consensus among all social partners (Radaelli 2002, 218; Ferrera and Gualmini 2004, 68), and tripartite agreements with the unions and employers facilitated reforms in an era of tainted politics. Amato and his technocratic successors continued during the 1990s to build consensus with their social partners in this way.

All these measures were taken to meet the Maastricht criteria (Ferrera and Gualmini 2004, 142; Graziano and Jessoula 2011, 162) and were made possible by the sense of emergency caused by the suspension of the lira from the ERM. The Maastricht timetable encouraged the unions to work with the government (Negrelli and Pulignano 2010, 143) and facilitate Italy's entry to the EMU. The collapse of the First Republic and the *partitocrazia* helped bring in a technocratic government and strengthen the executive. This was the beginning of the institutional transformation of the Italian political economy.[11] However, of all the measures introduced during the Maastricht decade, "the most permanent and significant" were those on fiscal discipline (Sbragia 2001, 87). Although the deficit and debt levels had not yet fallen, the Amato reforms were the beginning of a process of genuine fiscal consolidation.

The Ciampi Government: Austerity, Full Steam Ahead

But Amato's government was being weakened by judicial investigations, and its Cabinet lost seven ministers in the ongoing *mani pulite*. The prime minister resigned in April 1993 after a series of referenda that reflected mass discontent with the political system. Both the press and public opinion agreed that the new prime minister must absolutely *not* be a politician.

The president then appointed Carlo Azeglio Ciampi, a former governor of the Bank of Italy, as prime minister. Ciampi was the ideal caretaker candidate. The financial markets saw in him a leader deserving of their confidence. Free from the restrictions of partisan politics, Ciampi staffed his government with explicitly non-partisan, technical specialists (Pasquino and Vassallo 1995, 58–9).

The Mini-Budget, the Budget for 1994, and the "Ciampi Protocol"

Ciampi continued Amato's policies of austerity: he was intent on keeping to the Maastricht targets. Having personally represented Italy during the treaty negotiations as the governor of the Bank of Italy, he also felt obliged to get the persistent deficit and the debt under control (Pasquino and Vassallo 1995, 62). The first move his government made was to announce a corrective budgetary manoeuvre in May 1993 to rein in the runaway deficit. Despite the reform measures that Amato had brought in, there was still a shortfall in revenues due to an unforeseen cyclical weakness – higher social security spending. The EU loan that Italy had requested earlier would be granted if the European Commission approved these measures, but due to this weakness in the Italian economy, the loan was limited to around 0.8 per cent of GDP (OECD 1993, 46–7).

The government presented the new multi-year DPEF in July 1993. Based on the revised Italian convergence program, it emphasized the need for increased fiscal restraint. It aimed to reduce the budget deficit to 6.8 per cent of GDP in 1996 and stabilize the public debt by 1995 (OECD 1993, 48–9). It also aimed to cut the deficit to 8.7 per cent by 1994. According to the new budget, the proposed deficit reduction was based almost entirely on cuts to public spending, which was in sharp contrast with past practice. Among the planned cuts, ITL 5 trillion was to come from cuts in old age pensions and between ITL 3 and 5 trillion from cuts to health care (*Reuters News*, 12 July, 13 July 1993). The government announced that the proceeds from privatization were not included in the budget to comply with Maastricht Treaty rules (OECD 1993, 89; *Financial Times*, 10 September 1993). Ciampi had promised to unveil his budget earlier than usual – in July; however, the government faced tremendous opposition and decided to postpone debate on it in Parliament.

In a significant break with past practice, none of the political parties was consulted during the budgetary process. In fact, when the budget was being debated in Parliament, the technocratic prime minister told reporters, "I work here in the same manner I worked at the Bank of Italy – without the distractions of political alchemy" (*Wall Street Journal*, 16 September 1993). Ciampi faced strong opposition in Parliament to his plans to cut welfare and pensions, not only from the opposition parties but also from the other governing parties. He was challenged time and again. A number of deputies asked that funds be set aside to finance an increase in pensions for former state employees. The unions demanded that more funds be allocated to public-sector pay increases and unemployment benefits. Ciampi's response was the standard line about "external constraint" (Felsen 2000, 163).

While the budget was being drawn up, to remind everyone of the imperative of Euro-austerity for Italy's EMU entry, the budget and Treasury ministers repeatedly threatened to resign if the announced limits on spending (especially on pensions) were challenged (*Reuters News*, 27 October 1993). The government had already made concessions, but it refused to bend further (ibid., 3 November 1993). Although hundreds of amendments to the budget bill were presented, the austerity budget passed in both Houses of Parliament on schedule – but only after a deal was struck among the coalition and opposition parties. Under the deal, Ciampi agreed to support four blocks of amendments that would soften the restrictive impact of some of the most unpopular austerity measures (ibid., 30 November 1993). The compromise was reached after other funds were diverted to measures supporting employment, pensions, and welfare (ibid., 3 December 1993).

Like Amato, Ciampi sought legitimacy beyond Parliament in pushing his austerity measures through, continuing the direct negotiations with the trade unions that Amato had initiated. He feared potential disruptions, like those that had taken place the previous autumn, when millions of workers from all sectors had held demonstrations. Already that May, some groups were calling for work stoppages to oppose the austerity measures (*Reuters News*, 25 May 1993). In July, however, Ciampi managed to finalize a social pact on important structural reforms with objectives similar to those of Amato: abolish wage indexation, privatize employment and placement services, and reform collective bargaining (Regini and Colombo 2011). According to the "Ciampi Protocol," the social partners committed themselves to work with the government to frame budgetary policies that would meet the Maastricht parameters (Ferrera and Gualmini 2004, 68; Pasquino and Vassallo 1995, 65).

*Partial Implementation of Amato's Pension Reforms
and the 1994 Budget*

Ciampi's consensual style was not enough to prevent fierce opposition to such stringent austerity measures. When the 1994 budget was unveiled, it was clear that the cuts were focused on pensions. For example, pension privileges were reduced for early retirees in accordance with the Amato reforms, and postponing the start date for the new pension regime was to be suspended. Given the severity of these proposals, the unions called a general strike in late October in protest. The strike paralyzed Italian public services, banks, and much of industry.

After rounds of demonstrations and strikes, the unions obtained significant concessions. When the government was due to announce cuts in pensions and health care benefits and a freeze on public-sector wages, the unions lobbied and managed to overturn the freeze. The pension-reform measures passed by the Amato government were scheduled to take effect with the 1994 budget, but to stave off potential opposition, some were significantly diluted, and the date on which the most stringent measures would be introduced was postponed further (Economist Intelligence Unit, 1994, 13). Meanwhile, the unions' strong lobbying efforts had succeeded in persuading the government to divert more resources to pensions (*Financial Times*, 29 October 1993). Although the Amato government's 1993 budget decision to deny pension benefits to those seeking early retirement was meant to apply over the next few years, the 1994 budget lifted the ban, costing the government approximately ITL 4 trillion. Moreover, it raised the reference salary used to calculate pension benefits. The rate of this revaluation of earnings was also raised, to about 1.5 per cent, higher than the Amato reform had envisaged (1 per cent per year).

These changes in pensions (through Legislative Decree No. 373/1993) *reversed* about two-thirds of the entire range of cuts introduced by the Amato government in 1992 (Pizzuti 1998, 47). They also aimed to contain the costs of the unemployment benefits program, which the government had expanded under pressure from the unions. Provisions for exemptions on basic health payments were re-introduced (*Financial Times*, 11 September 1993).[12]

As a result of all these adjustments, the discrepancy between social security contributions and social welfare payments exceeded the government's target by over ITL 7 trillion. More than two-thirds of the beneficiaries were still under sixty years of age, indicating that the reform measures that aimed to reduce this number had not actually been implemented according to the original plan. It was evident that the savings from the reform would accrue only in the long term. Moreover, local health authorities accumulated a deficit of ITL 8 trillion, derived from the government's failure to implement its proposed cuts to health care (Economist Intelligence Unit, 2nd Quarter 1994, 19).

The budget bill in its original draft form had envisaged the fiscal adjustment to come almost entirely from spending cuts. The government had insisted on keeping the adjustment to ITL 32 trillion, but, after bringing in its changes, it realized that this was no longer possible unless it made cuts in other areas or raised new revenues. It stated repeatedly that it would not resort to introducing new taxes. In its final form, however, the budget covered only two-thirds of the fiscal adjustment through spending cuts; the remaining third had to be covered by raising new revenues, despite the government's promises to the contrary (*Financial Times*, 20 December 1993).

Instead of making cuts primarily in social expenditure items, therefore, the budget sought to increase savings by alternative means. First, the government initiated a comprehensive reform of the public administration. Each ministry was asked to find across-the-board cuts amounting to 3 per cent; some ministries were reduced in size or abolished altogether. Second, the government adjusted VAT payments, reduced the scope of tax write-offs on government investment, and refined the controversial "minimum tax" (*Financial Times*, 10 September, 11 September 1993). Third, it increased taxes to the tune of ITL 6.7 trillion (*Reuters News*, 27 December 1993). Finally, the proceeds from the privatization program, which had been originally left out of the calculations, were put back into the budget, boosting revenues by around ITL 5 trillion (ibid., 22 December 1993).

The Ciampi government achieved most of the austerity goals that it had set for itself. In addition to continuing to roll back the mounting deficit, it introduced other reforms, such as a wide-ranging privatization program and a new electoral law. Notwithstanding the limitations of a caretaker government, Ciampi continued relentlessly to eliminate the structural causes of Italy's budget deficit. However, despite the fact that he and Amato had managed to introduce wide-ranging budget cuts and structural reforms, their success in correcting Italy's fiscal balances was limited. The deficit remained stubbornly above 9 per cent of GDP.[13] The fiscal austerity drive was far from over if Italy wished to join the euro.

Berlusconi: Austerity without Welfare Reform

Ciampi resigned in January 1994, and Italians went to the polls in March for the first time since the fall of the First Republic. Berlusconi's Forza Italia attracted the largest number of votes but needed the support of three other parties to form a majority government: the federalist Lega Nord, the neo-fascist Alleanza Nazionale, and the smaller Christian Democratic Centre. The coalition government was finally formed in May. While it was divided on many issues, the economic ministers, particularly Lamberto Dini as Treasury minister, instilled confidence in the financial markets.

After a few months in office, the new government approved the new DPEF, prepared in July for The Year of the Euro (1997). Although its forecast was still not consistent with the Maastricht requirements, the fiscal austerity envisaged for 1994 and 1995 was sizeable (Ferrera and Jessoula 2007, 434). It targeted a reduction in the budget deficit to 8.0 per cent of GDP in 1995 (excluding proceeds from privatization) and a further 5.6 per cent in 1997 (OECD 1994, 45). In September, the government presented the 1995 budget bill, which broadly followed the objectives of the DPEF. The bill incorporated spending cuts and tax increases. On the expenditure side, the government planned most of the cuts to come from health care and pensions. According to the DPEF, reforming the pension system was necessary to meet the Maastricht fiscal criteria (Pitruzzello 1997, 1611).

Before introducing the budget in Parliament, Berlusconi attempted to garner support for his plan by conveying an image of cooperation with his social partners. His minister of labour and welfare, Clemente Mastella, set up an ad hoc commission under the chairmanship of Professor

Castellino to work out the details of the pension reforms. The commission consisted of academics, bureaucrats, and experts appointed by the unions and Confindustria, and it received wide media attention. However, because it represented such a range of interests, it could not arrive at a compromise and failed to produce any recommendations, leading to the final breakdown of the already weak dialogue between the government and the unions (Antichi and Pizzuti 2000, 89; *EIRR* 1994, 250: 9).

Regardless of its disagreements with the unions, the government presented a set of measures in the budget bill in late September. Compared with the original plan unveiled in July, the 1995 budget brought about a modest easing of the cuts in pension spending (ITL 3 trillion). But these were compensated for by additional revenue-raising measures. The government proceeded with a two-pronged strategy. First, it passed a decree blocking all new pension applications for four months and freezing the indexing of pensions in 1995; and, second, it drafted a law (at the request of President Scalfaro), to be annexed to the budget, setting out the main thrusts of the reforms. These measures, which would bring about savings of ITL 9 trillion, included the following (OECD 1994, 47; *EIRR* 1994, 250: 9):

- Reduce the accrual rate of pensions from 2.0 per cent per year to 1.75 per cent in 1996, falling to 1.5 per cent in 2001 for those with more than fifteen years of experience at the end of 1992.
- Speed up the increases in the minimum retirement age initiated by Amato, with the final date of completion brought forward from 2002 to 2000.
- Institute penalties for taking early retirement by 3 per cent for every year of shortfall for those with less than forty years of contributions (the previous number of years was thirty-five).
- Abolish all pension privileges of public-sector employees.
- Freeze the CPI indexing of all pensions in 1995 for twelve months, until January 1996, and switch to a less generous indexation method tied to targeted inflation.

These measures called for immediate cuts in spending. In principle, neither the unions nor the government's coalition partners disputed the need for austerity measures to meet the Maastricht benchmarks, but they disagreed on the *content* of the measures. They also criticized the government's radical approach and advocated more balance between spending cuts and revenue increases. In particular, they favoured smaller spending cuts and a gradual approach, accompanied by a more effective fight against tax evasion. They also demanded pension reform that would be sustainable in the long term. They maintained that reform should be distinct from short-term budgetary considerations by decoupling it from the budget process (Braun 1996, 212).

But the government went ahead with its reform proposals without taking into consideration the suggestions made by the unions, which were increasingly upset about the government's unilateral and exclusionary approach. They demanded direct negotiations with Berlusconi (Pitruzzello 1997, 1613, 1615), and these demands (along with those from the opposition parties) turned into an uproar. After countless strikes and demonstrations in September, Berlusconi met with the unions and promised smaller pension cuts. Although the unions called off the general strike, disagreements remained. They rejected the reform plan and announced that they would call a general strike in mid-October.

Now the government adopted a harder line. Berlusconi announced that he was withdrawing some of the concessions granted earlier (*Financial Times*, 30 September 1994). The period from September to December witnessed the largest protests and general strikes in Italian post-war history, a reminder of the events of the "hot autumn" of 1969 (Braun 1996, 212). During the general strike in October, about three million people demonstrated against the reform measures in the streets of all major cities and towns.

In the meantime, divisions among the coalition partners were deepening. Although it had voted unanimously in favour of the budget, Berlusconi's coalition partner Lega Nord began to distance itself from his welfare reform agenda, and it formally broke away from the coalition in late October. When the government refused to negotiate with them, the unions mobilized a new mass demonstration in Rome in mid-November. This second general strike brought together two million demonstrators from all across Italy. When Berlusconi threatened to use a vote of confidence to coerce the Lega into giving up its position, the party sided with the unions, and the unions threatened to go on strike again in early December. They would revoke their strike decision only if the government negotiated the reform proposals with them. At the same time, the Lega promised the unions that it would postpone the pension reforms.

As a result, an accord on pensions was signed in early December, after twenty-four hours of negotiations between the government and the unions. The government essentially had no choice but to postpone debate on the draft pension-reform law to avoid another strike. It also either deleted most of the measures that were to be inserted into the 1995 budget or significantly softened them. The proposed strike was called off, although the unions repeated their commitment to the budget's objectives (*Reuters News*, 1 December 1994). Eventually, all sides agreed that the government should not collapse before passing the budget (*Agence France-Presse*, 20 December 1994).

After overcoming the unions' veto, Parliament approved the revised 1995 budget bill in late December. The revisions were remarkable since the budget had already been approved in the Chamber. The *Financial Times* observed that the unions "have imposed change even when legislation ha[d] been endorsed by one chamber of parliament, and reinforced their role as interlocutors" (3 December 1994). The bill contained the absolute minimum in cuts to pensions, and Berlusconi announced that the pensions accord would not affect the budget (*Reuters News*, 1 December 1994). The Constitutional Court had ruled in June 1994 that the state should reimburse certain pensioners for having downgraded their benefits after Amato's pension reforms of 1992 came into effect. However, this would have a serious effect on public finances and undermine the projections for the additional fiscal effort needed to prepare for the 1995 budget (ibid., 14 June 1994). No action was taken to cover the costs of this decision for the 1995 budget year, but Treasury Minister Dini announced that the government would take further measures in early 1995 to finance any potential higher expenditure (ibid., 9 December 1994).

Because of the fragility of the coalition and Berlusconi's choice to reject negotiations with the unions, the coalition government could not pass the pensions component of the budget law (Ferrera and Jessoula 2007, 435; Negrelli and Pulignano 2010, 144). Berlusconi was fiercely opposed as he had broken all the unwritten rules that had always governed negotiations among the state, business, and the unions (Regini and Regalia 1997). In late December, after facing three separate motions of no confidence, the government resigned after just seven months in office. This was seen as Berlusconi's surrender; in fact, his government's fate had been sealed when the Lega Nord withdrew from the coalition (Radaelli 2002, 219). The president called on Treasury Minister Dini to lead a caretaker government.

Dini: Another Technical Government

Lamberto Dini formed the third *governo dei tecnici* in January 1995, a government composed entirely of technocrats. He also carried on the responsibility of the Treasury portfolio. The government was mandated to continue to reduce the deficit to meet the Maastricht fiscal criteria and carry out pension reform (Felsen 2000, 163–4; Pasquino 1996, 140). Immediately after taking office, Dini announced that his priority was to pass a supplementary budget. The fact that the Italian lira had fallen dramatically in late January, hitting a record low against the German mark and other major currencies, sped up the process. In February, the government unveiled its mini-budget, which proposed additional fiscal restraint measures amounting to 1.1 per cent of GDP. In a spirit of financial emergency like that of the Amato government, these measures aimed to meet the deficit target for 1995 and stabilize the public debt-to-GDP ratio. The budget would derive savings from a combination of new revenues and spending cuts, most of which would be carried out through a decree law (OECD 1995, 44; *Capital Markets Report*, 19 February 1995). In justifying this fiscal austerity, Dini referenced the treaty requirements, declaring that Italy would "do everything in its power" to be part of the EMU core group *(Dow Jones News Service*, 8 March 1995).

Thanks in large part to the technocratic nature of the government, its commitments were considered credible, and the supplementary budget – which was just strict enough to meet the DPEF targets – was approved in March without much difficulty (Pasquino 1996, 142). The *vincolo esterno* was omnipresent in the government's everyday discourse during the budget negotiations. For example, in passing the supplementary budget, Budget Minister Masera referred to the Maastricht timetable as requiring a "bullish consolidation" (*Capital Markets Report*, 17 May 1995). Moreover, the DPEF justified the government's efforts to reduce the deficit to 3 per cent of GDP by making explicit reference to the treaty (OECD 1995, 45; *Wall Street Journal of Europe*, 31 May 1995).

Reforming Pensions through Concertazione: *The Dini Social Accord*

During Berlusconi's final days in office, the unions had signalled that they supported the idea of a technocratic Cabinet under Dini. They had even written formal letters to the parliamentary groups, asking for the creation of a government that would be able to address "pressing economic and social issues and urgent reforms" (Braun 1996, 213). Dini had proved his goodwill towards the unions despite Berlusconi's hard-line approach to pension reform. He now realized that, with the breakdown of the conservative coalition, the unions and the left-wing parties would have to be brought into the reform process (Baccaro 2002, 419). The government then began a consultation process for reforming the pension system. Acting on the agreement reached in December 1994, the minister of labour and welfare, Tiziano Treu, initiated negotiations with the government's social partners in early February 1995. The negotiations were open: the government side never came forward with ready-made solutions that would signal to the unions that their participation was merely pro forma. In the long and complex process of preparing the reform bill, union representatives participated at each stage (Natali and Rhodes 2008; Regini and Colombo 2011).

Although the main aim of the bill was to improve the long-term fiscal sustainability of the pension system, the reform was mainly shaped by short-term considerations of fiscal stress, and reforming pensions was once again chosen as the cost-containment option. The responsibility for designing and implementing the Amato reform had been transferred from the Ministry for Labour and Social Protection to the Prime Minister's Office and the Ministry of Treasury. This transfer revealed the main motivation underlying the reform: enhancing executive power in the pursuit of Euro-austerity (Franco 2002, 240). Exercising Euro-austerity also meant that the government should strike a better balance between the contributions paid by pensioners and the benefits they received.

The negotiations culminated in an agreement in early May 1995; it was signed by the government, the three main trade union confederations, and the smaller trade unions and organizations representing the self-employed. The employers represented by Confindustria, however, did not sign the pact on the grounds that the reform did not go far enough (Antichi and Pizzuti 2000, 90–1; Baccaro 2002, 417). The reform was predicated on the principle of solidarity – the revised system would treat all workers as equally as possible. The main features of the reform are the following (Franco 2002, 221–2; Antichi and Pizzuti 2000, 83–7):

– Separate the state pension system from the rest of the social security system. This implied a more strict division between "insurance benefits," financed by contributions, and "assistance benefits," financed by the general budget.
– Switch from a defined-benefit system to a "notional" defined-contribution system and link the contributions made over an individual's entire lifetime with the sum of the benefits the individual receives when retiring.
– Consolidate the state pension system to end the multiple separate schemes. Coverage of private- and public-sector employees and the self-employed would be brought under a single scheme.
– Equalize the retirement ages of men and women, and introduce a flexible retirement age. Employees would be allowed to choose a retirement age between fifty-seven and sixty-five.
– Create a framework for introducing complementary pension schemes as a compensatory instrument in addition to the basic state pension scheme.

– Tie old-age pensions to the contributions made over an individual's entire working life up to the age of retirement. The minimum number of years of contribution required was reduced to five.

The government expected the bill to pass smoothly. However, during debate in Parliament, about 3,500 amendments were proposed, most by the Rifondazione Comunista. In response, contrary to its original intent, the government called three votes of confidence to bypass debate on these amendments. During its consultations with other parties, the government had reached a compromise with the Lega Nord and Forza Italia. To avoid watering down the reform any more, the government convinced Parliament that the bill was the outcome of a social pact signed with the unions and that it could not be altered further (*EIRR* 1995, 258: 24). The reform bill (Law No. 335) passed in both Houses of Parliament, with a few minor amendments, in August (*EIRR* 1996, 264: 33; Antichi and Pizzuti 2000, 91).

Although the new measures required sacrifices on the part of the unions, they continued to support the government's initiative, but their efforts did not stop there. Just after the accord was announced, they organized a referendum, from 29 May to June 1 1995, in which they asked all workers and pensioners to express their opinions on the draft reform and mounted a major campaign on the need to contain rising costs. Almost two-thirds of the four million Italians who voted, voted Yes to the proposals; the level of agreement for the reform was particularly high among pensioners (Baccaro 2002, 418; Ferrera and Gaulmini 2004, 145). Despite some internal dissatisfaction among union members, this result was considered a vote of confidence in Dini's reforms (Braun 1996, 214; Ferrera and Jessoula 2007, 438).

Strikingly, the government had secured the agreement of the same unions that had effectively blocked Berlusconi's reforms just a few months before. They conceded because of the technocratic nature of Dini's government and the consensual approach it had used (Pasquino 1996, 143; Braun 1996). They abandoned their veto and softened their position once the government dropped the Berlusconi draft reform in favour of their draft reform as the point of departure for negotiations (Ferrera and Gualmini 2004, 138). In fact, the reform process had been initiated by a proposal from the union side (Reynaud and Hege 1996, 65). This was an important victory for the Dini government, whose cooperative style contrasted with Berlusconi's unilateral approach (Radaelli 2002, 231). At the same time, the fiscal constraints imposed by the Maastricht Treaty and the threats from international financial markets were instrumental in mobilizing consensus for reform (Baccaro

2002, 419; Ferrera and Gualmini 2004, 138; Ferrera and Jessoula 2007, 437; Graziano and Jessoula 2011, 162; Quaglia and Radaelli 2007, 929).

Unlike Berlusconi's failed frontal assault, the Dini reform refrained from fundamentally challenging the existing system, despite the institutional changes it aimed to carry out. Including the unions in the negotiation process meant that no socially or politically unacceptable reform item would be inserted into the text. The unions had proposed that the reform take an extraordinarily gradual approach, allowing a long time to phase in the new pension scheme. The new system created three categories of workers: newcomers (workers who would begin to contribute in 1996), workers with less than eighteen years of contributions as of 1996, and those with eighteen years or more. Of these three categories, only the first came entirely under the new system. The second category was subject to the old system for rights acquired until 1996 and to the new system thereafter. The third remained entirely under the old system (Reynaud and Hege 1996, 70).

Postponing the measures proved extremely useful in garnering support for the reform, as had been the case for the Amato reform. The long transition period was the key condition for bringing the unions to the table (Regini and Regalia 1997, 217; Ferrera and Jessoula 2007, 437; Natali and Rhodes 2008, 37). But political support came with a cost. Because of the lengthy transition period, the reform could bring only limited savings in the short term. Although the measures were designed to put social spending on a sound footing in the longer term, the extent to which the reform would improve long-term expenditure trends was questionable. For example, it was estimated that about 40 per cent of those currently employed would retire under the pre-1992 pension formula; the reform would increase the incentive for them to retire early by signalling that retirement conditions would be tightened later. By distorting the incentives, the reform encouraged many to retire early. Thus, despite the increase in the age limit for old age pensions, the effective retirement age would not significantly increase over the next fifteen years, and neither would the replacement rate be reduced. This situation would increase pension spending even further (Franco 2002, 225).

An important aspect of the politics of the reform process was the use of obfuscation, used by both the Dini and the Amato governments. For example, the pension formulas that were introduced were not officially published anywhere. Second, most of the cuts were designed to come from changes to indexing; they would take effect not only gradually but also invisibly, and this helped ensure that these measures passed. Third, the reformers avoided revealing the cuts in replacement rates. In addition to concealing these measures, both governments justified the reform packages in the name of euro entry. Both used the *vincolo esterno* as a very successful "credit-claiming device" (Bonoli 2012, 96–7). All these techniques helped pass the reforms, something that would otherwise have been impossible (Franco 2002, 241).

Other strategies that proved useful in minimizing resistance to reform included an uneven distribution of the burden of changeover. These measures were designed to avoid creating a united front against reform by placing the burden disproportionately on two segments of the beneficiary population. The first group, pensioners and older workers, saw their benefits cut only marginally, if at all. Even these minor cuts were designed to be phased in over an extended period of time. Some grandfather clauses protected the acquired rights of older workers, who would remain in the old system, thereby retaining their seniority pensions. The second group, composed of younger workers, was heavily affected by the cuts, which introduced sudden increases in the minimum age for eligibility for old age pensions (Franco 2002, 241). The reform successfully divided these two groups by erecting an "artificial barrier between younger and older workers" and explicitly favoured the older workers (Fargion 2003, 321). The good, old divide-and-rule tactic helped minimize any potential opposition to reform (Ferrera and Jessoula 2007, 437).

The government made a tremendous budgetary effort to put Italy's financial house in order and prepare the country for the EMU. However, because of the long transition periods and other amendments, the 1995 reform failed to bring in any of the savings so desperately needed within the Maastricht time frame. In a short while, it became evident that meeting the fiscal benchmarks would require further efforts to contain costs. But these would have to wait until the next (Prodi) government introduced yet another round of welfare reform.

The 1996 Budget and the Commitment to the EMU

When he was working on the 1996 budget, Dini relied on the same strategy that he had pursued during the pension-reform process: he built consensus with the unions before taking the budget to Parliament. Both sides had agreed on the acute need for fiscal consolidation. To maintain the cooperation of the unions, Dini had approved many of their demands. For example, the new budget would not rely exclusively on spending cuts (which could have centred on social security), but rather take a balanced approach to spending and revenues. Most importantly, it would introduce measures to fight against tax evasion. This was a demand that the unions had made of all governments (Braun 1996, 214–15). Parliament, however, remained sceptical of the budget.

In September, meanwhile, addressing the Bundestag, Germany's Finance Minister Waigel remarked that the state of public finances in Italy would make it impossible for that country to join the EMU[14] (*Reuters News*, 20 September 1995). These comments revealed Germany's profound distrust of Italy's commitments. And the 1996 budget almost confirmed Waigel's expectations: the estimated deficit for 1997 stood at 4.4 per cent of GDP, well above the 3 per cent Maastricht benchmark (Dastoli 1996, 174–5). Waigel's comments were precisely what Dini needed; they helped him persuade the deputies of the need to pass such an austere budget. In presenting his budget, he repeated his commitment to Maastricht. He then defied those who thought Italy would not be able to meet the EMU requirements: Italy was "on the road to Europe," and "reducing the public debt is called for by Italy's EU partners, and … this budget is moving the country in the direction of the requirements of the Maastricht Treaty" (*Dow Jones International News*, 3 October 1995).

According to the revised timetable agreed at the Madrid European Council, Italy's eligibility for the EMU would be assessed in early 1998. Dini reminded the deputies that, in the final assessment, the most decisive reference point would be the country's budget deficit. He also warned them that it was time to face the situation regarding the deficit since failure to do so could prevent Italy from joining the EMU in the first wave. He added that, for Italy to qualify for the EMU, he would have to bring the deficit reduction plan forward by one year (*Dow Jones News Service*, 5 December 1995). With the pressure of austerity looming, the Chamber of Deputies gave Dini its full support (Dastoli 1996, 177). The Senate then swiftly approved the 1996 budget. It was marked by austerity, with savings coming largely from extra revenues (OECD 1997, 59; *Reuters News*, 22 December 1995).

Prodi: Walking through Narrow Gates towards the EMU

By passing the 1996 budget, Dini's government had fulfilled its mandate, and Italians went to the polls in April 1996. The election put an end to the transitional period of technocratic governments, and a centre-left coalition, the Ulivo, came to power under Romano Prodi. The new government was made up of the post-communist PDS and centrist parties drawn from the left wing of the then-defunct Christian Democratic Party, with outside support from the Rifondazione Comunista.

Although Italian politics returned to normalcy with the coming to power of an elected government, Prodi, like several of his Cabinet ministers, was not a career politician; he was an academic who had been invited into public service. In this respect, the Prodi government represented continuity with the technocratic governments of Ciampi and Dini. In fact, Ciampi himself became in charge of the Treasury, and Dini became minister of foreign affairs. The financial markets saw these appointments as a positive sign that the government intended to pursue austerity to meet the Maastricht deadline. An observer commented that "the regrouping of the ministers is a sign that (the government) has made a priority the attainment of the criteria laid down for Italy's entry into the single currency in 1999" (*Agence France Presse*, 17 May 1996).

From the Creation of a "Super Ministry" to Eighteen Months of Austerity

Ciampi demanded the merger of the Ministry of Treasury and the Ministry of Budget and Economic Planning as a condition for accepting the portfolio of Treasury minister. This long-debated merger had been put on the agenda several times in the past, but to no avail. Prodi approved Ciampi's demand, enabling Ciampi to lead a newly created economic "super ministry," merged under the Ministry of Treasury through Law No. 94 in April 1997. This formal restructuring augmented the Treasury's role as the chief guardian of public spending, and its executive power over budgetary spending increased tremendously at the expense of the spending ministries (Felsen 2000). This development, in the eyes of many, "symbolized the ascendancy that the public finance reformers had achieved since the collapse of the *partitocrazia*" (Sbragia 2001, 91). It was a turning point in Italian fiscal policy and politics and reflected the process of strengthening the executive vis-à-vis both Parliament and the spending ministries (Stolfi 2008, 561). The government successfully used the fiscal austerity of the EMU to bring about institutional changes in fiscal policymaking (ibid.).

The government's main challenge was Italy's participation in the EMU. According to Prodi, the EMU was the great unifying force in Italy (*Dow Jones International News*, 12 August 1996). In fact, Ulivo's key campaign promise had been to ensure its participation, and observers took the party's election as the Italian public's endorsement of this policy objective (Hine and Vassallo 1999, 35). In his first Cabinet meeting, referring to the Maastricht deadlines, Prodi announced eighteen months of austerity to "tackle the great national priorities, that is unemployment and rescuing the public finances, goals we cannot abandon if we want

Italy to play its full role in Europe" (*Agence France Presse*, 17 May 1996). In fact, Prodi repeated his government's commitment to meeting the Maastricht criteria in the Senate before the vote of confidence on his government (*Dow Jones International News*, 22 May 1996).

In the meantime, however, the optimistic projections of the Dini government for Italy to meet the fiscal criteria had not been met. Because of slowing growth rates, higher-than-projected interest rates, and the implementation of the rulings of the Constitutional Court in March on the back payment of certain pension rights, the financial prospects for the 1997 budget looked bleak (Sbragia 2001, 91; *Dow Jones International News*, 26 March 1996). In response, immediately after coming to office, the government presented a *manovrina* (mini-budget), which was approved in June. It brought about additional spending cuts and revenue gains aimed at keeping the deficit to 5.9 per cent of GDP for 1996.[15] So as not to offend the unions, these measures did not include any welfare cuts or tax breaks on employers' social security contributions. The government believed that these measures would suffice for safe entry to the third stage of the EMU.

From drei Komma null *to Valencia: Prodi's Ordeal*

The government announced its three-year macroeconomic targets in the DPEF and "expressed its firm will" to reach the Maastricht criteria (*Reuters News*, 4 July 1996). With a planned deficit of 4.4 per cent of GDP for 1997, also announced in the DPEF, it became apparent that Italy would not be able to meet the deficit criterion that year; it could be met only in 1998 (OECD 1997, 62). The decision reflected the government's concern that harsher austerity measures in the 1997 budget would risk social unrest. The government also assumed, optimistically, that Italy would still be able to make it to the third stage with the help of a "political interpretation" of the deficit parameter (*Financial Times*, 28 June 1996; Walsh 1998, 99–100; Radaelli 2002, 223). The government was "caught between the limits of its powers due to the weakness of its parliamentary majority and the constraints of the Maastricht parameters" (D'Alimonte and Nelken 1997, 25). Despite all this, Prodi continued to reiterate, "Our strategy of going into Europe is without alternative" (*Dow Jones International News*, 12 August 1996).

The government's hopes for a flexible interpretation of the fiscal criteria, however, were shattered when German Finance Minister Waigel rejected any such broad interpretation by famously referring to the *drei Komma null* rule (*Reuters News*, 18 September 1996). The urgency for additional measures became even more evident when Prodi visited

Spanish Prime Minister José María Aznar in Valencia a few days after Waigel made his comments. The press reported that the purpose of Prodi's visit was to discuss the possibility of a joint initiative to negotiate relaxing the entry criteria with the Germans and the French. Aznar told Prodi that Spain would be able to meet the criteria and that he would "ask for no discounts" (Quaglia and Radaelli 2007, 928). Thus, Prodi failed in his bid to secure Spanish support for softening the fiscal criteria (*Market News International*, 19 September 1996). Denying this, and announcing that Italy's late entry to the EMU had never been an option, Prodi rushed to unveil a tougher-than-expected budget just five days after the Valencia summit (Chiorazzo and Spaventa 1999, 132–3; Radaelli 2002, 224; D'Alimonte and Nelken 1997, 25–6).

To lower the budgetary target required to meet the criteria by the next year, the government revised the DPEF by reducing the 1997 deficit target to 2.6 per cent of GDP (OECD 1997, 65). By almost doubling the size of the planned fiscal adjustment, the new budget package relied on raising taxes (despite Prodi's election pledge not to do so) and other measures. The government had reversed course and brought the 3 per cent deficit target forward by one year. In the budget negotiations, Prodi repeatedly insisted that being left out of the EMU in the first wave would "mean the economic ruin of Italy" and that he would "certainly not be the prime minister who leaves Italy, a founding member of Europe, outside the new European Union" (*Reuters News*, 25 September 1996).

Intervento per l'Europa, *the Euro-Tax, and the 1997 Budget*

The 1997 budget package called for severe austerity measures to reduce the deficit by 3.2 percentage points. Some represented an ordinary fiscal adjustment; however, more than 40 per cent of the adjustment would be secured by a supplementary deficit cut as part of what the DPEF called "*intervento per l'Europa*" ("extra effort for Europe"). In fact, these supplementary measures were added to the budget after a report was released in November 1996 by the European Parliament's Task Force on Economic and Monetary Union, which stated that "it is unlikely that Italy will meet the criteria for entry into stage III of Economic and Monetary Union by the 1997 deadline." The report identified the Italian budget deficit as the main reason for this. That same week, as part of its supplementary measures, the government introduced a one-year, progressive "tax for Europe" (Savage 2005, 129).

Prodi's Euro-tax received wide support from the political establishment as well as the unions. Ciampi played a key role as Treasury minister, and his highly competent advocacy of Italy's participation in the

EMU helped Italy re-enter the EMS that year. The PDS leaders, Massimo D'Alema and Walter Veltroni, supported Prodi's efforts in Cabinet, and the leaders of all the main unions were extremely helpful in persuading their membership to accept the austerity measures. Even the leader of the Rifondazione Comunista, Fausto Bertinotti, refrained from sabotaging the efforts. Underlying such wide support for Prodi's austerity efforts was perhaps the strongly progressive nature of the tax. His careful and repeated refusal to launch a frontal attack on social security clearly worked to his advantage (Ginsborg 2003, 305).

The very name of the tax reflected its purpose, which was presented as being "imperative" if Italy were going to enter the EMU. This was "the first such measure identified by name with the race to join the EMU" among all the EMU candidates. It was, in a way, one of "the most cynical fiscal policy schemes undertaken by any EU member state to comply with the Maastricht criteria" (Savage 2005, 128, 130).[16] Chiorazzo and Spaventa (1999, 134) summarize the political significance of the Euro-tax: it was, first, "the ultimate signal of the government's commitment to gain admission, for, after imposing a levy aimed at achieving this objective, the government would be compelled to resign in case of failure." Second, the need for such extraordinary measure was accepted by the Italian public as a "symptom … that the aim of not being left 'outside Europe' was widely shared in the country."

By introducing the Euro-tax, the government could postpone any bitter austerity measure such as retrenching pensions. When Prodi announced an early review of the pension scheme as part of his fiscal effort, even his own Cabinet ministers questioned it. The Rifondazione Comunista required Prodi to put aside plans to reform any aspect of the Italian welfare state if he wished to obtain their support for the extraordinary budget. Prodi, in turn, reassured it and the unions that the issue of pension reform would not be discussed until 1998.

Prodi defended his austerity measures on every occasion by referring to the EMU. He made it clear that the tough 1997 budget would ensure that Italy became a founding member of the EMU (*Reuters News*, 27 September 1996; *Market News International*, 24 October 1996). At the same time, however, he was intent on preserving welfare benefits. Although "reconciling budget toughness with preservation of welfare benefits" had affected the entire structure of the budget, Prodi chose to remain loyal to Ulivo's election manifesto, which had declared "as the first and foremost issue that the social state should not be touched" (Pakaslahti 1997, 21). In fact, to counterbalance any adverse impact of the austerity measures, he introduced a complementary program to reduce unemployment. In due course, the media reported that underlying these new measures to defend social protection and promote employment was the government's attempt to compensate for the sacrifices Italians were making (*Le Monde*, 29 September 1996, quoted in Pakaslahti 1997, 24). After agreeing with its European partners, the government announced in the second convergence program of July 1997 that the pension reform would be tackled later, in the context of the 1998 budget (d'Ercole and Terribile 1998, 193–4).

The press reported that, despite the tremendous effort at austerity, the government was "cooking the books" to catch the Euro-train. Referring sarcastically to the fudges as "Roman numerals," the *Financial Times* claimed that the government's intention was clear: "to present the illusion of fiscal rigor without the associated pain" (20 November 1996). Years after Italy joined the EMU, the Commission revealed that there had actually been some "creative accounting involved" in reporting the Italian deficits (*Agence Europe*, 10 December 2004; *ANSA*, 8 January 2003).

In carrying out his austerity program, Prodi was careful to maintain consensus with the unions. He recognized them as institutional interlocutors even more than the union-friendly technocratic governments of Ciampi and Dini. Although this approach was seen, by some, as a "weakness" (Parker 1997, 138–9), it was actually part of a rational strategy on the part of the left-leaning Ulivo to convince the unions of the desperate need for reform. This strategy is in line with the Nixon-goes-to-China hypothesis (F. Ross 2000): parties on the left can mobilize support for bitter reforms since they are perceived to be defenders of the welfare state. This strategy was vital for a government that had been formed under emergency conditions.

However, the government and the unions could not agree on the government's 1997 budget bill, and in late October, the unions announced a general mobilization against the austerity measures. But this round of confrontation with the Prodi government had no comparison with the previous round against Berlusconi's attack on pensions. The government did not budge on austerity, however. The 1997 budget was one, in the eyes of the international press, "tailor made to meet the Maastricht Treaty" (*Financial Times*, 21 October 1996). For keen observers, it was the ultimate fiscal manoeuvre "to which were attached the last hopes of joining in the project for a common European currency" (D'Alimonte and Nelken 1997, 25). In November, the Chamber of Deputies approved the budget, and the same month, to prove the government's commitment to the EMU, Ciampi announced that the lira had re-entered the ERM.[17]

These developments were seen as making significant progress towards "the single most important and defining policy objective of

Prodi's government" – EMU membership (Parker 1997, 136). After the crucial budget for the EMU and the lira's participation in the ERM had been approved, to reinforce his government's credibility, Prodi openly pledged to resign if Italy were not among the first wave of EMU participants (Chiorazzo and Spaventa 1999, 134). The budget was safely approved in the Senate in December. Thus, the extraordinary 1997 budget, which included the Euro-tax, passed "with remarkably little fuss," despite an immense jump in the overall tax burden from 41 to 44 per cent of GDP (Bardi and Rhodes 1998, 30).

Never-Ending Pension Reform: The Onofri
Commission Report

When the 1997 budget was being debated in the Senate, it became clear that the budget deficit for 1996 had exceeded the official prediction. The slippage had occurred mainly due to back payments under the Constitutional Court ruling and repayment of tax credits by issuing government bonds (OECD 1997, 62). Drastic and urgent steps were needed to bring the deficit down to the Maastricht benchmark, such as making new cuts in pensions. The exceptional pressure of the Maastricht ordeal, the government believed, could permit a review of the Dini reform a year earlier than planned. Therefore, in January 1997, the government appointed a commission of experts under the chairmanship of Professor Paolo Onofri to identify measures for comprehensive welfare reform.

The final report of the Onofri Commission presented an elaborate plan for reform. It did not aim to reduce social spending but, instead, emphasized the need to rebalance the *stato sociale* (social state). However, it questioned the compatibility of current spending with the need to bring down the deficit in line with the Maastricht criteria. In fact, Onofri stated initially that Italy would miss the Maastricht target if it did not cut pensions (*Financial Times*, 25 March 1997). He later announced that any immediate cut did not have to fall on pensions or health care, adding that "the pension problem must not be read as a figure to be written into the 1998 budget" (*Reuters News*, 27 April, 12 May 1997). The Commission proposed the following measures (Ferrera and Gualmini 2004, 114–16):

– Take additional measures to retrench and rationalize public
   pensions: the phasing in of the new pension system introduced by
   Dini was too slow and was overburdening the younger generations;
   consolidate the new regime more rapidly.

- Reform unemployment benefits and employment promotion schemes: establish three tiers of unemployed and emphasize active measures.
- Rationalize the incentive structure within the National Health System: accelerate the self-financing of the regions, with particular emphasis on the division of competencies between central and regional administrations.
- Reform social assistance: emphasize a balance between universalism (in terms of beneficiaries) and selectivity (with respect to benefits provision); redefine needs and benefits based on citizenship; empower local governments.

Meanwhile, the government proposed passing the 1998 budget earlier than usual, in April or May 1997, as a token of Italy's commitment to the EMU. This budget would follow the Onofri Commission's recommendations. The Rifondazione Comunista quickly responded by threatening to bring down the government "if the welfare state would be touched" (*Dow Jones International News*, 10 February 1997). Walking a tightrope, the government withdrew its proposal on an early budget.

Prodi also had to pull back from reforming the welfare state. Instead, the government carefully crafted a mini-budget for March, after Ciampi and Prodi had promised not to include any measures on pensions or health care (Walsh 1998, 102). The rationale behind this mini-budget was given in a statement from the Prime Minister's Office: "This budget ... will allow Italy to meet the necessary objectives needed to fully satisfy the Maastricht Treaty" (*Reuters News*, 19 February 1997). As "the latest dose of bitter medicine" "in the name of European integration," the mini-budget was severely criticized by the opposition and Prodi's own allies (ibid., 6 May 1997). To speed up approval, the government had to reduce the amount of revenue it had planned to raise. In fact, only then could the government secure a vote of confidence in the Chamber of Deputies (ibid.).

In April, while the mini-budget was being negotiated, the European Commission released a report stating that Italy (along with Greece) was missing the Maastricht targets for the EMU. Italy was running a deficit of 3.2 per cent of GDP in 1997, and it would reach 3.9 per cent in 1998. The government received the report with fury and lobbied the Commission so intensely that the report had to be rewritten three times (Walsh 1998, 102). In the final version, referring to the March mini-budget, the Commission added that the 3.2 per cent "may become 3.0 percent of GDP if the [budgetary] measures already taken have full effectiveness and, if necessary, additional measures are introduced" (*Reuters News*,

23 April 1997). The report put additional pressure on the government and opposition parties supporting Italy's EMU bid. At the same time, because the date to assess the convergence criteria was fast approaching, financial market actors were locked into watching the performance of all the EMU candidates. Italian interest rate spreads were closely following the probabilities assigned by market participants to the prospect that Italy would meet the criteria on time (Chiorazzo and Spaventa 1999, 143).

Almost immediately after the mini-budget was approved, the government announced the three-year DPEF. The document predicted that Italy would be included in the first wave of the EMU in January 1999. It emphasized the main target: a deficit of 2.8 per cent of GDP. In response, a statement from Prodi's office was clear: "The commitment that today is asked of this government is that of completing what has already been started … in time to allow Italy to take part from the start in the construction of economic and monetary union" (*Reuters News*, 30 May 1997). In July, the government submitted its second convergence program (1998–2000), which had been requested by the ECOFIN Council as part of a series of recommendations on excessive deficits. Based on the DPEF, the ambitious program established a set of medium-term targets and the measures needed to achieve them. The Council endorsed Italy's program after Ciampi reassured his colleagues that Italy would take further measures to qualify for the EMU, if need be (ibid., 7 July 1997).

From Prodi's Resignation to Limited Pension Reform

During the summer months, negotiations on the 1998 budget continued between the employers and the unions. The government was planning to raise ITL 15 trillion in savings in 1998 to qualify for the EMU, and these savings included cuts to the welfare state. There was a common perception that Italy's chances of joining the EMU would be very low unless it brought down social spending. In the meantime, the government entered into negotiations with the unions based on the recommendation of the Onofri Commission, and, in response to their reactions, the government made some concessions. Eventually, the two parties reached an agreement to include welfare reforms in the 1998 budget, but the government was forced to significantly scale back its ambitions. For example, following a recommendation in the Onofri report, its DPEF had specified a spending cut of ITL 6 to 7 trillion in the area of pensions. After the negotiations with the unions, however, this figure was reduced to ITL 5 trillion.

Prodi presented the 1998 budget in late September, reaffirming the objectives of the DPEF. The government had been pressed to insert many of the Onofri Commission's recommendations into the budget, which, to correct the country's fiscal imbalances, called for sizeable cuts in pension and other social security spending. Throughout this process, none of the political parties ever questioned the legitimacy of the European goal. The issue was framed by many, such as the leader of left-wing coalition member PDS, Massimo D'Alema, as "neither of the left nor of the right, but simply as an inevitability" (Bardi and Rhodes 1998, 22). Moreover, the government successfully framed "being left out" of the EMU's first wave as a question of "life or death" (Radaelli 2002, 226).

Only the Rifondazione Comunista strongly objected to achieving the "European imperative" in this way and considered the concessions that the government had made inadequate. It announced that it would oppose a budget proposal incorporating any change in pensions beyond those agreed with the Dini government in 1995. But its support was crucial for Ulivo to pass any legislation in the Chamber of Deputies. Leader Bertinotti warned, "If the government takes concrete action (on pensions), the break will be definite" (*Reuters News*, 27 August 1997). The first week of October saw extremely tense arguments between the two parties; in the meantime, negotiations with the unions were suspended. The Rifondazione Comunista announced that it would continue to oppose the budget when Prodi presented it in the Chamber on 9 October.[18]

Facing a standoff, Prodi tendered his resignation to the president. The attempt at pension reform sounded the death knell for Ulivo; in Italy, this political crisis was perceived to be the "crisis of Europe" (Legrenzi 1998, 58). The media reported on the crisis by repeating Ciampi's words: "Missing the euro will mean years of sacrifices" (ibid.). These sacrifices "would lose their justification if the government were about to fall, the budget were rejected and, consequently, the conditions for being within the famous Maastricht parameters vanished" (ibid., 64).

Given public support for the EMU project, the Rifondazione Comunista was fiercely criticized not only by the government and the PDS but also by the media and the unions. Bertinotti was accused of torpedoing Italy's efforts to join the EMU, and his party dropped in popularity. He had apparently underestimated the significance of participating in the euro for Italian policymakers, interest groups, and the electorate (Felsen 2000, 164). Facing intense pressure to cooperate, he conceded to Prodi that he would accept the budget, but only with smaller cuts to pensions and a reduction in the work week. Negotiations between the government and the Rifondazione Comunista resumed. The resulting compromise included a government pledge to gradually reduce the work week to thirty-five hours in 2001 for firms with more than fifteen employees, an exemption for manual labourers from the restrictions on early retirement, and a further reduction in cuts in pension spending to ITL 4 trillion (Walsh 1998, 103; d'Ercole and Terribile 1998, 195). In return, the Rifondazione Comunista agreed to approve the budget with these minor changes. After the deal was reached, the president revoked Prodi's resignation. The government secured a vote of confidence, thereby putting Italy back on course for the EMU.

In November 1997, negotiations with the unions resumed after months of painful dialogue and political stalemate. The negotiations produced the following set of amendments to pensions, introduced in Law No. 449 in December (Ferrera and Jessoula 2007, 441):

- Tighten the eligibility rules for seniority pensions.
- Introduce a one-year freeze on indexing pensions.
- Increase basic pensions.
- Work toward partial compatibility of incomes from pensions and employment.

In the end, the government was able to insert some cuts to seniority pensions, raise the contributions of the self-employed, and put a temporary freeze on indexation. However, these cuts were modest in comparison with the government's original intentions. Although the Ministry of Treasury quickly announced that these measures contributed 0.2 per cent of GDP to meeting the deficit targets for 1998, they did almost nothing to change the underlying trend in social spending up to 2007 (*Market News International*, 25 November 1997). Most strikingly, the most significant element of the Onofri report – a more rapid phasing-in of the Dini reform – was not inserted into the budget due to fierce opposition from the Rifondazione Comunista. The budget included no other significant proposals from the Onofri Commission. In the area of unemployment insurance, for example, no reform measure was passed.

In the area of health care, a measure was passed in June 1999, establishing new financing rules, regulating the relationship between doctors and the National Health Service, and instituting a new framework for supplementary health insurance funds (Ferrera and Gualmini 2004, 116–17). The unions and the Rifondazione Comunista were successful in forcing the government to withdraw a proposal to eliminate early retirement packages altogether. Thus, like all the other structural reforms proposed by the government, pension reform was modified to secure the support of left-wing groups. In fact, the conflict over pension reform nearly brought down the Prodi government; its survival was secured only by softening its reform measures (Bardi and Rhodes 1998, 30). Although the amendments passed only after a set of quid pro quos, Prodi hailed the accord as "historic" and characterized it as "a decisive step toward the re-equilibrium of public finances and for entry into the single currency" (*Reuters News*, 1 November 1997).

Italy Finally Meets Its Maastricht Targets

The austerity strategies of successive Italian governments during the Maastricht decade resulted in consistent primary surpluses. The Italian deficit was brought down from 6.7 per cent of GDP in 1996 to 2.7 per cent in 1997 – a level equal to that of Germany! The largest budgetary consolidation effort during this period was realized in budget year 1997, when the deficit was reduced by no less than 4.0 percentage points of GDP. Interest rates came down due, in large part, to the government's commitment to the EMU and the perception thereof in financial markets. Lower interest payments, in turn, contributed to the deficit reduction process. In this consolidation period, government expenditures declined, and revenues increased slightly. As a result, the primary balance recorded surpluses, beginning with the convergence process and rising from 0.1 per cent of GDP in 1991 to a sizeable 6.8 per cent of GDP in 1997! The ever-increasing primary surpluses during the 1990s and the decline in deficits also set in motion a gradual reduction in the enormous public debt. At the same time, non-social spending items (such as production subsidies, capital transfers to enterprises, and government investment) were reduced. Despite waves of welfare reform, however, social expenditures remained essentially unchanged.

The literature on Italian fiscal policy and politics emphasizes, in hindsight, the unequivocal Maastricht effect on Italian fiscal behaviour (Quaglia 2013). Scholarly observations made during the Maastricht decade, too, pointed to the EMU effect. Reviewing the changes in the budgetary area in the penultimate year of the run-up to the EMU, Felsen (2000, 171) observed, "With the Maastricht convergence criteria serving as public finance targets, and persistent EU scrutiny, successive governments were able to pursue budget policies which further reduced public expenditure and deficit levels." Hine and Vassallo (1999, 34) concurred by arguing that "pressures for European convergence, both within and beyond the Maastricht economic and monetary convergence criteria were responsible for the main institutional modifications and sectoral reforms introduced by the Prodi government."

In January 1998, the ECOFIN Council concluded that Italy's 1998 budget complied with the convergence program it had submitted in July 1997, which had projected a deficit lower than the Maastricht reference value (*Agence Europe*, 20 January 1998). In early March 1998, Ciampi presented the details of the 1998 budget to his colleagues in Brussels in the wake of the publication of the convergence reports by the European Commission and the EMI. In the meeting, Ciampi won approval for Italy's fiscal austerity plan to reduce the deficit and debt (*Associated Press Newswires*, 9 March 1998). However, the ministers demanded that the DPEF be passed in the Italian Parliament before they could make a decision about Italy joining the EMU (*Reuters News*, 9 March 1998).

Ciampi announced his government's decision to have Parliament pass the DPEF. The Dutch government stated that it would vote against Italy's participation in the EMU "if the Italian parliament does not support the government's proposals regarding its draft budget" (*Financial Times*, 16 April 1998). Tightening the deficit target for 1998 to 2.6 per cent of GDP and further accelerating the planned decline of the debt-to-GDP ratio, the revised DPEF set more ambitious targets than the original 1997 DPEF. The budget commissions in the Chamber and the Senate approved the DPEF "in a move deemed crucial to Italy's plan to become a founder member of the European Monetary Union" (ibid.). Although the Rifondazione Comunista and the Greens were very reluctant to continue with the austerity measures, Parliament approved the DPEF in April, several weeks ahead of schedule (ibid.). The European Commission and the EMI, in separate reports, stated that Italy now fulfilled the conditions necessary for adopting the single currency.

All these decisions came just in time for the EU summit that would identify the first wave of EMU participants (*Financial Times*, 1 May 1998). The special European Council met in May to make the final decision on the eligible candidates and announced that Italy was allowed to join the EMU, along with ten other candidate countries. This was a dramatic success for a country whose fiscal balances had been in a shambles just a few years before.

Bertinotti Withdraws Support

Prodi's success in pushing Italy into the EMU was not enough to secure the survival of his government. From the start, "the need to 'join the single currency'" by bringing the deficit ratio into line with the Maastricht parameters had "enabled the Prodi government successfully to press for a high degree of policy-making autonomy from the parties in the Ulivo alliance, in order to bring Italy into line with the Maastricht conditions" (Fabbrini 2000, 123; see also Stolfi 2010, 121). After all, it was the very climate generated by "the absolute necessity of the convergence criteria" that had sanctioned the cohesion in the face of an otherwise precarious coalition (Hine and Vassallo 1999, 34). Suddenly, there seemed to be no reason to sustain the Prodi government (ibid. 33, 39, 41). Once Italy's entry to the EMU was confirmed in May 1998, the Ulivo, "having reached the European finishing post," lost its *raison d'être* (Massari and Parker 2000, 50).

By the summer of 1998, the launch of the EMU was imminent. But Italy's 1999 budget still needed to be approved as a matter of paramount urgency. Prodi continued to seek support for this budget, which would bring more austerity. The party leaders in Ulivo demanded some changes to soften its impact, yet Prodi remained firm. For its part, the Rifondazione Comunista, always critical of Prodi's austerity policies, repeatedly called for the government to make a "concrete 'signal' of a leftward policy turn" to address social issues (Ferrera and Gualmini 2004, 71). The party had declared its intention to refuse to support even the previous 1998 budget, which would take Italy to the EMU, but it was forced to reconsider its position.

During the summer of 1998, Bertinotti's position on the budget grew even more hard line, and, in August, he put forward the irrevocable conditions for his party's support for the budget. Prodi showed no sign of compromise, however, and Bertinotti realized that he would not secure any concessions. In fact, Prodi continued to press for passing the budget before the launch of the EMU. In his address to the Chamber in early October, he appealed to the *vincolo esterno* again by stating that "Italy cannot enter monetary union weakened or uncertain" (*Reuters News*, 7 October 1998).

In response to Prodi's move, Bertinotti declared that he had not seen "any change in the government's economic policy" (Fausto Bertinotti, quoted in Fabbrini 2000, 130) and announced that he was withdrawing his party's support for the coalition. Prodi brought the 1999 budget to the Chamber in October 1998 nonetheless. Bertinotti and a majority of Rifondazione Comunista deputies were intent on "escaping from the policy straight-jacket imposed by Maastricht" and refused to give a vote of confidence to Prodi's government (Hine and Vassallo 1999, 35). The draft 1999 budget bill did not pass, and the Prodi government fell.

Two unsuccessful attempts were made to form a new government. A technocratic government led by Ciampi and another government led by Prodi could not gain parliamentary support. Massimo D'Alema, the leader of the PDS, the largest party in Ulivo, formed a government shortly after. He retained Ciampi in his government as Treasury minister. The new government's program was very similar to that of Prodi's. In December, Parliament approved the 1999 budget bill, which contained no fundamental changes from the earlier version. Italy had now secured its place in the EMU.

Euro-Austerity and the Political Economy of Welfare State Reform in Italy

When Italy's deficit and debt levels were so far from the Maastricht targets, its governments were operating in an environment of ever-increasing structural budgetary pressure. Especially after the lira was ousted from the EMS in 1992, pensions occupied centre stage in Italian politics, indicted for being responsible for Italy's mounting fiscal problems. All governments that came to power during the 1990s aimed to meet the Maastricht criteria by containing costs. For almost everyone, this meant cutting pensions. The EMU provided politicians with a trump card with which they could justify any reform whatsoever – or so they thought. They expected that, as a powerful *vincolo esterno*, the EMU would strengthen their hand in containing costs, while shielding them from opposition. Assuming that they could hide behind the Maastricht imperative, and facing enormous fiscal pressure, each government, in its election campaign and everyday political discourse, declared that it was determined to carry out long-overdue pension reform.

The Italian case shows that every government that came to power during the Maastricht decade hoped to push through a reform of the pension system. And, at each round, the Amato, Berlusconi, Dini, and Prodi governments faced waves of strikes, demonstrations, and protests opposing the reforms. Likewise, when the Ciampi government intended to implement reforms that had been legislated earlier by the Amato government, reaction mobilized by the unions resulted in the reversal of the strictest measures. Opposition to reform initiatives by organized labour, opposition parties in Parliament – even parties in coalition governments – put any radical retrenchment strategy beyond reach.

In fact, only one radical reform plan was tabled, by Berlusconi, and it was scrapped even before it was introduced in Parliament. When he insisted on passing the plan, the unions responded in an uproar and organized rounds of massive general strikes. When social unrest reached its peak – the worst industrial unrest since the 1970s – Berlusconi's coalition partner Lega Nord (which had fervently supported the draft bill) defected and dropped its support. The bill had already been passed in the Chamber with the support of all coalition partners, but the opposition mounted by organized labour and the middle class was so strong that the bill had to be withdrawn. As if this were not enough, the government was forced to resign.

In other cases, as the Ciampi and Prodi reform episodes show, governments did not have the nerve to even initiate reform when they were intimidated by the potential threat, if not outright demonstration, of massive popular unrest. Some governments were compelled (if not forced) to reverse some of the previously legislated cuts. For instance, in the case of the caretaker Ciampi government, when the time came to begin implementing the Amato pension reforms, rounds of union lobbying forced the government to change course. The harshest measures, which would have raised the savings so desperately needed for euro entry, were postponed, and the only measures that were implemented were those that had been toned down. In the end, negotiations with the unions resulted in reversing about two-thirds of the cuts legislated by the Amato government.

Later in the Maastricht decade, when the Prodi government commissioned an independent study on alternative reform options, even technocratic protection did not help. Opposition from the unions as well as the Rifondazione Comunista, the government's supporter, prevented the government from pursuing its original reform proposals, and the reform measures were passed in much diluted form – but only after Prodi had threatened to resign, which might have meant the end of Italy's dream for eurozone entry.

In the three instances where reforms were passed, success hinged on two conditions: scaling down the measures and consultation. All three instances occurred when these two conditions co-existed; Euro-austerity alone was not enough to make reform happen. Whenever a government's attempt at social security reform was perceived as a frontal attack on the welfare state, organized labour staged massive protests and demonstrations. Through formal or informal consultation mechanisms, the unions were always successful in coercing governments to significantly rewrite their reform measures. Only after the unions had won significant concessions was it possible for governments to pass their reform bills. By the end of negotiations, at the insistence of opposition groups and the political parties close to them, implementation of the measures had been delayed, indexation freezes had typically been dropped, maximum pension ceilings had been pushed up, and overall cuts had been watered down. Even when governments were in a more advantageous position and successfully introduced their budgets in Parliament (as in the case of the Amato reform), coalition partners themselves felt obliged to ask the reformers to water down their planned cuts.

All in all, after a decade of reform initiatives, any radical reform of the Italian pension system had proved elusive. By the time Italy entered the EMU, its basic principles were not much different than when the Maastricht Treaty was signed. Although governments introduced a series of parametric changes, hoping to bring in savings that would meet the EMU targets, come implementation, savings lagged far behind targeted levels. The recurring strategy of postponing the bitter impact by prolonging transition periods paid off by making the reforms more palatable and enabling governments to pass their reform measures. However, in no single case were these reforms even *barely* effective at meeting the immediate budgetary goals. Paradoxically, the savings that were to accrue to budgets on the road to the EMU had absolutely no short-term, ameliorating impact on Italy's budgets.

The Italian case demonstrates that governments succeeded in introducing an exceptional fiscal retrenchment program during the 1990s. Every government strived for budgetary austerity, and Italy corrected its large fiscal imbalances with the help of its convergence programs. As table 12 shows, although public debt remained very high, budget deficits declined from 11.3 per cent of GDP in 1991 to 1.8 per cent by 1999. Governments tried to introduce welfare state reforms, too, but when they realized that they could not do so as they had initially intended, they were forced to find alternative strategies to increase savings to meet the Maastricht requirements. They counted on savings from pension reforms, but these reforms were either shelved altogether or passed in substantially revised form, thereby postponing their budgetary impact. In the end, virtually no savings were made. To reach the deficit targets in their convergence programs, governments had to resort to alternative revenue-raising measures. For example, the Ciampi government made concessions to the unions and their allies by relaxing some of the measures introduced by Amato as long as they accepted an overall austerity budget. Prodi pursued a similar strategy of defending social protection while imposing generalized budgetary austerity. When welfare reforms were watered down, the unions generally agreed that the government could raise extra revenues to compensate for the forgone savings. They did not object if they were promised that social security benefits would not be scaled down or that cuts would be limited.

To compensate for losses, governments resorted to a number of strategies. As the table suggests, they first raised revenues. Successive governments increased taxes despite their election promises to the contrary; they also eliminated tax breaks and write-offs and cracked down on tax evasion. Additionally, they introduced new emergency

Table 12. Italy: General Government Accounts, Social Expenditures, and Privatization Revenues (% of GDP)

	1991	1992	1993	1994	1995	1996	1997	1998	1999	2000	2001
Total government expenditures	53.0	54.5	55.4	52.7	51.7	51.7	49.6	48.3	47.4	45.4	47.5
Social expenditures	21.0	21.7	22.0	21.9	21.0	21.4	22.2	22.3	22.8	22.6	22.9
Non-social expenditures	32.0	32.7	33.4	30.8	30.8	30.2	27.4	26.0	24.7	22.8	24.6
Total government revenues	42.4	44.7	46.0	44.2	44.6	45.0	46.6	45.3	45.6	44.2	44.1
Privatization receipts	–	0.1	0.4	1.0	1.1	1.1	2.3	1.4	2.3	0.9	0.2
Government deficit	–11.3	–10.3	–10.0	–9.0	–7.3	–6.7	–3.0	–3.0	–1.8	–1.3	–3.4
Public debt	97.6	104.7	115.1	121.2	116.9	116.3	113.8	110.8	109.7	105.1	104.7

Source: OECD (2002, 2016a, 2016b, 2017a, 2017c); European Commission (2017); privatization figures: author's calculations.
Note: A dash (–) denotes zero or a negligible amount.

taxes, such as Amato's minimum tax (which was also implemented by Ciampi) as a quid pro quo for postponing welfare cuts or keeping them to a minimum. The Euro-tax introduced by Prodi as a requirement for EMU entry was another example. It was imposed only after its coalition partner, the Rifondazione Comunista, forced it to scrap Prodi's upcoming pension reform, thereby putting Italy's chance of qualifying for the EMU in jeopardy.

As a result of these revenue-raising measures, total government revenues rose from about 42.4 per cent of GDP in 1991 to 45.6 per cent in 1999 and declined only after Italy's EMU entry had been secured. At the same time, governments recorded sizeable privatization receipts towards their budget deficit and debt. At the beginning of the decade, they planned not to include these receipts in their budgets, but, starting with the Ciampi government, as the Maastricht deadline loomed, they were budgeted repeatedly. As table 12 shows, privatization proceeds contributed immensely to the fiscal consolidation effort, producing immediate savings for current budgets. But once EMU entry was guaranteed, privatization proceeds declined sharply.

In a second cost-containment strategy, Italian governments were highly successful in cutting back total outlays. Government expenditures declined drastically, from 53.0 per cent of GDP in 1991 to 45.4 per cent by 2000. It was widely expected that such savings would come from social expenditures: cuts in costly pensions programs. Table 12 shows, however, that it was actually *non-social* expenditures that bore the brunt of Euro-austerity. While social expenditures as a percentage of GDP remained stable throughout the Maastricht decade, non-social items were curtailed sharply, from 32.0 per cent of GDP in 1991 to 22.8 per cent by 2000.

These trends suggest that governments believed that social priorities had to be protected even under the severe circumstances of Euro-austerity. Moreover, Italian interest rates were declining sharply during the Maastricht decade; they contributed to the consolidation effort and helped make EMU entry possible. Finally, although there is some evidence that Italian authorities engaged in creative accounting manoeuvres, these alone cannot account for the fourfold decline of the deficit ratio, from 11.3 per cent of GDP in 1991 to 3.0 per cent of GDP by 1998.

This chapter helps us test the Euro-austerity hypothesis. Scholars and policy practitioners (foreign as well as Italian) expected Italy, facing the imperative of fiscal cutbacks in exchange for EMU membership, to go through one of the most radical welfare-retrenchment scenarios in all of Europe. True, Italy was a prime candidate for draconian fiscal surgery during the Maastricht decade, and many expected that this pressure would seriously undermine the Italian welfare state, forcing governments to cut social expenditures, especially in its pensions program. At the same time, Italian politicians assumed that they had been blessed with the euro card to retrench bloated pensions. The evidence presented in this chapter demonstrates that these scenarios were partly right and partly wrong. They were right with respect to the emergence of austerity pressure stemming from the EMU and the discursive opportunities that the euro afforded governments. They were largely wrong, however, with respect to the actual outcomes. Even during the extraordinarily intense Maastricht decade, the EMU could not bring about the widely expected massive retrenchment of the Italian welfare state.

7 Euro-Austerity and the Comparative Political Economy of Reform

Social trends of development repeatedly come up against counteracting factors that may slow them down or divert, modify or halt them. Societies observe the trends at work in them and react to them. In doing so, they display an inventiveness far beyond anything imagined by social scientists, even by those who have correctly identified the (socially contentious) underlying trends.

Streeck 2014, xiii–xiv

Europe's welfare states have been living under the shadow of Euro-austerity for almost three decades. With its draconian macroeconomic requirements, through economic and monetary integration, the EU institutionalized austerity at a pan-European level. In this era, the most intense austerity episodes were the 1990s and the post-2008 crisis period. During Euro-austerity – Episode I, with which this book is concerned, the drive for the euro meant that the EMU candidates came under inexorable structural, macroeconomic constraints imposed by the EMU. At the same time, the EMU gave reform governments a powerful *vincolo esterno*, which, many assumed, would shield them from any opposition whatsoever in their retrenchment efforts. Have these expectations been proved correct? This chapter uses a comparative perspective to summarize the main findings about the impact of Euro-austerity on Europe's generations-old welfare states during the Maastricht decade.

The chapter is organized in four sections to address the first six research questions posed in the introductory chapter. (The final question will be addressed in the next chapter.) It begins by summarizing the evidence from the indicators of social expenditure and replacement rate data and brings in the case study material presented in chapters 4 to 6 to compare the patterns of reform in the EMU candidates. In doing so, it addresses the first three questions raised in chapter 1: (1) What does the empirical evidence on comparative welfare reform reveal about the domestic reform outcomes in the EMU candidates? (2) If there was no radical retrenchment during the Maastricht decade, was there no welfare state reform at all? And, relatedly, (3) How was radical retrenchment averted in spite of not only the EMU's material pressure but also the discursive opportunities it afforded to ruling governments?

Next, the chapter asks, (4) What were the intervening factors that cushioned the otherwise intense impact of the EMU on welfare reform paths? and (5) If EMU entry did not bring about sizeable savings from welfare reforms, what alternative strategies did governments rely on to meet their fiscal targets? The chapter then addresses the next question: (6) Under what conditions were incisive reforms possible, and what role did the EMU play in these processes?

Patterns of Reform under the Damoclean Sword of Euro-Austerity

This book presented two sets of empirical evidence on what Pierson (2011, 11) calls the "single most pressing question": How much change has there been in welfare states? It did so by exploring the dynamics of welfare state reform in what is commonly referred to as the Maastricht decade. The first set of evidence is based on quantitative indicators of social expenditures and replacement rates. These data show that, despite the dramatic pressure of the Euro-austerity imperative, the Maastricht decade saw much less systematic social expenditure retreat and massive cutbacks in entitlements than originally expected. The evidence suggests that the welfare reform effort, however operationalized, remained largely stable – a finding overwhelmingly at odds with the Euro-austerity hypothesis. Most strikingly, social spending among the EMU candidates remained relatively stable, even though EMU-*cum*-austerity produced draconian cuts in total public expenditures. Thus, the share of the welfare state represented in these countries' budgets grew dramatically vis-à-vis other expenditure items. Facing intense pressure to contain costs, most member states (particularly the EMU candidates) preferred to place the burden of fiscal austerity on non-social spending items.

Such a striking shift in priorities away from non-social goals and towards social goals attests to the increasing salience of the welfare state in public budgets even in times of (and perhaps even more so under) Euro-austerity. At the same time, the fact that social spending per dependent remained stable in real terms demonstrates that social standards were largely maintained. Additionally, summary measures constructed on the basis of program-level spending data indicate that there was more programmatic upsizing than downsizing.

The book also presented evidence on replacement rates in unemployment insurance, sick pay insurance, and standard pensions programs. The stability of these replacement rates during the Maastricht decade corroborates the findings on social expenditures. All this evidence demonstrates that the convergence process towards the EMU was characterized much less by retrenchment in Europe's welfare states than by stability. As chapter 3 discussed, for the Euro-austerity hypothesis to have any bearing above and beyond the fact that a few EMU candidates seem to have undergone some form of retrenchment suggested by some indicator, it should point to clear trends towards sizeable cuts. The evidence presented in that chapter, however, shows that even when an indicator pointed to some retrenchment in a given country, alternative indicators suggested otherwise. More significantly, that discussion shows that there is no clear evidence that the EMU candidates behaved any differently than the non-EMU candidates in the direction of change predicted by the Euro-austerity hypothesis.

The second set of evidence presented in the book is based on qualitative case studies of welfare reform in the three fiscally profligate EMU candidates – Belgium, Greece, and Italy. The Euro-austerity hypothesis implies that, had there been any EMU pressure on the welfare state in any candidate, it would have been on them. According to the logic of testing the "most likely" "crucial cases," if one does not find the predicted pattern of welfare retrenchment because of the EMU here, one is very unlikely to find it in any other case (Gerring 2007).

The evidence shows that the Belgian, Greek, and Italian governments *did* push through fiscal austerity during the Maastricht decade. All the governments that came to power during the 1990s – those on the left, on the right, and in the centre – were committed to the Maastricht criteria. Moreover, when they came to power, all, albeit to varying degrees, intended to push through fiscal austerity by cutting social expenditures. Welfare states (especially pensions programs) were typically indicted in political debates as the main reason for the severe financial problems that could forestall EMU entry. At the same time, the EMU gave these governments a convenient pretext for justifying any cost-containing welfare reform. Facing the Maastricht imperative, all governments – in their election campaigns, government declarations, budget speeches, and daily discourses – stated that they were determined to scale back their welfare programs to secure the otherwise impossible EMU entry.

The evidence from the three case studies shows that pushing for austerity was never easy. The structural pressure and discursive opportunities stemming from Euro-austerity helped these governments achieve dramatic reversals in fiscal policy and behaviour; however, when they pressed for welfare state cutbacks, they foundered on the treacherous shoals of reform. They always justified their reform plans by appealing to the impending Maastricht deadlines. However, they faced a powerful, broad-based bloc of organized interests that opposed the cuts. This bloc included, but was not limited to, organized labour (led by the main union confederations), interest groups (such as women's organizations in Belgium), traditionally protected groups (mainly in Greece, but also, to a lesser extent, in Italy and Belgium), professional groups (especially in Greece and Italy, but also in Belgium), opposition parties in Parliament, coalition partners in government, external supporters (especially the Wallonian Socialists in Belgium and the Rifondazione Comunista in Italy), and even Cabinet ministers (in the case of Greece under PASOK).

Some reform attempts were scrapped even before they were introduced in Parliament. Examples include the repeated attempts at pension reform by ministers Willockx and Colla under Belgium's Dehaene governments – once in 1993, twice in 1994, and again in 1997. Other attempts were brought before Parliament, but could not be passed, even after the lower chamber had passed the bill – for instance, by Colla in 1994 in Belgium and Berlusconi in 1994 in Italy. On certain occasions, ruling governments did not dare to introduce significant reform because they were intimidated by opposition threats or potential electoral retribution. The Ciampi and Prodi governments in Italy, and the Papandreou and Simitis governments in Greece, withdrew their reform plans altogether after realizing that they would face powerful resistance and that any further move was futile. Although all political parties planned to introduce reform, those that formally proposed radical plans were severely punished in elections. The Liberal Party in Belgium is a case in point, in spite of the fact that its opponents in the 1995 election were dogged by scandal.

Do these findings mean that the Maastricht decade saw no welfare state reform at all? The answer is no. In fact, this decade of Euro-austerity was one of permanent reform. Introducing reform, however, was possible only when the initial, radical ambitions of governments were dramatically scaled back – in some cases, to the point that the national press made a mockery of it. In virtually all episodes of reform, governments initially intended to introduce comprehensive revisions to the welfare state, but made do with mini-reforms instead. In Belgium, the Dehaene governments' original reform measures in 1993–4 and 1996 were seriously scaled back after not only demonstrations and protests but also the first massive general strike in sixty years. In Italy, when Amato (1992), Dini (1995), and Prodi (1997) attempted to reform the Italian social security system, they were successful only after making substantial concessions to opposing groups in the form of social pacts. In Greece, even the reform measures that were introduced by conservative Mitsotakis in 1990–2 were only watered-down versions of the original plans.

After waves of protests and strikes, harsh reform packages boiled down to a handful of weaker and, hence, less contested measures. When Simitis intended a comprehensive reform consolidating Greece's three-hundred-plus pension funds in 1998, after opposition from the unions the process resulted in only modest cutbacks. In fact, as the Maastricht deadlines approached, governments in all three EMU candidates resorted to extraordinary decree powers to push through reform: Dehaene in 1996 with the Social Framework Law, Prodi in 1997 in the *intervento per l'Europa*, and Simitis in 1998 through emergency powers. But each time, the mountain became a molehill.

None of these reforms raised significant savings for state coffers, for several reasons. First, all reforms passed only after their impact had been pushed forward onto future generations, mainly by increasing transition periods. Second, governments postponed, if not reversed altogether, measures that had previously been passed. Examples are the deliberate non-implementation of reforms under the Ciampi, Prodi, and Simitis governments. Finally, the Constitutional Courts of Greece and Italy imposed institutional "veto players" and ruled against cuts legislated by incumbent governments. All these outcomes were, ironically, time-inconsistent – governments aimed to introduce cuts to increase savings *before* the Maastricht deadline, but they would come into effect only in the longer run, *beyond* the Maastricht horizon. Moreover, any impact in the longer run would come only when the reforms were actually implemented, and this would depend on the preferences and power of future domestic political actors.

Although governments in all three countries introduced expanded benefits here and there in a program for certain groups, only Greece implemented a series of systematic, large-scale reforms that led to an expansion of benefits. Paradoxically, Greece was the EMU candidate that faced the greatest budgetary pressure. In fact, the pressure was so great that Greece was not even considered to be in the running! Its reforms explicitly aimed to appease the growing popular opposition to fiscal austerity undertaken in the name of Euro entry. The Mitsotakis and Simitis governments resorted to such measures to buy public submission to budgetary austerity. In fact, the reform of 1998 (the Simitis package) actually *augmented* program benefits to quell unrest that would otherwise not only derail the entire fiscal consolidation process but also threaten the life of his government.

The evidence in these three crucial cases (where, under the Euro-austerity hypothesis, we would expect the largest retrenchment of all the EMU candidates) clearly shows that, even after rounds of reform, across-the-board welfare state retrenchment did not occur. The convergence period was marred by successive episodes of mass mobilization of the unions against pension reforms, which diluted the reform measures. Opposition parties (or even political parties that were partners in governing coalitions or that gave them external support) prevented governments from pushing through far-reaching reforms. The middle class took to the streets to protest against plans for welfare cuts. In some cases, initiatives were shelved entirely, while in others, governments' ambitions were scaled back, with the result that their reforms were much more modest than originally planned.

These findings are strongly corroborated by the general conclusion of an earlier, influential work on the impact of the EMU on the European social model: welfare states escaped draconian retrenchment under the Damoclean sword of Euro-austerity. Radical reforms were averted by "political constellations" characterized not only by "strong and slowly changing cleavage patterns, rooted in evolving deep social structures and organized by parties with their respective ideological orientations in the context of distinct and durable state traditions" but also by "new constituencies built up around components of social models" (Martin and Ross 2004, 15). The case studies on the political economy of reform and the statistical findings based on social expenditures and replacement rates presented in this book, firmly support these claims.

Standing Up to Euro-Austerity: "New Politics," "Old Politics"

The evidence from the case studies on Belgium, Greece, and Italy demonstrates how a set of institutional variables refracted the externally imposed Euro-austerity on domestic welfare states. These institutions represent conditions that make up a configuration. These clustering conditions effectively precluded any radical departures from a path, such as overhauling generations-old social security systems. One of these institutional variables is organized interest groups – beneficiaries of maturing welfare state programs. These beneficiaries were well placed politically to defend their interests, and they played an instrumental role in sustaining welfare state programs. Despite the fact that every social security reform initiative in these countries was justified on the basis of Euro-austerity, many of these interest groups (which enjoyed the protection of well-entrenched "acquired rights") succeeded in thwarting radical retrenchment plans. Governments, given fierce electoral competition, were always wary of the ever-present potential of voter retribution. Unprotected private-sector employees bore the brunt of reform processes, while highly protected public-sector employees experienced only a few cuts.

A second institutional variable is program maturity. Old programs are often seen as fiscal black holes, and they are the prime targets when a government needs to find savings. However, the case studies show that, paradoxically, overhauling these big-ticket items was never within governments' reach. In Belgium, Greece, and Italy, social security systems are based on pay-as-you-go pensions. They are structurally locked in because they are based on intergenerational contracts, whereby the contributions of current workers finance the retirement pensions of previous generations. There are also grandfather clauses, which further solidify existing liabilities, rendering retrenchment institutionally more difficult. As these systems mature, they amass a large debt as a result of the standing benefits payable to current pensioners. Thus, contributors must continue to pay social security premiums to fund both their own future pensions and the standing debt. Servicing this debt becomes more difficult, especially in an environment of increasing dependency ratios. These systems were very difficult to reform since any reform of intergenerational contracts would need to be sanctioned by organized labour as well as the electorate. Therefore, rather than overhauling existing systems, Belgian, Greek, and Italian governments resorted to more politically viable, parametric changes aimed at maintaining the sustainability of their welfare state systems.

A third institutional variable concerns rules in legislative processes when welfare state reform is introduced. To render reforms politically acceptable, social security laws are generally designed to affect later cohorts of beneficiaries. Therefore, implementation, in principle, takes place in a deferred period. Despite the acute need to raise immediate savings under Euro-austerity, new pieces of legislation passed by Belgian, Greek, and Italian governments were rarely fully retroactive. In some cases, incoming governments deliberately did not pass secondary measures to implement the retrenchment legislation enacted by outgoing governments. In general, the newly introduced legislation covered individuals who would be entering the labour force in the future. Facing strikes, demonstrations, protests, and potential electoral backlash, governments were forced to continue to grant grandfather clauses protecting the rights of current beneficiaries. At the end of the day, it was always younger cohorts that bore the brunt of adjustment.

A final institutional variable that mediated the impact of Euro-austerity on welfare states was the existence of veto players. Reforms may be inhibited or delayed by institutional veto players whose consent may be necessary to pass new policies. The evidence from the three case studies points to the role played by key actors in maintaining the status quo: Upper Houses, whose approval was required to pass reform (such as in the case of Italy); coalition parties, which could veto reform because any legislative change relied on the consensus principle (especially in Belgium, but also in Italy); and constitutional courts, which reversed previous legislation (as in Greece and Italy). Existing institutions and past commitments effectively locked in particular paths of reform, while preventing others.

The key roles that institutional variables played in precluding the retrenchment scenarios in Belgium, Greece, and Italy are in line with the variables emphasized in the literature on the "new politics of the welfare state" (Pierson 1996). Although these variables are significant, other findings in the case studies point to some blind spots in this literature. First, in proclaiming the emergence of a new politics, Pierson (and others after him) claimed that "it is difficult to identify examples where unions took the lead role in the mobilization against programmatic cutbacks" (Pierson 1994, 165). The Belgian, Greek, and Italian case studies clearly demonstrate that the socio-political forces shaping the old politics of welfare state expansion were alive and well, even at the peak of Euro-austerity. As a key socio-political force defending the welfare state, labour unions and their allies, organized under union leadership, invariably played key roles in all the reform processes. Their strength and organizational capacity acted as conditions that effectively blocked radical reforms, even when they were justified on the basis of the otherwise omnipotent *vincolo esterno*.

Second, the new politics literature expects that, in the age of "permanent austerity," the effect of partisan politics on welfare state development vanishes and all parties converge on similar programs. The findings presented in the case studies may be interpreted to support these claims: all political parties that came to power – no matter their political leaning – *did* attempt radical reform during the Maastricht decade. However, they approached welfare reform in markedly different ways: the actions by Papandreou's and Simitis's Socialist PASOK, Prodi's centre-left Ulivo, Dehaene's coalition of Christian Democrats and Socialists contrasted with those by Mitsotakis's conservative ND, Berlusconi's conservative coalition under Forza Italia, and Verhofstadt's Flemish Liberals.

In terms of style and methods, right-wing and left-wing governments differed systematically and significantly in their negotiations with the unions and other societal groups. While centre-left coalitions and technocratic governments sought more formal forms of consultation (such as the Amato, Dini, Prodi, Willockx, and Colla reform initiatives), centre-right governments either tried informal negotiations, from which the unions eventually walked out (the Souflias, Fakiolas Committee, and Sioufas reform proposals) or opted for a largely go-it-alone strategy (the Berlusconi and Giannitsis reform proposals).

Moreover, in terms of scale, welfare state retrenchment efforts were much more modest under left-wing governments than under centre-right governments. As the case studies demonstrate, there was a sharp contrast between the intentions (as well as the discourse) of centre-right and left-wing governments: Berlusconi's frontal attack on the Italian welfare state and Mitsotakis's insistence on radical solutions signalled that they wanted to do too much all at once. In contrast, the left-wing Prodi and Simitis governments, and the centre-left-leaning technocratic governments of Amato and Dini, carried out parametric reforms in the name of either *risanamento* (in Italy) or putting the fiscal house in order for future generations (in Greece).

The case studies on Belgium, Greece, and Italy demonstrate that, however great the pressure from Euro-austerity during the Maastricht decade, the political colour of the governments in power and their very partisan preferences determined whether the pressure was vigorously resisted, openly welcomed, or strategically taken advantage of. These conclusions are in line with the state-of-the-art work on the impact of partisan differences on welfare state reform under Euro-austerity (Dolvik and Martin 2015a).

Alternative Paths to Euro-Austerity: The Politics of Plan B

The three case studies also show that, despite all odds, Belgian, Greek, and Italian governments managed to improve their budgetary performance on the road to the EMU. All governments attempted to reform their welfare states, but their attempts generally failed to produce the much-hoped-for savings when they were useful – that is, before the Maastricht deadline. As the deadline approached, governments knew they needed to find alternative fiscal strategies to meet the requirements. These strategies were premised on increasing fiscal and non-fiscal revenues, reducing non-social expenditures, and resorting to creative accounting.

Perhaps the most striking aspect of the Belgian, Greek, and Italian fiscal consolidation efforts during the Maastricht decade was their bold declarations about raising public revenues. These declarations found their way into tax reforms. Almost all governments introduced large-scale tax reforms and other measures for improving tax compliance, broadening the tax base, and modernizing and updating the tax administration. As a result, the tax burden increased in all three cases: by about 7 per cent in Belgium (making the Belgian tax burden the highest of all OECD countries), about 13 per cent in Italy, and more than 30 per cent in Greece (by far the largest increase in the EU).

As for non-tax measures, all three EMU candidates initiated very large privatization programs when they believed it was necessary. They saw privatization as perhaps the most convenient revenue-raising instrument for securing EMU entry without having to rely on either politically treacherous social security cutbacks or unpopular tax increases. Greece relied most heavily on privatization receipts in its fiscal consolidation strategy, and just before the Council assessed its EMU membership, the proceeds exceeded a full 4.0 per cent of its GDP. Italy and Belgium, too, budgeted to raise immense amounts from asset sales. More strikingly, when EMU entry was guaranteed in each case, these privatization processes came to a sudden halt. Greece also received sizeable monetary transfers from the EU, a significant source of revenue that contributed to the upward trend in social expenditures at a time when its budget was facing harsh Euro-austerity.

In addition to raising revenues, counting on the *vincolo esterno*, successive governments announced time and again that they *had* to curtail public expenditures in the name of Euro-austerity. In fact, all attempts at welfare state reform were justified by the imperative of reining in expenditures. Thus, cutting spending became an end in itself. After many reforms were scaled back, however, it turned out that these measures had not produced any significant savings. The evidence from the case studies corroborates the statistical findings on the absence of significant and systematic social expenditure retreat in Belgium, Italy, and Greece: while social-spending levels (as a share of GDP) remained stable in Belgium, they increased sizeably in Italy and Greece.

As a result, when these governments faced draconian Euro-austerity, they had to find savings in other expenditure areas. This can be seen in the remarkable increases in the share of social spending within total public outlays in all three countries. Greece and Italy recorded the highest levels of increase in the budget share of social spending in the EU; Belgium recorded substantial increases as well. These findings attest to the continued salience of welfare goals in public budgets. More interesting is the fact that real social spending per dependent increased in all three countries despite adverse demographic and labour market developments. The evidence suggests, therefore, that with respect to all the measures analysed in chapter 3, the three welfare states did *not* follow the direction that the Euro-austerity hypothesis points to. Although these countries embarked on severe (mostly revenue-based) fiscal consolidation to pass the Maastricht test, none of them scaled back social spending. All in all, Euro-austerity was *the* inexorable constraint determining the direction and timing of welfare state reforms during the Maastricht decade. It also gave Belgian, Greek, and Italian governments a prime opportunity for reform (Featherstone 2004). It just did not determine the actual policies for getting there.

The Power of the EMU as the *Vincolo Esterno* for Reform

The case studies on Belgium, Greece, and Italy clearly demonstrate that the drive for euro membership led to severe pressure to carry out budgetary austerity. They also show that this draconian pressure did not translate into systematic and radical welfare state retrenchment. However, permanent Euro-austerity during the Maastricht decade did mean permanent welfare state reform. So did the drive for Euro-austerity play any role in "successful" reform processes? And if so, how?

First, the case studies show that all governments used the *vincolo esterno* time and again as an instrument of "blame-buffering." But they did so with varying degrees of success. The technocratic governments were especially successful. For example, technocrats in Italy, who were seen as neutral and credible policymakers, justified the 1990–2 and 1994 welfare reform by playing the EMU card.

Second, all governments used the *vincolo esterno* as a "credit-claiming device," particularly in reform episodes that occurred close to the Maastricht deadline. Examples of such empowerment were the Dini and Prodi reforms in Italy, Simitis's mini-reform in Greece, and the Dehaene government's Social Framework Law in Belgium. Popular support for European integration in general and EMU entry in particular played a conditioning role in relieving electoral pressure on ruling governments.

Third, the EMU helped justify welfare state reforms by playing a powerful agenda-setting role. Once the treaty had institutionalized the Euro-austerity agenda, the EMU effectively justified all reform attempts. Policy agendas were set in the name of genuinely preserving (Prodi's reform), modernizing (Dehaene's Social Framework Law), making sustainable (Dehaene's Social Framework Law), and improving the organization of (Simitis's mini-reform) welfare state programs.

Fourth, with its institutionalized surveillance procedures, the EMU acted as a catalyst in times of acute domestic financial crisis. The *vincolo esterno* compelled governments to put their financial house in order and allowed them to use extraordinary measures to do so. Dehaene's crisis tax of 1993, Amato's emergency powers in 1992 (after the lira had been ousted from the ERM), and the subsequent pension reform in the same year are examples of Euro-austerity as an invaluable catalyst.

Fifth, the overarching EMU goal also helped broker bargains between governments and their social partners. Among the reform episodes analysed in Belgium, Greece, and Italy, the Italian technocratic governments of Amato and Dini as well as the Prodi government relied on formal consultation mechanisms to pass pension reforms. Maastricht's strictures and the associated deadlines played a key role in bringing partners together around the negotiating table.

Sixth, the EMU helped governments when the proposed reform measures included modest parametric changes and compensation mechanisms. However, radical reform proved futile everywhere; reform was possible only when governments could convince the unions and their allies that the proposed measures were incremental. Moreover, quid pro quos quelled opposition when governments promised to expand some programs while retrenching others. Examples include Mitsotakis expanding benefits to families; Papandreou extending farmers' pensions, childcare, and benefits to the lowest-paid segments of society; Simitis expanding farmers' pensions and the social solidarity pension supplement; and the minimum pension right incorporated into Dehaene's Social Framework Law.

Finally, when governments faced intense opposition to cutting entitlements, meeting the Maastricht criteria helped legitimize increasing social security contributions. Fiscal targets were presented as the rationale for securing actuarial balances and strengthening the link between social security contributions and benefits. All these uses of the EMU in social security reform processes are broadly consistent with using the EU in employment and other policy reforms (Woll and Jacquot 2010; Sotiropoulos 2011).

Lessons for Comparative Political Economy

The comparative political economy of reform in the three cases under investigation shows that the causal link between the EMU and welfare state reforms is not as strong as we all assumed back in the 1990s. It goes without saying that the EMU *did* prove to be an imposing structural constraint on domestic political choices, but these constraints were mostly what governments made of them. The same is true for the discursive opportunities afforded by the EMU. Therefore, we see that domestic actors did not take a back seat; on the contrary, they opted for differing strategies, like those Streeck (2014) would have expected. The case studies presented in this book show varieties of *politicization*: inviting, welcoming, directly transposing, taking advantage of, turning a blind eye to, covering up, deflecting, resisting, compensating for all these structural constraints as well as the discursive opportunities that the EMU provided. They also show that welfare state reform, as one keen observer puts it, has always been about "compromise, accommodation and contestation" (Wincott 2008, 359).

What lessons, then, can we draw for the comparative political economy literature in analysing overwhelming external constraints? The evidence from Euro-austerity – Episode I reminds us to beware of two fallacies that can impair our analysis of the consequences of Euro-austerity – Episode II on Europe's welfare states. The first fallacy is that we find ourselves tempted to focus exclusively on the incentive structures and the goals of the policymakers, whom we consider to have been either coerced or empowered by crisis conditions. We then brush off the welfare reform outcomes because we are either overwhelmed or delighted by austerity's severe structural constraints and powerful discursive political opportunities.

The evidence presented in this book, however, suggests that we should beware of overestimating the power of Euro-austerity as a *material constraint* on the welfare states. Euro-austerity as a structural force alone could not and cannot foreclose all political options. During Episode I, many were mesmerized by the severe restrictions on budgets, tied to tight deadlines. These constraints seemed so real that it was easy to overlook the fact that they defined only caps on budget deficits and not even expenditure or revenue levels or their composition. In an era when the Conservative Revolution had just transformed domestic politics, most of us expected the burden of adjustment to be borne by our welfare states. We simply could not imagine governments resorting to alternative methods to meet the Maastricht criteria.

The case studies show, however, that the impending material constraints compelled all governments to seek alternatives: to curtail spending, they devised strategies to cut non-social expenditure items; to raise revenues, they increased direct taxes, rationalized the tax administration, increased privatization receipts, and maximized their absorption of EU funds. All these strategies resulted in diverting budgetary pressure from their welfare state budgets. Even in the most desperate of cases (e.g., Greece, which in the early 1990s had no hope of qualifying for the EMU), extraordinary developments took place: successive governments had to *expand* some welfare state programs as a means of buying off submission to budgetary austerity.

At the same time, most of us overestimated the power of Euro-austerity as a *discursive opportunity* to bring about welfare reform. All three case studies demonstrate that the *vincolo esterno* emphatically served the governments in question. The EMU proved to be an all-purpose instrument: blame-buffering tool, credit-claiming device, reform catalyst, and reform broker. Empowered by the opportunities offered by the overarching goal of joining the euro, governments managed to introduce strict tax reforms (even in countries such as Belgium, where the tax burden was already extremely high), large-scale privatization programs (even where it had been taboo just a short time before), and even additional rounds of wage freezes (even after having introduced previous rounds of freezes) – all to alleviate the pressure of austerity on their public budgets. When governments attempted to find sizeable savings in welfare programs for the same purpose, however, the otherwise omnipotent *vincolo esterno* failed to help them deliver radical reform. In hindsight, therefore, any argument that Euro-austerity, whether as a material constraint or as a discursive opportunity, will directly retrench the welfare state should be considered with caution.

In contemplating the impact of austerity on welfare states, our one-sided emphasis on the constraints of Euro-austerity leads us to a second fallacy: we tend to overlook the very mechanisms through which austerity is politically constructed. When judging the impact of the current wave of austerity (Episode II), we must be careful not to underestimate the power of the resistance by societal actors to welfare retrenchment initiatives. The past episode of Euro-austerity provides ample evidence that there are still remarkably powerful organizations and constituencies that support welfare state programs. These actors include a large constellation of societal groups: first and foremost, organized labour and others mobilized by them, such as organized societal actors (traditionally protected groups, professional groups, and other civil society organizations) and ordinary individuals representing the middle and working classes taking to the streets. These groups were sometimes supported not only by opposition parties in Parliament but also by senior members of ruling coalitions. In most cases, such resistance led to the complete shelving of reform plans; in others, it led to limited, modest changes in welfare state programs.

At the same time, while centre-right governments capitalized on the discursive shield offered by Euro-austerity to push their neoliberal agendas forward, left-wing governments were not helpless. The

Belgian, Greek, and Italian case studies show that governments enjoyed (the rarely recognized) significant degree of manoeuvring around their policy choices, especially their budgetary policies. Even centre-right governments pursued alternative means of curtailing spending and/or raising revenues when they believed their welfare reform options had been thwarted cut off by effective opposition forces. More significantly, when they realized that acting otherwise could bring them down, governments chose to embark on fiscal strategies other than retrenching social programs.

The evidence presented in the case studies compels us to remain measured, cautious, and tentative when we interpret the consequences of external constraints on evidently path-dependent welfare states (Martin and Ross 2004, 3). The welfare state reform outcomes reflect *less* the imprints of neoliberal ploys and frontal attacks on the welfare state, even when structural pressure and discursive opportunities point strongly in that direction. The outcomes of permanent reform represent *more* the very choices that governments make in playing day-to-day political games. They also reflect *more* the strength of societal actors aligned against reforms, the power of veto players, the popularity of welfare state programs, the level of mass support for euro entry, the degree of commitment of the ruling elite to European integration, the nature of regime-typical compromises, the difficulty of making bargains based on quid pro quos, the severity of path-dependent, accumulated maladies, the imprint of reform-enabling and/or -constraining national policymaking traditions, the nature of welfare state and labour market regimes, the frequency of past policy reversals and cul-de-sacs, and the availability of Plan Bs.

These welfare states proved to be like heavy-duty water balloons. They took in all sorts of pressure, particularly from Euro-austerity. And their shapes certainly changed. But they did not burst, as the Euro-austerity hypothesis had expected.

8 Euro-Austerity – Episode II

Glancing over one's shoulder ... may help temper some of the assumptions about the uniqueness of our own times. ... Perhaps there is no wave of future, only many small ripples; no decisive watersheds, only a variety of slippery slopes.

Heclo 1981, 383

Ever since the Maastricht Treaty was signed, Europeans have feared the potential effects of "the single most important and supranational step in European integration on the single most important area still reserved to national politics" (Martin and Ross 2004, 17). This single most important step is the point of departure of this book because it ultimately and firmly institutionalized Euro-austerity at the EU level. Europeans were very concerned on the road to the EMU, and it was only after their country's entry was secured that this concern began to fade. After a decade into the EMU, however, Europeans find themselves embroiled in yet another episode of austerity. This must be what Pierson (2001) meant about two decades ago by "permanent austerity."

But should Europeans be worried about the impact of austerity? Is Euro-austerity – now in Episode II – likely to bring about the end of the welfare state as we know it? This chapter addresses the seventh and final question posed in the introductory chapter: What insights do the first episode of Euro-austerity offer us for assessing the consequences of the second episode? Following Heclo's (1981, 383) lead, this chapter looks at "our present circumstances in light of the past" in the hope of gaining "some perspective on what the future of the welfare state may portend."

What have we learned about the impact of Euro-austerity on Europe's welfare states? Comparative political economists have responded with only a few empirical studies. On the one hand, there is an ever-growing literature on the financial crisis, the Great Recession, the so-called sovereign debt crisis, and their links to the EMU. On the other, the literature on comparative welfare state reform continues to thrive as we experience one crisis after another. Interestingly, however, despite the intensity of the debate on the impact of EMU-*cum*-Euro-austerity on contemporary welfare states, we have yet to accumulate a mass of empirical research that directly tackles this causal link.

Whenever studies on welfare states point to the impact of a crisis, they do so only tangentially and indirectly. With recession and unemployment everywhere across the eurozone, influential comparative political economists have focused on developments in economic policy (Bermeo and Pontusson 2012; Kahler and Lake 2013) as well as labour markets and the consequent rise in inequality (Dolvik and Martin 2015a). We know, in the words of a prominent welfare state specialist, "surprisingly little" about the impact of the current crisis on the welfare state (Kvist 2013, 93; see also Steinebach, Knill, and Jordana 2019). Researchers complain that "existing knowledge about the effects of economic hardship on social policy is both sparse and contradictory" (Steinebach and Knill 2017, 1164). Others are concerned that "there is no literature specifically on the causal impact of the EMU on (welfare) reform efforts in the present crisis context" (de la Porte and Heins 2016, 6).

This literature has thus far been so quiet that, in exploring the impact of crises on welfare states, comparativists Starke, Kaasch, and van Hooren (2013, 12) felt the need to remind us that "the welfare state *is* relevant as an object of research in the context of crisis" (emphasis added). However, it seems that this is only natural. A veteran comparativist helps explain why there is no room for "black swans" (sudden and unexpected crises) in our research (Castles 2010, 91, 92). These crises naturally "affect the character of welfare state interventions and welfare state development." Their impact, however, generally "flies well below [our] intellectual radar" due to our disciplinary training and curiosities (ibid., 96).

Alternatively, it may simply be that not enough time has passed for us to have a clear understanding of the consequences of the current episode of Euro-austerity on Europe's welfare state. Mario Draghi, president of the European Central Bank from 2011 to 2019, announced a few years ago that "the crisis is behind us" and that "the recovery of the Eurozone is solid" (*ANSA*, 18 May 2017). Although the eurozone is returning to pre-crisis levels of output (Frieden and Walter 2017, 372), we are certainly not seeing an end to Euro-austerity. Political economists who keep an eye on how politics is "structured," not only in space but also in time, may feel uneasy about passing judgment on a still unfolding, multi-dimensional, complex phenomenon. Scholars, however alarmed they may be, may be concerned that their claims will turn out to be premature when there is still some risk that new evidence *ex post facto* might point in other directions.

Thus, instead of prognosticating on the future of the welfare state based on the limited evidence we have, the best strategy may be to "place today's headlines in a substantially broader context" (Pierson 2011, 21). After all, the headlines that are capturing the popular imagination today are surprisingly similar to those we read at the height of Euro-austerity – Episode I. So let us take a step back and reflect on the impact of this current episode of austerity based on we have learned from the impact of the EMU on welfare states.

What lessons can we draw from the first episode of Euro-austerity? Here we are aiming at an inference, in Mahoney's (2009) words, "past the past." We explore "how (and if) causal findings about the past can be generalized beyond the past" (ibid., 3; see also Tilly 2006). After all, as one leading economic sociologist taught us, we "can understand which state [a] system has reached only by looking at its history" (Granovetter 1992, 9). In this line of thinking, Mahoney (2009, 3) reminds us, "most social science predictions are *conditional predictions* – that is, predictions that assert that an outcome will occur if other things happen first." These conditional predictions "allow researchers to try to specify the conditions that would bring about desirable outcomes" (ibid., 5). Once these are specified, researchers may conclude that "findings from the study will hold up provided that some other events establish conditions that are similar to those that are stipulated in the argument's scope[1] statement" (ibid., 4, 7).

To make conditional generalizations, therefore, we need to make valid analogical comparisons. *Analogies*, as we define them here, are "assertions of repetition"; they involve "the creation of analytic categories in relation to which the researcher decides whether two or more cases are instances of the same phenomenon" (Collier and Mazzuca 2006, 472). The validity of any such comparison hinges on the similarity of the contexts and the conditions we are dealing with across time and space (Falleti and Lynch 2009; Hall 2016). Let us explore the extent to which the contextual and other conditions we are concerned about today are similar to those of yesterday.

In terms of the overall *contextual condition*, there seems to be a general continuity since the 1990s. Both episodes of Euro-austerity, in the 1990s and the post-2008 crisis period, are clearly enveloped in the general context of neoliberalism (Hall and Lamont 2013; Blyth and Matthijs

2017). There is a consensus in the comparative political economy literature that *neoliberalism*, defined as the "macroeconomic regime" in place
since the 1980s, does not seem to go anywhere (Crouch 2011; Schmidt
and Thatcher 2013; Mirowski 2014). It continues to be, in the words of
Blyth and Matthijs (2017, 208), "the main target variable for a country's
macroeconomic policy." It also "necessarily shapes states' institutional
choices" (ibid.; see also Evans and Sewell, Jr. 2013).

For any conditional prediction about the impact of Euro-austerity to
hold any sway today, the neoliberal macroeconomic regime (as context)
should have remained unchanged. However, there are signs that the
regime is not as resilient as it was. There is wide consensus that the 2008
crisis has revealed the "inconsistencies and incoherence of 'neoliberalism'" (Farnsworth and Irving 2018, 477). Many observe that the neoliberal regime has been increasingly "politically contested" (Streeck 2017).
Signs of contestation appear not only in the critical literature but also in
the establishment. For example, the IMF's own publication, *Finance &
Development*, featured a 2016 research piece titled "Neoliberalism: Oversold?," in which senior IMF staff pointed to cumulative evidence on
what neoliberalism had failed to deliver and announced that the IMF
had reached a point of "reconsideration." They warned that "policymakers, and institutions like the IMF that advise them, must be guided
not by faith, but by evidence of what has worked" (Ostry, Loungani,
and Furceri 2016, 41; see also Farnsworth and Irving 2018).

These contestations suggest that neoliberalism is no longer the only
game in town; rarely do we hear the "there is no alternative" salvos
from the establishment. Therefore, the structural context epitomized by
neoliberalism is not as uncontested as it was before the Great Recession
began. This brings us to the overall *contextual condition*: as long as the
current neoliberal regime is a continuation of the one that characterized
Euro-austerity in the 1990s, any adverse effect it has today may be only
as powerful as the effects it had yesterday.

Do the conditions under which the welfare states of the 1990s stood
up to Euro-austerity hold today? The cases presented in this book suggest that those conditions made up a configuration. Therefore, as long
as they continue to cluster as a configuration, we can expect the welfare state resilience of the 1990s to hold in the current episode of Euro-
austerity. There are two arguments in favour of this.

First, this book showed that, among the conditions of the 1990s, *organized interests*, along with *public support*, played a key role in successfully
defending welfare state programs – despite the frontal attacks on the
welfare state in the name of the EMU. Interest groups (such as the beneficiaries of mature welfare programs), progressive forces (labour unions

and political parties, especially those with a left-leaning or labour orientation), and, at times, even coalition partners in ruling governments defended social rights, playing roles such as veto players precluding reform options and groups fighting for protected rights and equitable outcomes through concerted action. Organized functional interests also used political opportunity structures, including social pacts, and mobilized other groups in pursuit of their goals. We need detailed case studies to evaluate whether these forces are as determined and as powerful today as they were during the 1990s.

The case studies also show that the level of public support for the welfare state significantly shaped the politics of reform. Public support was significant not only during elections but also between elections, when citizens, as members of civil society and social movements, held their elected representatives accountable for their actions. Contemporary political and public debates show that, as a central pillar of the European social model, the welfare state still enjoys very high levels of support among citizens throughout Europe. In fact, in the face of such popularity, contemporary political parties in government or opposition across Europe refrain from directly linking the fiscal austerity imperative to welfare state reform.

This situation is strikingly different than the previous episode of Euro-austerity, in which welfare state downsizing (or, in their minds, rightsizing) was a top priority for all conservative parties. The election programs of the leading political parties in the EU show that, between September 2008 and March 2017, only 1.2 per cent of programs promised welfare state limitation[2] as one of their top five policy priorities,[3] while 61 per cent featured welfare state expansion as one of their top five policy priorities. Moreover, 94 per cent of all leading political parties emphasized welfare state expansion more often than welfare state limitation.[4] These data show that, even under the severe circumstances of Euro-austerity – Episode II, the overwhelming majority of the EU's leading political parties maintained a stance favouring welfare state expansion. This finding aligns nicely with most recent empirical research on European party manifestos (Eger and Valdez 2018).

Clearly, in the eyes of Europeans, it is Euro-austerity itself – not the welfare state – that is highly unpopular, so that, since 2008, conservative governments cannot use the magic wand – the *vincolo esterno* – that did the trick earlier. No longer are there carrots such as EMU entry on the table, only sticks. Faced with Euro-austerity – Episode II, popular resistance has given way to electoral volatility; one after another, governments have fallen across Europe. These turnarounds have been more dramatic in the hardest-hit eurozone members – such as Greece,

Portugal, Ireland, Spain, and Italy (G. Ross 2012, 185; Hutter, Kriesi, and Vidal 2018) – resulting in the electoral success of populist parties not only in Northern Europe but also elsewhere (Rodrik 2018; Foster and Frieden 2019, 23). Unsurprisingly, radical-left populist parties, which have attracted scores of voters, especially in Southern Europe, have strongly favoured expanded social protection (Hall 2017).

What is surprising is that, after the Maastricht decade, the "welfare chauvinist," radical-right populist parties have also adopted a pro-welfare discourse. As they have increasingly participated in government, many, which traditionally opposed welfare state expansion and advocated cutbacks for "undeserving" immigrants, have become concerned about the future of welfare state programs (Greve 2019). Their new discourse has favoured social protection, provided that the benefits do not go to immigrants (Eger and Valdez 2015). Research suggests that this is because increasing numbers of working-class voters have abandoned left-labour parties and begun to vote for radical-right populist parties. With this changing basis of political support, these parties are shifting to more pro-welfare positions (Gingrich and Häusermann 2015, 52; Kriesi et al. 2012, 121). This realignment of cross-party support for the welfare state has "stabilized the welfare state in the face of declining working-class support for the Left" (Gingrich and Häusermann 2015, 51).

However, more recent research points to a more nuanced impact. Although generally remaining pro-welfare, radical-right populist parties have begun to reorient the program structure of welfare states along with their welfare-chauvinist preferences. As they join governments, these parties *do* help expand core social insurance programs (such as pensions and health care) that generally cover the native-born. Yet they have also retrenched programs disproportionally used by outsider groups, such as social assistance and some social services (Swank and Betz 2019). Thus, although "a pro-welfare-state rhetoric" has recently dominated the political and public agenda across Europe (Vis, van Kersbergen, and Hylands 2011, 342–3), research suggests that new, emerging cleavages may undermine the very social solidarity that upholds its welfare states (Swank and Betz 2019; Gidron and Hall 2019; Häusermann et al. 2019). This brings us back to the first condition for the continued resilience of the welfare state: as long as pro-welfare-state support remains widespread and in solidarity, welfare states are likely to survive the second episode of Euro-austerity.

The second condition for resilience is the *institutional structures of welfare states*, which themselves shape reform processes. Europe's welfare states entered the new crisis era in 2008 having gone through numerous rounds of reform; a long list of endogenous pressures had created tectonic shifts within them. Despite the rhetoric to the contrary, a consensus has emerged that this crisis has not been a "crisis *of* the welfare state"; instead, rising debt ratios, stemming from "momentous developments and their economic consequences," have been largely *exogenous* to the welfare state (Dolvik and Martin 2015c, 4; see also Hay and Wincott 2012, 219; Dolvik and Martin 2015b, 380).

What matters most in the political economy of reform processes are the endogenous, institutional features of welfare states. European welfare states are generally based on the pay-as-you-go model, and its institutional features weakened the hands of the reformers who desperately and urgently needed to find savings to meet the Maastricht deadline during Euro-austerity – Episode I. Given the highly politicized nature of intergenerational contracts, grandfather clauses, and other lock-in mechanisms, governments found it virtually impossible to raise critical savings by retrenching social programs. Instead, they raised revenues and cut non-social expenditure items. Thus, the 1990s was a decade of resorting to Plan Bs as opposed to carrying out original ambitions for radical cutbacks. But permanent austerity has always meant permanent reform.

Some of these reforms, research shows, has led to changes in the institutional features of welfare states. As a result, European welfare states may now be less resilient to reform, especially to the fate of future contracts (Palier 2010, 387). In any event, the institutional structures of contemporary welfare states are essentially no different now than they were under Euro-austerity – Episode I. This brings us to the *second condition*: as long as these adjustments do not lead to a structural break in the politics of reform, evidence suggests that welfare state retrenchment is likely to remain a treacherous enterprise in Episode II.

Even if the contextual as well as the other conditions characterizing the first episode have remained more or less the same, the *nature* of EMU-*cum*-austerity may have changed, rendering any analogical comparisons invalid. After Euro-austerity was institutionalized in Episode I, the EMU was the broadest template for making macroeconomic as well as other policies across the eurozone. But even before it was launched, the EMU was vehemently criticized for its significant gaps and flaws.[5] It proved somewhat resilient during its first several years, until it was seriously tested with the eruption of the financial crisis on the other side of the Atlantic. It transmitted the deleterious effects of the largely exogenous financial and economic crises to the eurozone and even magnified them. After a Keynesian interlude, policymakers across the eurozone reverted to a "vicious circle of austerity and increasing debt ratios" against a background of another "vicious circle of banking and government crises" (Martin 2015, 43). The resulting institutional innovations in the governance of the EMU strengthened it, and helped remedy some of the gaps and flaws in its original design.

Political economists are still concerned – some despite, others because of, these institutional innovations. Many believe that, in domestic macroeconomic policymaking, the EU level assumes an excessively heavy role, more so now than ever (Dolvik and Martin 2015b; Heins and de la Porte 2016) and that this shift in power away from national governments narrows down the policy options for adjustment that they enjoyed during Euro-austerity – Episode I. The new policy template, many fear, leaves member states only one option: "internal devaluation" in a game of "regime competition" (Dolvik and Martin 2015b, 384). Furthermore, by subscribing to ever-deepening Euro-austerity and through multiplier effects, the EMU locks the eurozone into dampened economic growth and restrains employment creation, which will weaken the funding base of welfare states (ibid., 354).

These arguments reflect some of those we heard during the 1990s. As presented in the introductory chapter, many comparative political economists were concerned that the EMU would institutionalize a deflationary macroeconomic regime across Europe and, in due course, "sap the European models by stealth" (Martin and Ross 2004, 330). Now this scenario may be finally materializing, and there may be fewer options available for deflecting pressure from welfare state programs. All the most valuable assets may have been privatized, so there may be no more to sell off to raise revenues. Policymakers may believe that raising taxes would only exacerbate recessionary pressure or that this would be more politically treacherous than cutting expenditures.

All these possibilities could mean that the EMU-induced pressure may erode the economic and actuarial basis of Europe's welfare states much more seriously than before. This scenario brings us to the *third condition*: as long as Euro-austerity continues to function more like an *exogenous* constraint, and domestic policymakers continue to have room to manoeuvre as they make decisions about who gets what, when, and how, welfare reform scenarios are not likely to be preordained.

What should we think about the impact of Euro-austerity – Episode II on today's welfare states based on what we know about the previous episode? Revisiting Heclo (1981, 383), we ask, "Have the customary forces so changed or the representative powers of our normal social politics become so depleted that present problems point toward a new kind – or perhaps no kind – of welfare state in the future?" We see, in the limited evidence we have of the impact of Euro-austerity – Episode II, that structural pressure for welfare state reform has grown stronger with the financial crisis. Permanent austerity has truly meant permanent reform in the hardest-hit countries – not only in those under a formal memorandum of understanding (such as in Greece, Portugal, and Spain) but also in others (such as Italy) under "the shadow of conditionality" (Dolvik and Martin 2015b; de la Porte and Heins 2016). However, to relate the actual outcomes of welfare state reform directly to Euro-austerity, the existing evidence is far from conclusive.

The limited evidence we have suggests that, although the scope for policy choices for welfare reform seems to be narrowing, reform outcomes remain quite varied. We observe that some countries have been "better equipped to weather the crisis" (Dolvik and Martin 2015b, 381). Although we do not have conclusive evidence at this time, an influential study concludes that "the options available to cushion [the effects of the crisis] were frequently influenced by political choices and shifts in coalition-building" (ibid., 352) This means that domestic political choices, along with institutional factors, still shape the extent to which welfare states cushion these effects (ibid., 381; see also Beramendi et al. 2015, 398). Other research shows that, despite the cascading crises, "the core of the various social models is resilient" (Heins and de la Porte 2016, 209).

These preliminary findings nicely echo Hemerijck (2013, 217), who warned that welfare state futures have never been preordained, nor will they ever be. Politicized groups – organized or unorganized, progressive, reactionary, or obstructionist – will shape the very nature, scope, pace, and tempo of welfare state recalibration as well as retrenchment. And they will do so *at least as much as* what we perceive to be inexorable constraints. This is not to deny that Europe's welfare states are under intense pressure and that there is no retrenchment whatsoever; in fact, quite the contrary. Permanent reform leads to all sorts of retrenchment in some welfare state programs and to resilience in others.

The empirical effects-of-causes question that this book has concerned itself with, however, has been whether such retrenchment is *directly, causally* attributable to EMU-*cum*-austerity. The extent to which pressure is modified, muted, or even fully mitigated by counter-pressure has been and will continue to be contingent on the political economy of reform. This is where Polanyi (1944) helps us interpret our current circumstances: Euro-austerity was planned; reactions to it were, and will continue to be, not. In this political game of who gets what, when, and how, the relative resilience of European welfare states to date should serve as testimony to the enduring primacy of the political economy of reform over structural, rule-based, external constraints.

Notes

1. Euro-Austerity and Europe's Welfare States

1 An earlier version of this section appeared in Bolukbasi (2009).
2 In this book, I base my exploration of the political economy of reform under Euro-austerity on the rich comparative political economy literature, in which scholars emphasize "institutional differences between countries and the way that such differences have refracted political and economic responses to common economic shocks or opportunities" (Baccaro and Pontusson 2016, 2; see also Beckert and Streeck 2008). In doing so, I rely on Peter Gourevitch (1986, 19), who focuses on the "politics of support for different economic policies" and "politics of policy choice" "in response to large changes in the international economy." In addressing the research questions I raise, I also find myself thinking along the lines of Harold Lasswell (1936), who advises us to chase after who gets what, when, and how. These are key distributional questions shaping the areas of not only political economy but also public policy. In this book, I take *political economy* to refer to domestic interdependent institutional matrices "encompassing organizational relations among economic actors, the policy regimes supporting those relationships, and the international regimes in which they are embedded" (Hall 2013, 129). Following Polanyi (1944), I see these institutional matrices as historically constituted, socially embedded, and politically constructed.
3 In the methodological literature, asking effects-of-causes questions is generally associated with quantitative research. Recent research, however, shows that qualitative research (such as case studies) is just as amenable to asking effects-of-causes questions. Hypothesis-testing case studies focusing on the potential effects of causes may successfully isolate the specific effects of a variable of interest. Any causal argument based on this research strategy, this literature suggests, is based on "careful" case selection (Deters 2013, 76–7).

2. The Institutionalization of Euro-Austerity

1 This section draws on Italianer (1993).
2 This surveillance scheme was subsequently formalized and named the multilateral surveillance procedure.
3 These programs were subsequently formalized and named convergence programs.
4 In particular, research shows that it was the Bundesbank that insisted on the stringent rules (Kaltenthaler 1998, 79–84; Kaelberer 2001, 188–97). It was not party to the treaty negotiations, but it did manage to influence the Monetary Committee as well as the German delegation (Dyson 1994, 148–53).
5 As a result, the Commission, in its *Convergence Report* (1998), interpreted the exchange rate criterion as de facto exchange rate stability and absence of devaluation (as opposed to remaining within narrow ERM bands).
6 In tables 1 and 2, I took the figures for 1993–8 from the European Commission's (1998) *Convergence Report* because the Council's final decision on whether an EMU candidate satisfied the criteria was to be based on the data published in this report.
7 The treaty stipulated that, after the third stage had begun, the EDP would apply to *all* EU member states – eurozone member or not. However, it did not explicitly say whether the 3 per cent deficit rule would apply as the benchmark. Moreover, it left unclear what the procedures would be for applying sanctions if the rules were breached.
8 As a rule, such a downturn was defined as at least 2 per cent of GDP.
9 The Council also reached agreement on appointing Wim Duisenberg, former president of the Dutch Central Bank, as president of the ECB. The ECB was established in Frankfurt on 1 June 1998, succeeding the EMI, and became fully operational on 1 January 1999. In the meantime, on the insistence of the French, it was decided that Duisenberg would share the eight-year term with their candidate, Jean-Claude Trichet, each serving four years.
10 For Blavoukos and Pagoulatos (2008), the Maastricht fiscal criteria were only "push factors." Thus, they were "necessary but not sufficient" for sustainable fiscal adjustment.

3. From Euro-Austerity to Welfare State Retrenchment?

1 In the analysis below, some versions of the indicators that I rely on were proposed by Castles (2001, 2004).
2 The figures for the EMU members include those of Finland, which negatively biases the EMU average because it became an EU member only

after 1995. However, the likelihood of a direct impact of the EMU on the Finnish welfare state is low.

3 The categories of public spending for purposes other than social protection include general public services (including spending on public order and safety), defence, education, housing, community services, economic affairs, recreation, and culture as well as a residual category that includes debt-interest payments (Castles 2004; based on United Nations 1999). Although the data provided in table 5 represent spending for purposes other than those with a social purpose, some programs (such as education) can also be considered to have a social purpose.

4 The only exceptions were Finland, the Netherlands, and Ireland, where savings came from both social and non-social expenditure components.

5 These compensatory movements of expansion, along with dismantling, have been the focus of a growing literature on public policy (Jensen et al. 2014; Steinebach, Knill, and Jordana 2019) following Pierson's (1994) pioneering work.

6 I would like to thank Fritz Scharpf, who encouraged me to construct an upsizing index to detect *expansions* in welfare state programs in addition to Castles's downsizing index.

7 The denominators of the downsizing and upsizing eight-component indices are total public social spending for the base year of 1991 minus total expenditures on unemployment programs for the same year.

8 In fact, it is not only the impact of the business cycle that results in changes in unemployment program spending, hence the difference between the nine-component and eight-component indices. The differences could also reflect changes in unemployment benefit programs (eligibility rules, replacement ratios, etc.) independent of the fluctuations in the number of claimants resulting from the business cycle. However, *restrictions* in these programs (e.g., tighter eligibility rules) would *reduce* the difference between the nine-component and eight-component indices.

9 The rapid deregulation of the financial markets in Finland and Sweden led to an immense expansion of credit, resulting in a financial bubble and banking crisis. In the meantime, the boom of the 1980s had pushed up inflation rates and undermined the international competitiveness of these economies, and, as a result, these countries ran increasing current account deficits. Moreover, the increase in ongoing interest rates in 1990 and the sudden collapse of the Soviet export market came as asymmetric shocks and aggravated crisis conditions, especially in Finland (Jonung, Kiander, and Vartia 2009).

10 The population aged sixty-five and older increased by almost 30 per cent during that time, and the number of unemployed increased by more than 47.8 per cent.

11 There was a 21.3 per cent increase in those aged sixty-five and older, along with a 14.6 per cent decrease in the number of unemployed.
12 The population aged sixty-five and older increased by more than 15.7 per cent, accompanied by a rise in the number of unemployed of over 10 per cent.

4. Euro-Austerity and the Political Economy of Reform in Belgium

1 In Belgium, there are two groupings of budgetary units: Entity I consists of the federal government and the social security system, while Entity II encompasses the federated entities – i.e., the communities and the regions. The social security system is budgeted in a separate budget account in Entity I.
2 Government declarations are a Belgian institution in which coalition governments set out their objectives and aims. Before a government is formed, the coalition partners negotiate a program, and the resulting objectives and aims are presented to Parliament in the government's declaration. As a result, deviating from the declaration in any significant way becomes very difficult because it would require a new round of negotiations with the coalition partners.
3 This section draws on Hallerberg (2004).
4 The council was established as an advisory body to the Ministry of Finance in 1936 and had limited importance in Belgian fiscal policy and politics. It had three sections, one of which was assigned tasks in relation to fiscal policy. Representing "fiscal orthodoxy," this section had only ten members, drawn from the National Bank of Belgium, the Ministry of Finance, and the three regions.
5 Therefore, according to the treaty, Belgium's entire general government budget – i.e., the budgets of both Entity I and Entity II – would have to meet the deficit benchmark.
6 The government intended to raise BEF 65 billion in 1993–4 from the sale of state-owned assets. In fact, it managed to reach its borrowing requirement target for 1994 – BEF 315 billion – thanks to the sale of Belgacom.
7 The state had previously been obliged, under a 1991 law, to retain a 51 per cent majority stake in state companies.
8 Dehaene decided not to proceed with the pact because he did not think it necessary to have the social partners' approval for the austerity measures. The government was a grand coalition, with both the Socialist and the Christian Democratic Parties controlling 120 seats of the 150-seat Parliament. Although the government was rather fragile due to linguistic divisions, Dehaene did not require the agreement of the social partners to pass the legislation once the coalition partners in the government had agreed on a policy matter. See Baccaro and Lim (2006), who claim that the Dehaene government did not need to strike a pact.

9　A social security deficit of BEF 110 billion was predicted for 1996, and the new measures were aimed to reduce this to nil by then.

10　The government continued to do so in the following years; see Savage (2005) for more details.

11　See footnote 2 above on the distinction between the federal government budget and the social security budget.

12　Dehaene had emphasized earlier the importance of reducing the social security contributions paid by employers for the creation of low-paid jobs. He had added that his government had been looking into alternative means of financing the social security system, including imposing a withholding tax on interest income and a carbon tax (*Reuters News*, 20 September 1994).

13　Based on credible sources, the *Wall Street Journal Europe* (11 April 1995) called the budget figures a result of "voodoo arithmetic." The deficit figure for 1994 of 5.4 per cent of GDP, according to the newspaper, was "a clear underestimation" of the real deficit.

14　This was the result of a number of scandals, the most humiliating of which concerned bribes paid in the late 1980s by an Italian helicopter manufacturer to win a large military contract.

15　Qualifying for the EMU was an existential goal for Dehaene. Later, commenting on his rationale for calling the early election, he claimed, "The reason I called early elections was to get a new government on track to make a 1996 budget which gets us ready for the single currency" (*Reuters News*, 23 June 1995).

16　Waigel also warned about debt-ridden Italy and Spain.

17　The rationale for reducing the budget deficit every year in the run-up to the EMU (including 1996) was that, although the budgetary performance of the EMU candidates would be discussed in 1998 on the basis of the data for 1997, if the government succeeded in reducing the deficit, its debt-to-GDP ratio would have fallen for four consecutive years. This would enable the government to take advantage of the wording of the Maastricht Treaty, which allowed for a debt ratio higher than the reference values stipulated, provided that it was "sufficiently diminishing."

18　The Belgian Constitution allows the government to rule with special powers only under exceptional circumstances, such as a war or an economic crisis. Parliament gives the government a free hand to reach a preset policy goal without having to answer to Parliament. Special powers had last been used in 1982 by the Martens government, which, facing economic crisis, introduced austerity measures and devalued the franc.

19　Dehaene was quoted in the *Financial Times* (2 October 1996) that the 1997 budget "could be called a turning point budget."

20　*Financial Times* (3 October 1996).

5. Euro-Austerity and the Political Economy of Reform in Greece

1 Interestingly, the hawkish new minister, Manos, harshly criticized the program, claiming that the targets were not stringent enough. Insisting that it "was no more than a scrap of paper," he announced that he refused to submit to Brussels just "a patchwork of good intentions" (Economist Intelligence Unit, 2nd Quarter 1992, 14).

2 These transfers were extremely significant for the budget. Had they been excluded, the 1994 primary surplus of 2.1 per cent of GDP would have indicated a deficit of 3.4 per cent.

3 In fact, with the support of ND, the third Simitis government amended the Greek Constitution by inserting an explicit clause on the "social welfare state." The amended article read, "The principle of the social welfare state [is] guaranteed by the State." This move was seen as "the most important and far-reaching change" in the Constitution in years because it could be interpreted as giving the courts the power to check (and to reverse, if needed) any decision scaling back the welfare state (Eleftheriadis 2005, 320–1).

4 If Greece did not absorb all the CSF funds, the outstanding balance would likely be transferred to another program.

5 For example, referring to excessively generous replacement ratios, the report maintained that "the fact that total pensions often amount to more than 100% of income received during working years is preposterous" (13).

6 For example, the report argued that "the period up to the submission of the budget for 1999, in November 1998, can be utilized to devise measures and initiatives so that the social security system can play an important role in the attainment of the macroeconomic goals, on the basis of which the eligibility of EU Member States for participation in EMU will be assessed" (Greece. Spraos Committee, 31).

7 The GSEE complained that, first, the report treated the social insurance sector exclusively on the basis of revenue–expenditure. Second, it found the proposal for an increase in the retirement age arbitrary, unrealistic, and, therefore, unacceptable. Third, it considered it unlawful to propose the abolition of early retirement for those who had worked in unhygienic environments and the restriction of the number of pensions for the disabled (*Athens News Agency*, 17 October 1997).

8 The report also contested Italy's qualification, but the Italians were encouraged by a footnote stating that it was still possible for the country to hit its fiscal targets if some additional measures, still to be introduced, proved effective as well as, if necessary, some extra belt-tightening (*Financial Times*, 25 April 1997).

9 The financial daily *Kathimerini* wrote that the austerity budget, which was designed to enable Greece to enter the EMU by 2002, had even made the

front page of the *Financial Times* for the first time ever (*Kathimerini*, quoted in *Reuters News*, 13 November 1997).

10 Although the strikes appeared to be organized against a wide range of issues, including demands for inflation-indexed tax thresholds and a thirty-five-hour work week, it was the proposed social security reforms that sparked the biggest protests (*EIRR* 1999, 300: 7; 1999, 299: 7).

11 OECD (1999, 59).

12 These were confirmed by Eurostat and the Commission in 2004.

13 The Greek government had failed to protect Abdullah Ocalan, who had been charged by Turkey with carrying out terrorist acts. This provoked an uproar, and Kurdish demonstrators occupied and took hostages in thirteen Greek missions across Europe (Economist Intelligence Unit, 2nd Quarter 1999).

14 Some time after Greece qualified for the EMU, the European Commission and Eurostat announced that there had been "serious elements of budget irregularities" on the road to the EMU in Greece. After investigations, the deficit was revised upward, taking into consideration the following accounting problems: the off-budget recording of military expenditures financed through special defence borrowing had been consistently understated; the surplus recorded in the social security account had been overestimated; EU-funded capital transfers had been misreported; and the expenditures of Greece's privatization agency had been incorrectly recorded. At the same time, the debt had been revised upward to reflect the non-recording of capitalized interest obligations, inadequate debt consolidation, incorrect recording of some social security funds as part of the private sector, and non-recording of debt after calling in guarantees. The revised figures revealed large discrepancies with the originally reported deficit. In fact, according to the revised figures, Greece had *never* satisfied the deficit rule (IMF 2005).

6. Euro-Austerity and the Political Economy of Reform in Italy

1 Although the public sector deficit fell following its initial year of operation, the trend thereafter was to increase.

2 The Italian budget-making process begins in June with the preparation of the DPEF, which outlines the government's main approach to fiscal policy. In September, the government submits the finance bill (*legge finanziaria*) for the following fiscal year to Parliament. The bill provides the level and composition of the fiscal measures (revenues and expenditures) set out in the DPEF. Parliament discusses the bill and makes certain modifications. The bill is then approved by both Houses and, by December, becomes the budget law (*legge di bilancio*) for the following year.

3 Covering the period 1992 to 1994, the program was based on the multi-annual economic program presented by the Italian government (DPEF 1991), which had been published in May of that year.

4 The 1992 budget targeted a substantial cut in the deficit thanks to revenue gains and one-off measures (such as accelerated privatization, a tax amnesty, and a mandatory reassessment of corporate assets). Moreover, as a lasting measure, it was planned that increases in personal income tax and indirect taxes would contribute to the consolidation effort (OECD 1992, 44).

5 Economics and Financial Affairs Commissioner Henning Christophersen had issued an earlier warning that Italy had to take the decision to correct the budget deficit if it wanted to meet the fiscal targets (*Reuters News*, 26 March 1992).

6 See Pasquino and McCarthy (1993) for a detailed analysis of the crisis of the Italian political regime.

7 The fiscal correction relied on a combination of revenue gains – to be achieved from higher stamp duties, higher one-off taxes on real estate and bank deposits, and higher social security contributions paid by employees – and spending cuts, to be realized by freezing public employment, lowering transfers to local authorities, and reducing calls on social spending and defence expenditures. On the expenditure side, this special budget introduced savings from structural reform measures in the areas of health services, pension payments, local-authority finances, and the labour market. On the revenue side, the budget introduced new taxes, removed tax deductions, eliminated compensation for inflation-induced fiscal drag, and imposed other measures (OECD 1992, 45–6).

8 The deficit targets set in the first convergence program had been revised in light of the adverse developments during the previous year, predicting a reduction of 4.8 percentage points in three years, from 9.5 per cent in 1992 to 4.7 per cent in 1995 (European Commission 1993c, 61). The additional fiscal measures that had just been announced in September were also inserted into the revised program.

9 In fact, when Amato was preparing his Cabinet, there was talk of merging all the economic ministries (Treasury, Budget, and Finance) into a "super-ministry" as a sign of the new government's bold attack. However, he did not achieve this (Hellman 1993, 155).

10 In fact, even before he took office in June 1992, Amato had met with the unions. In July, a joint committee (government and unions) was formed in the Ministry of Labour to discuss the outlines of a pension-reform scheme.

11 This was the impression in Brussels, too. After having discussed the Italian convergence program with Amato, Commission President Delors stated, "Is this country imploding (to quote a journalist) or is it coming out of the shackles that up until now have been jeopardizing its reputation, its

influence in the world and its development? I would tend rather toward the second hypothesis, hence the tempered optimism I have" (*Agence Europe*, 19 February 1993).

12 In early January 1994, the government also approved a legislative decree allocating ITL 1.6 trillion in 1994 and ITL 4.2 trillion in 1995 and 1996 to mitigate the effects of the unemployment crisis, mainly by covering the costs of the early retirement programs provided and other measures (Economist Intelligence Unit, 1st Quarter 1994, 16).

13 Notwithstanding the austere measures, the deficit remained at 9.5 per cent of GDP in 1993, mainly due to the recession. At the same time, the rise in interest rates in the aftermath of the suspension of the lira from the ERM pushed interest payments to an unprecedented level.

14 Waigel also referred to debt-ridden Belgium and Spain. He probably did not Greece because the consensus at the time was that it would enter the EMU at a later date.

15 The greater part of this supplementary budget relied on spending cuts in transportation, education, defence, and health care. Revenue measures included higher excise duties and levies on lotteries and unleaded gasoline as well as higher taxes on bank deposits (OECD 1997, 60).

16 The Euro-tax was a withholding tax on income generated in 1996, which would be repaid in 1999; therefore, it seemed more like a non-interest-bearing advance to the government than a tax. The government deliberately did not write the repayment schedule into law, leaving repayment as a "political commitment." The reason was that the European Commission (through Eurostat) would allow deficit reduction only through tax increases, not advances. As a temporary measure, the tax was designed to have an immediate effect on 1997 public finances; it was paid back in 1999 only after the EMU deal was struck (Savage 2005, 128–31).

17 In fact, Waigel was repeatedly asking the Italian government to show evidence of commitment to fiscal consolidation – e.g., demanding that the Council examine the lira's return to ERM *after* the 1997 budget was approved (Chiorazzo and Spaventa 1999, 133).

18 Bertinotti rejected the budget by stating, "If this Europe that you talk so much about is asking us to cut pension spending in order to enter today, tomorrow it will ask for other welfare cuts to allow us to stay in" (*Dow Jones Online News*, 9 October 1997).

8. Euro-Austerity – Episode II

1 By *scope*, Mahoney (2009, 18) refers to "the context within which a given causal pattern can be expected to operate," outside of which "causal heterogeneity may arise, prohibiting generalization." Similarly, Hall

(2016, 33) emphasizes the significance of contexts that are "relatively stable for discrete periods" in showing how politics is structured across space and time. He warns that we need to specify "the scope conditions relevant to the analysis, defined partly in terms of the presence of … structural factors" when examining the "relevant interaction effects" of context and conditions (34). Collier and Mazzuca (2006, 473) define *context* as "history as period"; "political phenomena are located within some socially defined interval of time – world historical time." These "temporal scope conditions" are "the canonical form of introducing history (period) as context"; they "limit the period in which causal generalizations hold" (475).

2 In the Manifesto Project Dataset Codebook, *welfare state expansion* refers to "favorable mentions of the need to introduce, maintain or expand any public social service or social security schemes." In contrast, *welfare state limitation* refers to favouring "limiting state expenditures on social services or social security and favorable mentions of the social subsidiary principle" (Volkens et al. 2017).

3 These figures are taken from the Manifesto Project Database, which is based on quantitative content analyses of political parties' election platforms (Volkens et al. 2017). The database surveyed the number of political parties that had participated in national elections between September 2008 and March 2017 and had secured leading positions (with the first-, second-, or third-highest number of votes); the number was 163.

4 The scores attributed to each variable (policy area) in a given manifesto in the database are the relative share of statements in each category out of all the statements in the manifesto. As an example, in the election program of Mario Monti's Scelta Civica for 2013, *welfare state expansion* has a score of 7.7, and *welfare state limitation* has a score of 2.9. This means that 7.7 per cent of the manifesto was devoted to welfare state expansion and 2.9 per cent to welfare state limitation. Because parties can argue in favour of expansion in one policy area and limitation in another, it is common to see manifestos with scores in both categories. In this case, since the emphasis on welfare state expansion is greater, the manifesto is categorized as a "net welfare state expansionist" manifesto – as is the case with 94 per cent of all the EU's leading political parties between 2008 and 2017.

5 It was these very gaps and flaws that prompted many scholars to react to the EMU's potentially adverse consequences, as surveyed in the introductory chapter of this book. Copelovitch, Frieden, and Walter (2016) and Frieden and Walter (2017) provide lucid accounts of how the EMU exacerbated the adverse effects of the US financial crisis on Europe.

References

Amenta, E. 2003. "What We Know about the Development of Social Policy." In *Comparative Historical Analysis in the Social Sciences*, edited by J. Mahoney and D. Rueschmeyer, 91–130. New York: Cambridge University Press.

Anderson, K., S. Kuipers, I. Schulze, and W. van den Nouland. 2007. "Belgium: Linguistic Veto Players and Pension Reform." In *The Handbook of West European Pension Politics*, edited by E. Immergut, K. Anderson, and I. Schulze, 297–395. Oxford: Oxford University Press.

Andreou, G., and N. Koutsiaras. 2004. "Greece and Economic and Monetary Union." In *Greece in the European Union*, edited by D.G. Dimitrakopoulos and A.G. Passas, 86–109. London: Routledge.

Antichi, M., and F.R. Pizzuti. 2000. "The Public Pension System in Italy: Observations on the Recent Reforms, Methods of Control and Their Application." In *Social Dialogue and Pension Reform*, edited by E. Reynaud, 81–96. Geneva: International Labour Office.

Arcq, É., and E. Chatelain. 1994. "Bref sur vol des relations collectives, des origines au Plan global." In *Pour un nouveau pacte social, emploi, compétitivité, sécurité sociale*, edited by E. Arcq and E. Chatelain, 45–62. Brussels: EVO.

Baccaro, L. 2002. "Negotiating the Italian Pension Reform with the Unions: Lessons for Corporatist Theory." *Industrial and Labor Relations Review* 55 (3): 413–31. https://doi.org/10.2307/2696049.

Baccaro, L., and S.-H. Lim. 2006. "*Social Pacts as Coalitions of 'Weak' and 'Moderate': Ireland, Italy and South Korea in Comparative Perspective.*" Discussion Paper No. DP/162/2006. Geneva: International Institute for Labour Studies.

Baccaro, L., and J. Pontusson, J. 2016. "Rethinking Comparative Political Economy: The Growth Model Perspective." *Politics and Society* 55 (3): 1–33. https://doi.org/10.1177/0032329216638053.

Bardi, L., and M. Rhodes. 1998. "Introduction: Mapping the Future." In *Italian Politics: Mapping the Future*, edited by L. Bardi and M. Rhodes, 21–36. Boulder, CO: Westview Press.

Baskaran, T. 2009. "Did the Maastricht Treaty Matter for Macroeconomic Performance? A Difference-in-Difference Investigation." *Kyklos* 62 (3): 331–58. https://doi.org/10.1111/j.1467-6435.2009.00439.x.

Beckert, J., and W. Streeck. 2008. *Economic Sociology and Political Economy: A Programmatic Perspective*. Cologne: Max Planck Institute for the Study of Societies.

Begg, I., and F. Nectoux. 1995. "Social Protection and Economic Union." *Journal of European Social Policy* 5 (4): 285–302. https://doi.org/10.1177 /095892879500500402.

Beramendi, P., S. Häusermann, H. Kitschelt, and H. Kriesi. 2015. "Conclusion: Advanced Capitalism in Crisis." In *The Politics of Advanced Capitalism*, edited by P. Beramendi, S. Häusermann, H. Kitschelt, and H. Kriesi, 381–403. New York: Cambridge University Press.

Bermeo, N., and J. Pontusson. 2012. *Coping with the Crisis: Government Reactions to the Great Recession*. New York: Russell Sage Foundation.

Bini-Smaghi, L., T. Padoa-Schioppa, and F. Papadia. 1994. *The Transition to EMU in the Maastricht Treaty*. Princeton, NJ: Princeton University Press.

Blavoukos, S., and G. Pagoulatos. 2008. "The Limits of EMU Conditionality: Fiscal Adjustment in Southern Europe." *Journal of Public Policy* 28 (2): 229–53. https://doi.org/10.1017/s0143814x08000883.

Blyth, M., and M. Matthijs. 2017. "Black Swans, Lame Ducks, and the Mystery of IPE's Missing Macroeconomy." *Review of International Political Economy* 24 (2): 203–31. https://doi.org/10.1080/09692290 .2017.1308417.

Bolukbasi, H.T. 2009. "On Consensus, Constraint and Choice: Economic and Monetary Integration and Europe's Welfare States." *Journal of European Public Policy* 16 (4): 527–44. https://doi.org/10.1080/13501760902872551.

Bolukbasi, H.T., and K.G. Oektem. 2018. "Conceptualizing and Operationalizing Social Rights: Towards Higher Convergent Validity in SCIP and CWED." *Journal of European Social Policy* 28 (1): 86–100. https:// doi.org/10.1177/0958928717700565.

Bonoli, G. 2012. "Blame Avoidance and Credit Claiming Revisited." In *The Politics of the New Welfare State*, edited by G. Bonoli and D. Natali, 93–110 Oxford: Oxford University Press.

Braun, M. 1996. "The Confederated Trade Unions and the Dini Government: 'The Grand Return of Neo-corporatism?'" In *Italian Politics: The Stalled Transition*, edited by M. Caciagli and D.I. Kertzer, 205–21. Boulder, CO: Westview Press.

Buiter, H.W., G. Corsetti, and N. Rubini. 1993a. "Excessive Deficits: Sense and Nonsense in the Treaty of Maastricht." *Economic Policy* 8 (16): 32–58. https://doi.org/10.2307/1344568.

– 1993b. "Maastricht's Fiscal Rules." *Economic Policy* 8 (16): 57–100.

Burkitt, B., and M. Baimbridge. 1995. "The Maastrciht Treaty's Impact on the Welfare State." *Critical Social Policy*. 14 (3): 100–11. https://doi.org/10.1177/026101839401404208.

Busemeyer, M.R. 2004. "Chasing Maastricht: The Impact of EMU on the Fiscal Performance of Member States." European Research Paper Archives 8 (8).

Buti, M., and G. Giudice. 2002. "Maastricht's Fiscal Rules at Ten: An Assessment." *Journal of Common Market Studies* 40 (5): 823–48. https://doi.org/10.1111/1468-5965.00399.

Castles, F. 2001. "On the Political Economy of Recent Public Sector Development." *Journal of European Social Policy* 11 (3): 195–211. https://doi.org/10.1177/095892870101100301.

– 2002. "Developing New Measures of Welfare State Change and Reform." *European Journal of Political Research*. 41 (5): 613–41. https://doi.org/10.1111/1475-6765.00024.

– 2004. *The Future of the Welfare State: Crisis Myths and Crisis Realities*. Oxford: Oxford University Press.

– 2010. "Black Swans and Elephants on the Move: The Impact of Emergencies on the Welfare State." *Journal of European Social Policy* 20 (2): 91–101. https://doi.org/10.1177/0958928709358793.

Chiorazzo, V., and L. Spaventa. 1999. "The Prodigal Son or a Confidence Trickster? How Italy got into EMU." In *From EMS to EMU: 1979 to 1999 and Beyond*, edited by D. Cobham and G. Zis, 129–55. London: Macmillan.

Christodoulakis, N. 2013. "Market Reforms in Greece, 1990–2008: External Constraints and Domestic Limitations." In *From Stagnation to Forced Adjustment*, edited by S. Kalyvas, G. Pagoulatos, and H. Tsoukas, 91–116. Oxford: Oxford University Press.

Clasen, J., and N. Siegel. 2007. "Comparative Welfare State Analysis and the 'Dependent Variable Problem.'" In *Investigating Welfare State Change*, edited by J. Clasen and N. Siegel, 3–12. Northampton, MA: Edward Elgar.

Clayton, R., and J. Pontusson. 1998. "Welfare-State Retrenchment Revisited: Entitlement Cuts, Public Sector Restructuring, and Inegalitarian Trends in Advanced Capitalist Societies." *World* Politics 51 (October): 67–98. https://doi.org/10.1017/s0043887100007796.

Collier, R.B., and S. Mazzuca. 2006. "Does History Repeat?" In *Oxford Handbook of Contextual Political Analysis*, edited by R.E. Goodin and C. Tilly, 472–89. Oxford: Oxford University Press.

Copelovitch, M., J. Frieden, and S. Walter. 2016. "The Political Economy of the Euro Crisis." *Comparative Political Studies* 49 (7): 1–30. https://doi.org/10.1177/0010414016633227.

Council of the European Communities. 1991. "ECOFIN Council Decisions of 11–12 November 1991." Press Release. Brussels: Council of the European Communities General Secretariat. http://aei.pitt.edu/3241/1/3241.pdf.

– 1992. ECOFIN Council decisions of 19 May 1992.

Council of the European Union. 1991. *Conclusions of the Luxembourg European Council*. 28–29 June. DOC/91/2. https://ec.europa.eu/commission/presscorner/detail/en/DOC_91_2.

Couttenier, I. 1991. Belgian Politics in 1990. *Res Publica* 3–4: 357–73.

– 1992. Belgian Politics in 1991. *Res Publica* 3–4: 347–69.

– 1993. Belgian Politics in 1992. *Res Publica* 3–4: 363–87.

– 1997. Belgian Politics in 1996. *Res Publica* 3–4: 523–45.

Croci, O., and L. Picci. 2002. "European Monetary Integration and Integration Theory: Insights from the Italian Case." In *The Euro: European Integration Theory and Economic and Monetary Union*, edited by A. Verdun, 215–40. Lanham, MD: Rowman and Littlefield.

Crouch, C. 2011. *The Strange Non-death of Neoliberalism*. Cambridge: Polity Press.

Crowley, P. 1996. "EMU, Maastricht and the 1996 IGC." *Contemporary Economic Policy*. 14 (2): 41–55. https://doi.org/10.1111/j.1465-7287.1996.tb00612.x.

Dafflon, B., and S. Rossi. 1999. "Public Accounting Fudges toward EMU: A First Empirical Survey and Some Public Choice Considerations." *Public Choice* 101: 59–84. https://doi.org/10.1023/a:1018311911605.

D'Alimonte, R., and D. Nelken. 1997. "Introduction: A Year of Difficult Dialogue." In *Italian Politics: The Centre-Left in Power*, edited by R. D'Alimonte and D. Nelken, 17–32. Boulder, CO: Westview Press.

Danforth, B. and J.D. Stephens. 2013. "Measuring Social Citizenship: Achievements and Future Challenges." *Journal of European Public Policy* 20 (9): 1285–98. https://doi.org/10.1080/13501763.2013.822910.

Dastoli, P.V. 1996. "The Stone Guest: Italy on the Threshold of European Monetary Union." In *Italian Politics: The Stalled Transition*, edited by M. Caciagli and D.I. Kertzer, 169–85. Boulder, CO: Westview Press.

Dehaene, Jean-Luc. 1992. "Déclaration gouvernementale lue par le Premier ministre Jean-Luc Dehaene à la Chambre le 9 mars 1992 et au Sénat le 9 mars 1992." Government declaration presented to the Federal Parliament, Brussels. http://www.crisp.be/crisp/wp-content/uploads/doc_pol/gouvernements/federal/declarations/DG_Dehaene_I_9-3-92.pdf.

– 1995. "Déclaration gouvernementale prononcée devant le Parlement par le Premier minister Jean-Luc Dehaene le 28 juin 1995." Government declaration presented to the Federal Parliament, Brussels. http://www.crisp.be/crisp/wp-content/uploads/doc_pol/gouvernements/federal/declarations/DG_Dehaene_II_28-6-95.pdf.

de la Porte, C., and E. Heins. 2016. "Introduction: Is the European Union More Involved in Welfare State Reform Following the Sovereign Debt Crisis?" In *The Sovereign Debt Crisis, the EU and Welfare State Reform*, edited by C. de la Porte and E. Heins, 1–13. London: Palgrave.

Della Sala, V. 1997. "Hollowing Out and Hardening the Italian State: European Integration and the Italian Economy." *West European Politics* 20 (1): 14–33. https://doi.org/10.1080/01402389708425173.

Delors, J. 1989. "Report on Economic and Monetary Union in the European Community." Collection of papers submitted to the Committee for the Study of Economic and Monetary Union [preparatory paper for Delors Report]. Luxembourg: Office for Official Publications of the European Communities.

d'Ercole, M., and F. Terribile. 1998. "Pension Spending: Developments in 1996 and 1997." In *Italian Politics: Mapping the Future*, edited by L. Bardi and M. Rhodes, 187–207. Boulder, CO: Westview Press.

Deschouwer, K., and M. Deweerdt. 1994. Belgian Politics in 1993. *Res Publica* 3–4: 269–81.

Deschouwer, K., and M. Platel. 1996. Belgian Politics in 1995. *Res Publica* 3–4: 527–38.

Deters, H. 2013. "Process Tracing in the Development and Validation of Theoretical Explanations: The Example of Environmental Policy-Making in the EU." *European Political Science* 12, 75–85. https://doi.org/10.1057/eps.2012.11.

Dinan, D. 1994. *Ever Closer Union? An Introduction to the European Community*. London: Macmillan.

– 1999. *Ever Closer Union: An Introduction to European Integration*. 2nd ed. Boulder, CO: Lynne Rienner.

– 2004. *Europe Recast: A History of European Union*. New York: Palgrave Macmillan.

Dolvik, J.E., and A. Martin, eds. 2015a. *European Social Models from Crisis to Crisis: Employment and Inequality in the Era of Monetary Integration*. New York: Oxford University Press.

– 2015b. "From Crisis to Crisis: European Social Models and Labor Market Outcomes in the Era of Monetary Integration." In *European Social Models from Crisis to Crisis: Employment and Inequality in the Era of Monetary Integration*, edited by J.E. Dolvik and A. Martin, 325–85. New York: Oxford University Press.

– 2015c. "Introduction: European Social Models from Crisis to Crisis." In *European Social Models from Crisis to Crisis: Employment and Inequality in the Era of Monetary Integration*, edited by J.E. Dolvik and A. Martin, 1–19. New York: Oxford University Press.

Downs, W.M. 1996. "Federalism Achieved: The Belgian Elections of May 1995." West European Politics 19 (1): 168–75. https://doi.org/10.1080/01402389608425126.

Dyson, K. 1994. *Elusive Union: The Process of Economic and Monetary Union in Europe*. London: Longman.

– 2000. *The Politics of the Euro-Zone: Stability or Breakdown*. New York: Oxford University Press.

– 2002. "Introduction: EMU as Integration, Europeanization and Convergence." In *European States and the Euro: Europeanization, Variation and Convergence*, edited by K. Dyson, 1–27. New York: Oxford University Press.

Dyson, K., and K. Featherstone. 1996. "Italy and EMU as a '*Vincolo Esterno*': Empowering the Technocrats, Transforming the State." *South European Society and Politics* 1 (2): 272–99. https://doi.org/10.1080/13608749608539475.

– 1999. *The Road to Maastricht*. Oxford: Oxford University Press.

Dyson, K., K. Featherstone, and G. Michalapoulos. 1998. "Strapped to the Mast: EC Central Bankers between Global Financial Markets and Regional Integration." *Journal of European Public Policy* 2 (3): 465–87. https://doi.org/10.1080/13501769508406998.

Economist Intelligence Unit. 1990–2001. *Country Report: Belgium*. London: Economist Intelligence Unit.

– 1990–2001. *Country Report: Greece*. London: Economist Intelligence Unit.

– 1990–2001. *Country Report: Italy*. London: Economist Intelligence Unit.

– 1995. *Country Profile: Italy*. London: Economist Intelligence Unit.

Eger, M.A., and S. Valdez. 2015. "Neo-nationalism in Western Europe." *European Sociological Review* 31 (1): 115–30. https://doi.org/10.1093/esr/jcu087.

– 2018. "From Radical Right to Neo-nationalist." *European Political Science* 18: 379–99. https://doi.org.10.1057/s41304-018-0160-0.

Eichengreen, B. 1993. "European Monetary Unification." *Journal of Economic Literature* 31 (3): 1321–57.

Eichengreen, B., and C. Wyplosz. 1993. *The Unstable EMS*. Brookings Papers on Economic Activity. Washington, DC: Brookings Institution.

EIRR (European Industrial Relations Review). 1994–2000.

Eleftheriadis, P. 2005. "Constitutional Reform and the Rule of Law in Greece." *West European Politics* 28 (2): 317–34. https://doi.org/10.1080/01402380500059777.

EMI (European Monetary Institute). 1995. *Progress toward Convergence*. Frankfurt: European Monetary Institute.

– 1996. *Progress toward Convergence*. Frankfurt: European Monetary Institute.

– 1998. *Convergence Report*. Frankfurt am Main: European Monetary Institute. https://www.ecb.europa.eu/pub/pdf/conrep/cr1998en.pdf.

Esping-Andersen, G. 1990. *The Three Worlds of Welfare Capitalism*. Princeton, NJ: Princeton University Press.

European Commission. 1991. *Annual Economic Report 1991–1992: European Economy*. Brussels: Commission of the European Communities.

– 1993. *European Economy: Broad Economic Policy Guidelines and Convergence Report*. No. 55. Brussels: Commission of the European Communities.

– 1998. *Convergence Report*. Brussels: Office for Official Publications.

– 2004. *General Government Data: General Government Revenue, Expenditure,
Balances and Gross Debt, Part II: Tables by Series; Spring.* Brussels: Directorate
General ECFIN.

– 2009–14. *Eurobarometer: Social Climate.* Brussels: European Commission.

– 2013. *General Government Data: General Government Revenue, Expenditure,
Balances and Gross Debt, Part II: Tables by Series,* Autumn. Brussels:
Directorate General ECFIN.

– 2017. *General Government Data (General Government Gross Debt).* Brussels.

Eurostat. 1998. "Statistics on Convergence Criteria: Assessment by Eurostat."
March. Brussels: Eurostat.

Evans, P.B., and W.H. Sewell, Jr. 2013. "Policy Regimes, International Regimes,
and Social Effects." In *Social Resilience in the Neoliberal Era,* edited by P.A.
Hall and M. Lamont, 35–68. New York: Cambridge University Press.

Fabbrini, S. 2000. "From the Prodi Government to the D'Alema Government:
Continuity or Discontinuity." In *Italian Politics: The Return of Politics,* edited
by D. Hine and S. Vassallo, 121–38. Oxford: Berghahn Books.

Falleti, T.G., and J.F. Lynch. 2009. "Context and Causal Mechanisms in Political
Analysis." *Comparative Political Studies* 42 (9): 1143–66. https://doi.org
/10.1177/0010414009331724.

Fargion, V. 2003. "Half Way through the Ford: The Italian Welfare State at the
Start of the New Century." In *Changing Patterns of Social Protection,* edited by
N. Gilbert and R.A. Van Voorhis, 309–38 International Social Security Series
Vol. 9. London: Transaction Publishers.

Farnsworth, K., and Z. Irving. 2018. "Austerity: Neoliberal Dreams Come True?"
Critical Social Policy 38 (3): 461–82. https://doi.org/10.1177/0261018318762451.

Featherstone, K. 2003. "Greece and EMU: Between External Empowerment
and Domestic Vulnerability." *Journal of Common Market Studies* 41 (5):
923–40. https://doi.org/10.1111/j.1468-5965.2003.00469.x.

– 2004. "The Political Dynamics of External Empowerment: The Emergence
of EMU and the Challenge to the European Social Model." In *Euros and
Europeans: Monetary Integration and the European Model of Society,* edited by
A. Martin and G. Ross, 226–47. Cambridge: Cambridge University Press.

– 2005a. "Introduction: 'Modernisation' and the Structural Constraints of
Greek Politics." *West European Politics* 28 (2): 223–41. https://doi.org
/10.1080/01402380500058753.

– 2005b. "'Soft' Co-ordination Meets 'Hard' Politics: The European Union and
Pension Reform in Greece." *Journal of European Public Policy* 12 (4): 733–50.
https://doi.org/10.1080/13501760500160631.

Featherstone, K., G. Kazamias, and D. Papadimitriou. 2000. "Greece and the
Negotiation of Economic and Monetary Union: Preferences, Strategies, and
Institutions." *Journal of Modern Greek Studies* 18 (2): 393–414. https://doi.org
/10.1353/mgs.2000.0028.

– 2001. "The Limits of External Empowerment: EMU, Technocracy and Reform of the Greek Pension System." *Political Studies* 49 (3): 462–80. https://doi.org/10.1111/1467-9248.00321.

Featherstone, K., and D. Papadimitriou. 2008. *The Limits of Europeanization: Reform Capacity and Policy Conflict in Greece*. Basingstoke, UK: Palgrave Macmillan.

Felsen, D. 2000. "Changes to the Italian Budgetary Regime: The Reforms of Law No. 94–1997." In *Italian Politics: The Return of Politics* edited by D. Hine and S. Vassallo, 157–73. New York: Berghahn Books.

Ferrarini, T., K. Nelson, W. Korpi, and J. Palme. 2013. "Social Citizenship Rights and Social Insurance Replacement Rate Validity: Pitfalls and Possibilities." *Journal of European Public Policy* 20 (9), 1251–66. https://doi.org/10.1080/13501763.2013.822907.

Ferrera, M. 2017. "Mission Impossible? Reconciling Economic and Social Europe after the Euro Crisis and Brexit." *European Journal of Political Research* 56 (1): 3–22. https://doi.org/10.1111/1475-6765.12185.

Ferrera, M., and E. Gualmini. 2004. *Rescued by Europe? Social and Labour Market Reforms in Italy from Maastricht to Berlusconi*. Amsterdam: Amsterdam University Press.

Ferrera, M., and M. Jessoula. 2007. "Italy: A Narrow Gate for Path Shift." In *The Handbook of West European Pension Politics*, edited by E. Immergut, K. Anderson, and I. Schulze, 396–453. Oxford: Oxford University Press.

Festjens, M.J. 1997. *La réforme des pensions: Une nouvelle génération et un nouveau contrat*. Planning Paper 82. Brussels: Bureau fédéral du Plan.

Fiers, S., and M. Deweerdt. 1998. "Belgian Politics in 1997." *Res Publica* 40 (3–4): 377–96.

– 1999. "Belgian Politics in 1998." *Res Publica* 41 (2–3): 265–84.

Fitzmaurice, J. 1996. *The Politics of Belgium: A Unique Federalism*. Boulder, CO: Westview Press.

Foster, C., and J. Frieden. 2019. "Compensation, Austerity, and Populism: Social Spending and Voting in 17 Western European Countries." Paper prepared for "Seminar on the State and Capitalism since 1800," Center for European Studies, Harvard University, Cambridge, MA.

Franco, D. 2002. "Italy: A Never-Ending Pension Reform." In *Social Security Pension Reform in Europe*, edited by M. Feldstein and H. Siebert, 211–51. Chicago: University of Chicago Press.

Fratianni, M., and J. von Hagen. 1992. *The European Monetary System and European Monetary Union*. Boulder, CO: Westview Press.

Freitag, M., and P. Sciarini. 2001. "The Political Economy of Budget Deficits in the European Union." *European Union Politics* 2 (2): 163–89. https://doi.org/10.1177/1465116501002002002.

Frieden, J., and S. Walter. 2017. "Understanding the Political Economy of the Eurozone Crisis." *Annual Review of Political Science* 20: 371–90. https://doi.org/10.1146/annurev-polisci-051215-023101.

Garrett, G. 1994. "The Politics of Maastricht." In *The Political Economy of European Monetary Unification*, edited by B. Eichengreen and J. Frieden, 47–65. Boulder, CO: Westview Press.

Gerring, J. 2007. "Is There a (Viable) Crucial-Case Method?" *Comparative Political Studies* 40 (3): 231–53. https://doi.org/10.1177/0010414006290784.

Gidron, N., and P.A. Hall. 2019. "Populism as a Problem of Social Integration." *Comparative Political Studies*. https://doi.org/10.1177%2F0010414019879947.

Gill, S. 1998. "European Governance and New Constitutionalism: Economic and Monetary Union and Alternatives to Disciplinary Neo-liberalism in Europe." *New Political Economy* 3 (1): 5–26. https://doi.org/10.1080/13563469808406330.

Gingrich, J., and S. Häusermann. 2015. "The Decline of the Working-Class Vote, the Reconfiguration of the Welfare State Support Coalition and Consequences for the Welfare State." *Journal of European Social Policy* 25 (1): 50–75. https://doi.org/10.1177/0958928714556970.

Ginsborg, P. 2003. *Italy and Its Discontents: Family, Civil Society, State*. New York: Palgrave Macmillan.

Goertz, G., and J. Mahoney. 2012. *A Tale of Two Cultures: Qualitative and Quantitative Research in the Social Sciences*. Princeton, NJ: Princeton University Press.

Gourevitch. P.A. 1986. *Politics in Hard Times: Comparative Responses to International Economic Crises*. Ithaca, NY: Cornell University Press.

Grahl, J., and P. Teague. 1997. "Is the European Social Model Fragmenting?" *New Political Economy* 2 (3): 405–26. https://doi.org/10.1080/13563469708406315.

Granovetter, M. 1992. "Economic Institutions as Social Constructions: A Framework for Analysis." *Acta Sociologica* 35 (1): 3–11. https://doi.org/10.1177/000169939203500101.

Graziano, P., and M. Jessoula. 2011. "'Eppur si muoveva …' The Italian Trajectory of Recent Welfare Reforms: From 'Rescued by Europe' to Euroscepticism." In *The EU and the Domestic Politics of Welfare State Reforms: Europa, Europae*, edited by P. Graziano, S. Jacquot, and B. Palier, 148–74. Basingstoke, UK: Palgrave Macmillan.

Greece. 1999. *Update of the Hellenic Convergence Program (1999–2002)*. Athens: National Bank of Greece.

Greece. Spraos Committee (Committee for the Examination of Economic Policy in the Long Term). 1997. *Pensions and the Greek Economy: A Contribution to the Public Debate*. Athens: National Bank of Greece.

Green-Pedersen, C. 2004. "The Dependent Variable Problem within the Study of Welfare-State Retrenchment: Defining the Problem and Looking for Solutions." *Journal of Comparative Policy Analysis* 6 (1): 3–14. https://doi.org/10.1080/1387698042000222763.

Greve, B. 2019. *Welfare Chauvinism, Populism and Welfare Chauvinism*. Bristol: Policy Press.

Gros, D., and N. Thygesen. 1992. *European Monetary Integration: From the European Monetary System to the European Union*. London: Longman.

Guillen, A.M., and M. Matsaganis. 2000. "Testing the 'Social Dumping' Hypothesis in Southern Europe: Welfare Policies in Greece and Spain during the Last Twenty Years." *Journal of European Social Policy* 10 (2): 120–45. https://doi.org/10.1177/a012486.

Hall, P.A. 1986. *Governing the Economy: The Politics of State Intervention in Britain and France*. New York: Oxford University Press.

– 2013. "The Political Origins of Our Economic Discontents: Contemporary Adjustment Problems in Historical Perspective." In *Politics in the New Hard Times: The Great Recession in Comparative Perspective*, edited by M. Kahler and D.A. Lake, 129–49. Ithaca, NY: Cornell University Press.

– 2016. "Politics as a Process Structured in Space and Time." In *Oxford Handbook of Historical Institutionalism*, edited by O. Fioretos, T.G. Falleti, and A. Sheingate, 31–50. Oxford: Oxford University Press.

– 2017. "Understanding the Roots of Populism: An Interview with Peter Hall." Interviewed by Henning Meyer of Social Europe. Minda de Gunzburg Center for European Studies Harvard. Accessed 28 September 2017. https://ces.fas.harvard.edu/recordings/understanding-the-roots -of-populism-an-interview-with-peter-hall.

Hall, P.A., and M. Lamont. 2013. "Introduction: Social Resilience in the Neoliberal Era." In *Social Resilience in the Neoliberal Era*, edited by P.A. Hall and M. Lamont, 1–31. New York: Cambridge University Press.

Hallerberg, M. 2004. *Domestic Budgets in a United Europe: Fiscal Governance from the End of Bretton Woods to EMU*. Ithaca, NY: Cornell University Press.

Hallerberg, M., R.R. Strauch, and J. von Hagen. 2009. *Fiscal Governance in Europe*. Cambridge: Cambridge University Press.Häusermann, S., M. Pinggera, M. Ares, and M. Enggist. 2019. "The Limits of Solidarity: Changing Welfare Coalitions in a Transforming European Party System." Paper presented at the International Conference of Europeanists, Madrid, 20–22 June.

Hay, C. 2000. "Contemporary Capitalism, Globalization, Regionalization and the Persistence of National Variation." *Review of International Studies* 26 (4): 509–531. https://doi.org/10.1017/s026021050000509x.

Hay, C., M. Watson, and D. Wincott. 1999. *Globalisation, European Integration and the Persistence of European Social Models*. Brighton, UK: Sussex European Institute.

Hay, C., and D. Wincott. 2012. *The Political Economy of European Welfare Capitalism*. Basingstoke, UK: Palgrave Macmillan.

Heclo, H. 1981. "Toward a New Welfare State." In *The Development of Welfare States in Europe and America*, edited by P. Flora and A.J. Heidenheimer, 383–406. London: Transaction Books.

Heins, E., and C. de la Porte. 2016. "Depleted European Social Models Following the Crisis: Toward a Brighter Future?." In *The Sovereign Debt Crisis, the EU and Welfare State Reform*, edited by C. de la Porte and E. Heins, 207–21. London: Palgrave.

Heipertz, M., and A. Verdun. 2010. *Ruling Europe: The Politics of the Stability and Growth Pact*. Cambridge: Cambridge University Press.

Heisenberg, D. 1999. *The Mark of the Bundesbank: Germany's Role in European Monetary Cooperation*. Boulder, CO: Lynne Rienner Publishers.

Hellman, S. 1993. "Politics Almost as Usual: The Formation of the Amato Government." In *The End of Post-war Politics in Italy: The 1992 Landmark Elections*, edited by G. Pasquino and P. McCarthy, 141–59. Boulder, CO: Westview Press.

Hemerijck, A. 2013. *Changing Welfare States*. Oxford: Oxford University Press.

Hicks, A., and D. Swank. 1992. "Politics, Institutions, and Social Welfare Spending in Industrialized Democracies, 1960–1982." *American Political Science Review* 86 (3): 658–74. https://doi.org/10.2307/1964129.

Hine, D., and S. Vassallo. 1999. "Introduction: One Step toward Europe, Two Steps Back from Institutional Reform." In *Italian Politics: The Return of Politics*, edited by D. Hine and S. Vassallo, 33–46. Oxford: Berghahn Books.

Huber, E., C. Ragin, and J.D. Stephens. 1993. "Social Democracy, Christian Democracy, Constitutional Structure and the Welfare State." *American Journal of Sociology* 99(3): 711–49. https://doi.org/10.1086/230321.

Huber, E., and J.D. Stephens. 2001. *Development and Crisis of the Welfare State: Parties and Policies in Global Markets*. Chicago: University of Chicago Press.

Hughes Hallett, A., and J. Lewis. 2008. "European Fiscal Discipline before and after EMU: Crash Diet or Permanent Weight Loss?" *Macroeconomic Dynamics* 12 (3): 404–24. https://doi.org/10.1017/s1365100507070204.

Hutter, S., H. Kriesi, and G. Vidal. 2018. Old versus New Politics: The Political Spaces in Southern Europe. *Party Politics* 24 (1): 10–22. https://doi.org/10.1177/1354068817694503.

IMF (International Monetary Fund). 2002. *Greece: Selected Issue – An Overview of Pension Reform*. Washington, DC: IMF.

– 2005. *IMF Country Report: Greece No 05/42*. Washington, DC: IMF.

Ioakimidis, P.C. 2001. "The Europeanisation of Greece: An Overall Assessment." In *Europeanization and the Southern Periphery*, edited by K. Featherstone and G. Kazamias, 73–94. London: Frank Cass.

Italianer, A. 1993. "Mastering Maastricht: EMU Issues and How They Were Settled." In *Economic and Monetary Union: Implications for National Policy*

Makers, edited by K. Gretschmann, 51–113. Maastricht: European Institute of Public Administration.

Jensen, C. 2011. "Less Bad Than Its Reputation: Social Spending as Proxy for Welfare Effort in Cross-National Research." *Journal of Comparative Policy Analysis: Research and Practice* 13 (3): 327–40. https://doi.org/10.1080/13876988.2011.565917.

Jensen, M.D., C. Knill, K. Schultze, and J. Tosun. 2014. "Giving Less by Doing More? Dynamics of Social Policy Expansion and Dismantling in 18 OECD Countries." *Journal of European Public Policy* 21 (4): 528–48.

Jones, E. 1995. "The Transformation of the Belgian State." In *Disintegration or Transformation? The Crisis of the State in Advanced Industrial Societies*, edited by P. McCarthy and E. Jones, 153–77. New York: Palgrave Macmillan.

– 2002. "Consociationalism, Corporatism, and the Fate of Belgium." *Acta Politica* 87(Spring/Summer): 86–103.

Jonung, L., J. Kiander, and P. Vartia, eds. 2009. *The Great Financial Crisis in Finland and Sweden: The Nordic Experience of Financial Liberalization.* Cheltenham, UK: Edward Elgar.

Kaelberer, M. 2001. *Money and Power in Europe: The Political Economy of European Monetary Cooperation.* Albany: State University of New York Press.

Kahler, M., and D.A. Lake. 2013. *Politics in the New Hard Times: The Great Recession in Comparative Perspective.* Ithaca, NY: Cornell University Press.

Kaltenthaler, K. 1998. *Germany and the Politics of Europe's Money.* Durham, NC: Duke University Press.

Kopits, G. 1997. "Are Europe's Social Security Finances Compatible with EMU?" IMF Paper on Policy Analysis and Assessment. Washington, DC: International Monetary Fund, Fiscal Affairs Department.

Korpi, W. 2003. "Welfare-State Regress in Western Europe: Politics, Institutions, Globalization and Europeanization." *Annual Review of Sociology* 29, 589–609. https://doi.org/10.1146/annurev.soc.29.010202.095943.

Korpi, W., and J. Palme. 2003. "New Politics and Class Politics in the Context of Austerity and Globalization: Welfare State Regress in 18 Countries, 1975–95." *American Political Science Review* 97 (3). https://doi.org/10.1017/s0003055403000789.

Kostoris Padoa-Schioppa, F. 2001. "Budgetary Policies and Administrative Reform in Contemporary Italy." *Daedalus* 130 (2): 115–38.

Kriesi, H., E. Grande, M. Dolezal, M. Helbling, D. Höglinger, S. Hutter, and B. Wüest. 2012. *Political Conflict in Western Europe.* Cambridge: Cambridge University Press.

Kvist, J. 2013. "The Post-crisis European Social Model: Developing or Dismantling Social Investments." *Journal of International and Comparative Social Policy* 29 (1): 91–107. https://doi.org/10.1080/21699763.2013.809666.

Kypris, C. 1997. "Greece: Tax Reform." *European Taxation – Amsterdam* 37 (5): 204–6.

Lasswell, H.D. 1936. *Politics: Who Gets What, When, How.* Cleveland, OH: Meridian Books.

Leander, A., and S. Guzzini. 1997. "European Economic and Monetary Union and the Crisis of Social Contracts." In *The Politics of Economic and Monetary Union*, edited by P. Minkkinen and H. Patomäki, 133–63. Helsinki: The Finnish Institute of International Affairs.

Legrenzi, P. 1998. "The October Crisis of the Prodi Government." In *Italian Politics: Mapping the Future*, edited by L. Bardi and M. Rhodes, 57–71. Boulder, CO: Westview Press.

Leibfried, S. 2000. "National Welfare States, European Integration and Globalization: A Perspective for the Next Century." *Social Policy and Administration* 34 (1): 44–63. https://doi.org/10.1111/1467-9515.00177.

Leibfried, S., and P. Pierson. 2000. "Social Policy: Left to Courts and Markets?." In *Policy-Making in the European Union*, edited by H. Wallace and W. Wallace, 267–92. Oxford: Oxford University Press.

Levy, J. 2010. "Welfare Retrenchment." In *The Oxford Handbook of the Welfare State*, edited by F. Castles, S. Leibfried, J. Lewis, H. Obinger, and C. Pierson, 552–68. Oxford: Oxford University Press.

Liargovas, P. 2000. "The Changing Role of the Greek State in View of EMU." In Contemporary Greece and Europe, edited by A. Mitsos and E. Mossialos, 205–21. Aldershot, UK: Ashgate.

Maes, I., and A. Verdun. 2005. "Small States and the Creation of EMU: Belgium and the Netherlands, Pace-Setters and Gate-Keepers." *Journal of Common Market Studies* 43(2): 327–48. https://doi.org/10.1111/j.0021 -9886.2005.00558.x.Mahoney, J. 2009. "Comparative-Historical Analysis: Generalizing Past the Past." Paper presented at the ASA Mini-Conference "Comparing Past and Present," Berkeley, CA, 12 August 2009.

Marier, P. 2008. *Pension Politics: Consensus and Social Conflict in Ageing Societies.* Abingdon, UK: Routledge.

Martin, A. 2015. "Eurozone Economic Governance: 'A Currency without a Country.'" In *European Social Models from Crisis to Crisis: Employment and Inequality in the Era of Monetary Integration*, edited by J.E. Dolvik and A. Martin, 20–48. New York: Oxford University Press.

Martin, A., and G. Ross. 1999. "Europe's Monetary Union: Creating a Democratic Deficit?" *Current History* April: 171–6.

– 2004. "Introduction: EMU and the European Social Model." In *Euros and Europeans: Monetary Integration and the European Model of Society*, edited by A. Martin and G. Ross, 1–19. Cambridge: Cambridge University Press.

Massari, O., and S. Parker. 2000. "The Two Lefts: Between Rupture and Recomposition." In *Italian Politics: The Return of Politics*, edited by D. Hine and S. Vassallo, 47–63. New York: Berghahn Books.

Matsaganis, M. 2002. "Yet Another Piece of Pension Reform in Greece." *South European Society and Politics* 7 (3): 109–22. https://doi.org/10.1080/13608740708539635.

– 2004. "A Tale of Recurring Policy Failure? Tackling Retirement Pensions in Greece." Working Paper 3/2004. Moncalieri, Italy: URGE Research Unit on European Governance.

– 2006. "Muddling Through: The Trials and Tribulations of Social Security." In *Social Policy Developments in Greece*, edited by M. Petmesidou and E. Mossialos, 147–73. Aldershot, UK: Ashgate.

McNamara, K. 2003. "Globalization, Institutions, and Convergence: Fiscal Adjustment in Europe." In *Governance in a Global Economy: Political Authority in Transition*, edited by K. Miles and D. Lake, 332–60. Princeton, NJ: Princeton University Press.

Milesi-Ferretti, G.M., and K. Moriyama. 2006. "Fiscal Adjustment in EU Countries: A Balance Sheet Approach." *Journal of Banking and Finance* 30 (2): 3281–98. https://doi.org/10.1016/j.jbankfin.2006.05.010.

Mirowski, P. 2014. *Never Let a Serious Crisis Go to Waste*. London: Verso.

Moravcsik, A. 1998. *The Choice for Europe: Social Purpose and State Power from Messina to Maastricht*. Ithaca, NY: Cornell University Press.

Mosley, L. 2000. "Room to Move: International Financial Markets and National Welfare States." *International Organization* 54 (4): 737–73. https://doi.org/10.1162/002081800551352.

– 2004. "Government–Financial Market Relations after EMU: New Currency, New Constraints." *European Union Politics* 5 (2): 181–209. https://doi.org/10.1177/1465116504042443.

Mussa, M. 1997. "Political and Institutional Commitment to a Common Currency." *American Economic Review: Papers and Proceedings* 87: 217–20.

Natali, D., and M. Rhodes. 2008. "The 'New Politics' of Pension Reforms in Continental Europe." In *Pension Reform in Europe: Politics, Policies and Outcomes*, edited by C. Arza and M. Kohli, 55–75. Oxford: Routledge.

Negrelli, S., and V. Pulignano. 2010. "The Evolution of Social Pacts in Italy: Crisis or Metamorphosis." In *After the Euro and Enlargement: Social Pacts in the EU*, edited by P. Pochet, M. Keune, and D. Natali, 138–56. Brussels: European Trade Union Institute.

Obinger, H., and U. Wagschal. 2010. "Social Expenditure and Revenues." In *The Oxford Handbook of the Welfare State*, edited by F. Castles, S. Leibfried, J. Lewis, H. Obinger, and C. Pierson, 333–52. Oxford: Oxford University Press.

OECD (Organisation for Economic Co-operation and Development). 1991–2001. *OECD Economic Surveys: Belgium and Luxembourg*. Paris: OECD.

– 1991–2001. *OECD Economic Surveys: Greece*. Paris: OECD.

– 1992–2002. *OECD Economic Surveys: Italy*. Paris: OECD.

- 1994. *New Orientations for Social Policy*. Social Policy Studies, no. 12. Paris: OECD.
- 1997–2001. *OECD Economic Surveys: Belgium*. Paris: OECD.
- 1999. *EMU: Facts and Challenges*. Paris: OECD.
- 2000. *EMU: One Year On*. Paris: OECD. https://www.oecd-ilibrary.org /docserver/9789264181205-en.pdf?expires=1594011940&id=id&accname =guest&checksum=A422154FCDD4F754C490504BF523FD0B.
- 2002. OECD Privatization Database. Paris: OECD.
- 2004. *Social Expenditure Database (SOCX), 1980–2001*. Paris: OECD.
- 2005. *National Accounts of OECD Countries General Accounts 1993–2004*. Paris: OECD.
- 2013. Social Expenditure Database (SOCX), 1980–2009–2013. Paris: OECD.
- 2016a. Economic Outlook Database. Paris: OECD.
- 2016b. Social Expenditure Database (SOCX), 1980–2009–2013. Paris: OECD.
- 2017a. Economic Outlook Database. Paris: OECD.
- 2017b. *Labour Force Statistics*. Paris: OECD.
- 2017c. *OECD Factbook: Country Statistical Profiles*. Paris: OECD.
Ostry, J.D., P. Loungani, and D. Furceri. 2016. "Neoliberalism: Oversold?" *Finance and Development* 53 (2): 38–41.
Padoa-Schioppa, T. 1994. *The Road to Monetary Union: The Emperor, the Kings and the Genies*. Oxford: Clarendon Press.
Pakaslahti, J. 1997. *Does EMU Threaten European Welfare? Social and Political Implications of Its Transitional Stage in EU Member States*. Working paper 17. Brussels: Observatoire social européen.
Palier, B. 2010. "The Long Conservative Corporatist Road to Welfare Reforms." In *A Long Goodbye to Bismarck? Politics of Welfare Reforms in Continental Europe*, edited by B. Palier, 333–88. Amsterdam: Amsterdam University Press.
Papadimitriou, D. 2001. "In Search of an Advocacy Coalition: Reforming the Greek Pension System in the Eurozone." Paper presented to the Hellenic Social Policy Association Conference on Social Policy in Greece and the European Union: New Challenges, Trends and Reform Prospects. Democritus University of Thrace, Komotini, Greece, 9–13 May.
Papadopoulos, T.N. 1997. "Social Insurance and the Crisis of Statism in Greece." In *Social Insurance in Europe*, edited by J. Clasen, 177–203. Bristol: Policy Press.
Parker, S. 1997. "The Government of the Ulivo." In *Italian Politics: The Centre-Left in Power*, edited by R. D'Alimonte and D. Nelken, 125–41. Boulder, CO: Westview Press.
Pasquino, G. 1996. "The Government of Lamberto Dini." In *Italian Politics: The Stalled Transition*, edited by M. Caciagli and D.I. Kertzer, 137–52. Boulder, CO: Westview Press.

Pasquino, G., and P. McCarthy. 1993. *The End of Post-war Politics in Italy: The 1992 Landmark Elections*. Boulder, CO: Westview Press.

Pasquino, G., and S. Vassallo. 1995. "The Government of Carlo Azeglio Ciampi." In *Italian Politics: Ending the First Republic*, edited by C. Mershon and G. Pasquino, 55–74. Boulder, CO: Westview Press.

Petmesidou, M. 2000. "Social Protection in Greece in the Nineties: Reforming the 'Weak' Welfare State." In *Contemporary Greece and Europe*, edited by A. Mitsos and E. Mossialos, 303–30. Aldershot, UK: Ashgate.

Petmesidou, M., and M. Mossialos. 2006. "Introduction: Addressing Social Protection and Policy in Greece." In *Social Policy Developments in Greece*, edited by M. Petmesidou and E. Mossialos, 1–21. Aldershot, UK: Ashgate.

Pierson, P. 1994. *Dismantling the Welfare State: Reagan, Thatcher and the Politics of Retrenchment*. Cambridge: Cambridge University Press.

– 1996. "The New Politics of the Welfare State." *World Politics* 48 (2): 143–79. https://doi.org/10.1353/wp.1996.0004.

– 2001. "Coping with Permanent Austerity: Welfare State Restructuring in Affluent Democracies." In *The New Politics of the Welfare State*, edited by P. Pierson, 410–56. New York: Oxford University Press.

– 2011. "The Welfare State over the Very Long Run." Working papers of the Centre for Social Policy Research no. 02/2011. Bremen: Center for Social Policy Research.

Pitruzzello, S. 1997. "Social Policy and the Implementation of the Maastricht Fiscal Convergence Criteria: The Italian and French Attempts at Welfare and Pension Reforms." *Social Research* 64 (4): 1589–642.

Pizzuti, F.R. 1998. "Pension Reform and Economic Policy Constraints in Italy." *Labour* 12 (1): 45–66. https://doi.org/10.1111/1467-9914.00056.

Pochet, P. 2004. "Belgium: Monetary Integration and Precarious Federalism." In *Euros and Europeans: Monetary Integration and the European Model of Society*, edited by A. Martin and G. Ross, 201–25. Cambridge: Cambridge University Press.

Polanyi, K. 1944. *The Great Transformation: The Political and Economic Origins of Our Time*. Boston: Beacon Press.

Quaglia, L. 2013. "The Europeanization of Macroeconomic Policies and Financial Regulation in Italy." *South European Society and Politics* 18 (2): 159–76. https://doi.org/10.1080/13608746.2013.784434.

Quaglia, L., and C. Radaelli. 2007. "Italian Politics and the European Union: A Tale of Two Research Designs." *West European Politics* 30 (4): 924–43. https://doi.org/10.1080/01402380701500389.

Radaelli, C. 2002. "The Italian State and the Euro: Institutions, Discourse and Policy Regimes." In *European States and the Euro: Europeanization, Variation and Convergence*, edited by K. Dyson, 212–37. New York: Oxford University Press.

Regini, M., and S. Colombo. 2011. "Italy: The Rise and Decline of Social Pacts."
In *Social Pacts in Europe: Emergence, Evolution and Institutionalization*, edited
by S. Avdagic, M. Rhodes, and J. Visser, 118–47. Oxford: Oxford University
Press.

Regini, M., and I. Regalia. 1997. "Employers, Unions and the State: The
Resurgence of Concertation in Italy." *West European Politics* 20 (1), 210–30.
https://doi.org/10.1080/01402389708425182.

Reman, P. 1994. "Du pacte social de 1944 au Plan global de 1993: evolution
de la solidarité." In *Pour un nouveau pacte social, emploi, compétitivité, sécurité
sociale*, edited by É. Arcq, 125–35. Brussels: Éditions Vie Ouvrière.

Reynaud, E., and A. Hege. 1996. "Italy: A Fundamental Transformation of the
Pension System." *International Social Security Review* 49 (3): 65–74. https://
doi.org/10.1111/j.1468-246x.1996.tb01110.x.

Rhodes, M. 1996. "Globalization and West European Welfare States." *Journal
of European Social Policy* 6 (4): 305–27. https://doi.org/10.1177
/095892879600600403.

– 1997. "The Welfare State: Internal Challenges, External Constraints." In
Developments in West European Politics, edited by M. Rhodes, P. Heywood,
and V. Wright, 57–74. London: Macmillan.

– 1998. "Subversive Liberalism: Market Integration, Globalization and West
European Welfare States." In *Regionalism and Global Economic Integration:
Europe, Asia and the Americas*, edited by W.D. Coleman and G.R.D. Underhill,
99–121. London: Routledge.

Rodrik, D. 2018. "Populism and the Economics of Globalization." *Journal of
International Business Policy* 1: 1–22. https://doi.org/10.1057/s42214-018
-0001-4.

Ross, F. 2000. "Interests and Choice in the Not Quite So New Politics of Welfare."
West European Politics 23 (2): 11–33. https://doi.org/10.1080/01402380008425365.

Ross, G. 1995. *Jacques Delors and European Integration*. New York: Oxford
University Press.

– 2012. "Economic and Monetary Union Twenty Years after Maastricht: Case
Studies in European Union Intergovernmentalism." In *Revue québécoise de
droit international*. Special issue: Les 20 ans de l'Union européenne, 1992–2012
(December 2012): 173–85. Atelier Schuman 2012.

Rotte, R. 1998. "International Commitment and Domestic Politics: A Note on
the Maastricht Case." *European Journal of International Relations* 4 (1): 131142.
https://doi.org/10.1177/1354066198004001005.

Rotte, R., and K. Zimmerman. 1998. "Fiscal Restraint and the Political
Economy of EMU." *Public Choice* 94 (3/4): 385–406. https://doi.org/10.1023
/a:1005042015560.

Salvati, M. 1997. "Moneta unica, rivoluzione copernicana" [Monetary union,
Copernican revolution]. *Il Mulino* 1, 5–23.

Savage, J.D. 2001. "Budgetary Collective Action Problem: Convergence and Compliance under the Maastricht Treaty on European Union." *Public Administration Review* 61 (1): 43–53. https://doi.org/10.1111/0033-3352.00004.

– 2005. *Making the EMU: The Politics of Budgetary Surveillance and the Enforcement of Maastricht*. New York: Oxford University Press.

Sbragia, A. 2001. "Italy Pays for Europe: Political Leadership, Political Choice, and Institutional Adaptation." In *Transforming Europe: Europeanization and Domestic Change*, edited by M. Green Cowles, J. Caporaso, and T. Risse, 79–96. Ithaca, NY: Cornell University Press.

Scharpf, F. 2000. "The Viability of Advanced Welfare States in the International Economy: Vulnerabilities and Options." *Journal of European Public Policy* 7 (2): 190–228. https://doi.org/10.1080/135017600343160.

Schelkle, W., and Z. Barta. 2008. Belgium's Fiscal Performance in EMU: An Unlikely Success Story of the EU's Budget Surveillance. Brussels: NewGov (New Modes of Governance Project), Deliverable 19a/D4q.

Schmidt, V., and M. Thatcher. 2013. *Resilient Liberalism in Europe's Political Economy*. Cambridge: Cambridge University Press.

Scruggs, L. 2013. "Measuring and Validating Social Program Replacement Rates." *Journal of European Public Policy* 20 (9): 1267–84. https://doi.org/10.1080/13501763.2013.822909.

Scruggs, L., D. Jahn, and K. Kuitto. 2013. "Comparative Welfare Entitlements Dataset 2: Version 2013." Storrs: University of Connecticut; Greifswald, Germany: University of Greifswald.

– 2017. "Comparative Welfare Entitlements Dataset 2 Codebook: Version 2017-09." Storrs: University of Connecticut; Greifswald, Germany: University of Greifswald.

Siegel, N. 2007. "When (Only) Money Matters: The Pros and Cons of Expenditure Analysis." In *Investigating Welfare State Change*, edited by J. Clasen and N. Siegel, 166–97. Northampton, MA: Edward Elgar.

Sotiropoulos, D.A. 2004. "The EU's Impact on the Greek Welfare State: Europeanization on Paper." *Journal of European Social Policy* 14 (3): 267–84. https://doi.org/10.1177/0958928704044627.

– 2011. "Usages of 'Europe' in Welfare State Policies in Greece, 1981–2010." In *The EU and the Domestic Politics of Welfare State Reforms: Europa, Europae*, edited by P. Graziano, S. Jacquot, and B. Palier, 121–47. Basingstoke, UK: Palgrave Macmillan.

Starke, P., A. Kaasch, and F. Van Hooren, 2013. *The Welfare State as Crisis Manager*. Houndmills, UK: Palgrave Macmillan.

Steinebach, Y., and C. Knill. 2017. "Social Policy in Hard Times: Crisis-Coping Strategies in Europe from 1976 to 2013." *International Journal of Public Administration* 40 (14): 1164–74. https://doi.org/10.1080/01900692.2017.1317802.

Steinebach, Y., C. Knill, and J. Jordana. 2019. "Austerity or Welfare State Transformation? Examining the Impact of Economic Crises on Social Regulation in Europe." *Regulation and Governance* 13 (3): 301–20. https://doi.org/10.1111/rego.12174.

Stephens, J. 2010. "The Social Rights of Citizenship." In *The Oxford Handbook of the Welfare State*, edited by F. Castles, S. Leibfried, J. Lewis, H. Obinger, and C. Pierson, 511–25. Oxford: Oxford University Press.

Stergiou, A. 2000. "Greece." In *Social Security and Solidarity in the European Union: Facts, Evaluations and Perspectives*, edited by J.P.A. Van Vugt and J.M. Peet, 87–110. New York: Physica-Verlag.

Stolfi, F. 2008. "The Europeanization of Italy's Budget Institutions in the 1990s." *Journal of European Public Policy* 15 (4): 550–66. https://doi.org/10.1080/13501760801996733.

– 2010. "Testing Structuralist and Interpretative Explanations of Policy Change: The Change of Italy's Budget Reform." *Governance* 23 (1): 109–32. https://doi.org/10.1111/j.1468-0491.2009.01469.x.

Strauch, R., M. Hallerberg, and J. von Hagen. 2004. "Budgetary Forecasts in Europe: The Track Record of Convergence and Stability Programmes." Working Paper Series no. 307. Frankfurt am Main: European Central Bank.

Streeck, W. 2014. *Buying Time: The Delayed Crisis of Democratic Capitalism*. London: Verso.

– 2017. "A New Regime: The Consolidation State." In *Reconfiguring European States in Crisis*, edited by D. King and P. Le Galés, 139–57. Oxford: Oxford University Press.

Swank, D. 2002. *Global Capital and Policy Change in Welfare States*. New York: Cambridge University Press.Swank, D., and H.-G. Betz. 2019. "Do Radical Right Populist Parties Matter? The Case of the European Welfare State." Paper presented at the 2019 Annual Meetings of the American Political Science Association, Washington, DC, 29 August–1 September.

Teague, P. 1998. "Monetary Union and Social Europe." *Journal of European Social Policy* 8 (2): 117–37. https://doi.org/10.1177/095892879800800202.

Tilly, C. 2006. "Why and How History Matters." In *Oxford Handbook of Contextual Political Analysis*, edited by R.E. Goodin and C. Tilly, 417–37. Oxford: Oxford University Press.Tinios, P. 2003. "Pensions in Greece: The Economics of the Politics of 'Reform by Instalments.'" Paper presented at the LSE Conference "Pension Reform in Europe," London.

Triantafillou, P. 2005. "Pension Reform in Greece: The Impossible Concertation." Paper presented at the ESPAnet Young Researchers Workshop, "Organized Labour and the Welfare State: New Perspectives on an Old Couple," Paris, 30 June–2 July.

– 2007. "Greece: Political Competition in a Majoritarian System." In *The Handbook of West European Pension Politics*, edited by E. Immergut, K. Anderson, and I. Schulze, 97–149. Oxford: Oxford University Press.

United Nations. 1999. *Classifications of Economic Statistics*. New York: Department of Economic and Social Affairs, Statistics Division. https://unstats.un.org /unsd/classifications/Econ.

Venieris, D. 1996. "Dimensions of Social Policy in Greece." *South European Society and Politics* 1 (3): 260–69. https://doi.org/10.1080/13608749608539492.

– 2003. "Social Policy in Greece: Rhetoric versus Reform." *Social Policy and Administration* 37 (2): 133–47. https://doi.org/10.1111/1467-9515.00330.

Verdun, A. 2000. *European Responses to Globalization and Financial Market Integration: Perceptions of Economic and Monetary Union in Britain, France and Germany*. New York: Palgrave Macmillan.

– 2001. "The Political Economy of the Werner and Delors Reports: Continuity amidst Change or Change amidst Continuity?" In *From the Werner Plan to the EMU: In Search of a Political Economy for Europe*, edited by L. Magnusson and B. Strath, 73–96. Brussels: P.I.E.-Peter-Lang.

– 2002. "Merging Neofunctionalism and Intergovernmentalism: Lessons from EMU." In *The Euro: European Integration Theory and Economic and Monetary Union*, edited by A. Verdun, 9–28. Lanham, MD: Rowman and Littlefield.

– 2013. "The Building of Economic Governance in the European Union." *Transfer* 19 (1): 23–35. https://doi.org/10.1177/1024258912469343.

Vilrokx, J., and J. van Leemput. 1998. "Belgium: The Great Transformation." In *Changing Industrial Relations in Europe*, 2nd ed., edited by A. Ferner and R. Hyman, 315–47. Malden, MA: Blackwell.

Vis, B. 2013. How to Analyse Welfare States and Their Development. In *The Routledge Handbook of the Welfare State*, edited by B. Grieve, 274–82. Oxford: Routledge.

Vis, B., K. van Kersbergen, and T. Hylands. 2011. "To What Extent Did the Financial Crisis Intensify the Pressure to Reform the Welfare State?" *Social Policy and Administration* 45 (4): 338–53. https://doi.org/10.1111/j.1467-9515 .2011.00778.x.

Volkens, A., P. Lehmann, N. Merz, S. Regel, A. Werner, O.P. Lacewell, and H. Schultze. 2017. The Manifesto Data Collection. Manifesto Project. Berlin: Wissenschaftszentrum Berlin für Sozialforschung (Social Sciences Research Centre).

von Hagen, J., A. Hughes Hallett, and R. Strauch. 2001. *Budgetary Consolidation in EMU, European Economy*. Economic Papers 148. Brussels: European Commission, Directorate-General for Economic and Financial Affairs.

Walsh, J. 1998. "The Uncertain Path to Monetary Union." In *Italian Politics: Mapping the Future*, edited by L. Bardi and M. Rhodes, 93–110. Boulder, CO: Westview Press.

– 2000. *European Monetary Integration and Domestic Politics*. Boulder, CO: Lynne Rienner Press.

Weiss, L. 2003. "Introduction: Bringing Domestic Institutions Back In." In *States in the Global Economy: Bringing Domestic Institutions Back In*, edited by L. Weiss, 1–33. Cambridge: Cambridge University Press.

Wessels, W., A. Maurer, and J. Mittag. 2003. *Fifteen into One? The European Union and Its Member States*. Manchester: Manchester University Press.

Wincott, D. 2008. Welfare Reform In *The Euro at 10: Europeanization, Power, and Convergence*, edited by K. Dyson, 359–77. Oxford: Oxford University Press.

Woll, C., and S. Jacquot. 2010. "Using Europe: Strategic Action in Multi-level Politics." *Comparative European Politics* 8 (1): 110–26. https://doi.org/10.1057/cep.2010.7.

Index

European Union Studies

www.ingramcontent.com/pod-product-compliance
Ingram Content Group UK Ltd.
Pitfield, Milton Keynes, MK11 3LW, UK
UKHW041812020225
454515UK00002B/68/J

9 781487 507763